FREQUENT

Restaurants, ba... ...o ensure you get the most out of your guide, the app features all of our favourites, as well as the latest openings, and is updated regularly. Simply update your app when you receive a notification to access the most current listings available.

Shopping in Oman still revolves around the traditional souks that can be found in every town in the country – most famously at Mutrah in Muscat, Salalah and Nizwa, which serve as showcases of traditional Omani craftsmanship and produce ranging from antique khanjars and Bedu jewellery to halwa, rose-water and frankincense. Muscat also boasts a number of modern malls, although these are rare elsewhere in the country.

TRAVEL TIPS & DESTINATION OVERVIEWS

The app also includes a complete A to Z of handy travel tips on everything from visa regulations to local etiquette. Plus, you'll find destination overviews on shopping, sport, the arts, local events, health, activities and more.

HOW TO DOWNLOAD THE WALKING EYE

Available on purchase of this guide only.

1. Visit our website: www.insightguides.com/walkingeye
2. Download the Walking Eye container app to your smartphone (this will give you access to both the destination app and the eBook)
3. Select the scanning module in the Walking Eye container app
4. Scan the QR code on this page – you will be asked to enter a verification word from the book as proof of purchase
5. Download your free destination app* and eBook for travel information on the go

* Other destination apps and eBooks are available for purchase separately or are free with the purchase of the Insight Guide book

Contents

THE BEST OF LONDON: TOP ATTRACTIONS

At a glance, everything you won't want to miss, from long-established icons like Tower Bridge and Big Ben to exciting newer landmarks such as Tate Modern and the Shard.

◁ **Buckingham Palace.** The best time to see the palace is during Changing the Guard. If you would like to see inside, then you must time your visit to coincide with the Queen's annual trip to Balmoral (late July–early Sept) when some of the State Rooms of the palace, plus special exhibitions, are open to visitors. See page 80.

◁ **The London Eye.** For the best views in London take a trip on the London Eye on the South Bank. The stately observation wheel takes 30 minutes to rotate, allowing plenty of time for picking out London's sights – there are also information screens in each capsule. On a fine day you can see for up to 25 miles (40km). See page 172.

▷ **Big Ben and the Houses of Parliament.** The clock tower of this flamboyant Gothic-style building is a symbol of London. Guided tours of the Houses of Parliament can be arranged during the summer recess in August and September. See page 74.

▽ **The British Museum.** This immense museum contains some of the world's most important treasures from antiquity. See page 134.

◁ **Trafalgar Square.** London's best-loved square has fountains, huge lion statues and Nelson's Column, and is overlooked by the colonnaded National Gallery. See page 97.

▷ **St Paul's Cathedral.** Built after the Great Fire of London of 1666, St Paul's is Christopher Wren's greatest work. See page 162.

▽ **Tower Bridge.** The famous bascule bridge is a triumph of Victorian engineering. See page 181.

◁ **Piccadilly Circus.** Presiding over this gateway to the West End and Theatreland is the famous statue of Eros. See page 89.

▽ **Tower of London.** Established by William the Conqueror, the Tower has a long and bloody history. See page 164.

△ **Tate Modern.** For modern art in an inspired setting, visit this power station-turned-art-gallery on the South Bank. See page 182.

THE BEST OF LONDON: EDITOR'S CHOICE

Here are our ideas on what to do once you've seen London's top sights, plus some tips and tricks even Londoners won't always know.

BEST FOR CHILDREN

Museum of Childhood.

The Natural History Museum. The Darwin Centre allows children to examine specimens and watch scientists at work. See page 202.

The Science Museum. The Who Am I? section is a great hands-on experience. See page 198.

Museum of Childhood. This outpost of the V&A appeals to adults and children alike. See page 233.

London Zoo. One of the world's top zoos. See page 121.

The London Aquarium. Sharks, seahorses, touch pools and much more. See page 171.

HMS *Belfast*. A World War II battleship moored on the Thames. See page 180.

***Cutty Sark*.** The renovated historic tea clipper has exhibits and family events on its decks and in the new glass-fronted gallery, underneath. See page 239.

London Duck Tours. See London in an amphibious vessel used in WWII. See page 268.

Madame Tussauds. Kids love spotting their favourite celebrities, even if they are made of wax. See page 124.

The London Dungeon. Scary fun ideal for 10- to 14-year-olds. See page 171.

London Transport Museum. A huge hit with younger children. See page 103.

Ice-skating. In winter, ice rinks spring up outside the Natural History Museum, Tower of London and Somerset House. See pages 202 and 139.

Princess Diana Memorial Playground. With its pirate ship and teepees, this is one of the best playgrounds in central London. See page 197.

Hamleys. Seven floors to explore in the 'world's finest toy shop'. See page 115.

BEST VIEWS

The Shard. London's iconic skyscraper offers incredible views at a height of 1,016ft (310 metres). See page 180.

The London Eye. Unbeatable vistas whichever way you look. See page 172.

Monument. Climb the 311 steps for views over the City. See page 160.

Waterloo Bridge. Panoramas day and night. See page 173.

Westminster Cathedral. Take the lift to the top of the 273ft (82-metre) tower. See page 77.

Up At The O2. Wearing climbing gear and a helmet, a guided walk takes you over the top of The O2's roof for views of east London and The City. See page 243.

Richmond Hill. The pastoral view from here is protected by an act of Parliament. See page 223.

Parliament Hill. Far-reaching views across London from Hampstead Heath. See page 229.

Restaurants and bars with views. Try Tate Modern Restaurant (see page 182), Oxo Tower Restaurant (see page 175) and restaurants halfway up The Shard (see page 180).

The view from The Shard.

Deer grazing in Richmond Park.

BEST WALKS

Old and new London. An introductory walk, starting from Westminster Abbey, crossing Westminster Bridge, strolling along the South Bank past the London Eye, Shakespeare's Globe and Tate Modern, and then crossing the Millennium Bridge to St Paul's Cathedral. See pages 77, 172 and 147.

Hampstead Heath. Meadows, woods, lakes and ponds, with great views over London. See page 229.

Hyde Park and Kensington Gardens. Sculptures, fountains, gardens and playgrounds in the centre of the city. See pages 197 and 196.

Regent's Canal. Walk all or part of the 8.5 miles (14km) from Paddington to Limehouse, taking in Camden Lock and Little Venice. See page 228.

Richmond. Offers fabulous views, a deer park, interesting pubs and 17th-century Ham House. See page 223.

Changing the Guard.

ONLY IN LONDON

Harrods. The store that has everything. See page 180.

Shakespeare's Globe. The play's the thing, as in Elizabethan days. See page 176.

Royal Pageantry. The Changing the Guard ceremony at Buckingham Palace takes place daily at 11.30am May–July (alternate days rest of year). See page 82.

The Orbit. Take a lift to the top for a view over the Olympic Park. See page 236.

The V&A. The world's largest collection of decorative arts. See pages 190 and 200.

HISTORIC PUBS

The George. This 17th-century pub off Borough High Street is London's only galleried coaching inn. See page 179.

Black Friar. Built in 1875 on the site of the Black Friars Monastery, this is London's only pub from the Arts and Crafts movement. The marble interior carries bronze friezes depicting the activities of monks. See page 145.

Lamb and Flag. Traditional pub tucked down a tiny alleyway in the heart of Covent Garden.

The Grenadier. Hidden away in a quiet cobbled mews, this pub used to be the mess of the Duke of Wellington's officers.

Jerusalem Tavern. Once an 18th-century coffee shop, this is now an intimate pub with an open fire, Georgian-style furniture and ales from Suffolk's St Peter's Brewery.

The Mayflower. It was by this waterside pub in Rotherhithe that the Pilgrim Fathers moored their ship before setting off for Plymouth and thence the New World in 1620. See page 180.

Ye Old Cheshire Cheese. Famous olde-worlde pub off Fleet Street, rebuilt after the Great Fire but retaining its medieval crypt. Frequented by literary luminaries in the past, including Charles Dickens and Dr Samuel Johnson. See page 144.

Famous hotel The Savoy.

DISTINCTIVE HOTELS

The Savoy. Grand riverside hotel near Covent Garden, a favourite with Winston Churchill and Frank Sinatra. See page 101.

Brown's Hotel. Intimate luxury in the heart of Mayfair.

The Goring. Where Kate Middleton and her family spent the night before the Royal Wedding.

Hazlitt's. A characterful 18th-century property in Soho.

Enjoying a drink in The George's cobbled courtyard.

SUMMER IN THE CITY

River cruises. Cruise down to Greenwich or the Thames Barrier, or up to Hampton Court Palace. See page 264.

Open-air drama. Watch Shakespeare at the Globe Theatre on the South Bank or in Regent's Park. See pages 176 and 121.

The City in Bloom. See a carpet of spring flowers at Royal Botanical Gardens, Kew, or visit the lovely Rose Garden (June to late autumn) in Regent's Park. See pages 208 and 121.

Sporting greats. See tennis played at Wimbledon, cricket played at Lord's and cycling events at the Olympic Park. See pages 225, 122 and 236.

Cool off. Swim in the bathing ponds on Hampstead Heath, in the Serpentine in Hyde Park, or the 50-metre heated outdoor pool in London Fields. See pages 229 and 197.

Picnic in the park. London's parks, such as Green Park or St James's Park, are great for lunching al fresco. See pages 80 and 116.

Last Night of the Proms at the Royal Albert Hall.

BEST FESTIVALS

Notting Hill Carnival. This is Europe's biggest street festival, with Caribbean bands, extravagant costumes and floats. Held over the last weekend in August.

Chinese New Year. Dancing dragons and exotic food in Soho's Chinatown and Trafalgar Square. Late January/early February.

Trooping the Colour. The Queen rides out on Horse Guards Parade, with the Household Cavalry in red tunics and bearskin hats. The nearest Saturday to 10 June.

Lord Mayor's Show. The Lord Mayor rides out in his gilded coach from the Guildhall to the Law Courts. Second Saturday in November.

BBC Proms. Annual series of 'promenade' classical music concerts in Royal Albert Hall. From July to September.

Dancer at Notting Hill Carnival, held on the last weekend in August.

MONEY SAVING TIPS

Half-price Theatre Tickets The TKTS booth in Leicester Square sells same-day tickets for West End shows at up to 50 percent off, plus a service fee (Mon–Sat 10am–7pm, Sun 11am–4.30pm; www.tkts.co.uk). Tickets for some plays at the National Theatre can be purchased for £15 through the Travelex scheme (www.nationaltheatre.org.uk). Some theatres reserve a few tickets for under 26s to purchase on the day at greatly reduced prices.

Restaurant Discounts A number of restaurants, especially around Covent Garden, have special pre- and post-theatre menus at discounted prices. Check www.coventgardenlife.com for deals.

Museums and Attractions The national museums and galleries (including Tate Modern, Tate Britain, the National Gallery, National Portrait Gallery, British Museum, Science Museum, Natural History Museum, the Victoria & Albert Museum, Imperial War Museum and National Maritime Museum) are free. Most other museums and attractions have entrance charges.

The London Pass allows free entry to over 60 attractions. Prices for an adult pass range from £59 for a one-day pass (including travel on Tube and bus) to £172 for a six-day pass including travel. Tel: 7293 0972; www.londonpass.com

The **Where Pass** can be purchased ahead of arrival or while in London. This debit card can be loaded with spending money, and to used to buy discounted tickets and access great offers at attractions, restaurants and shops in a single currency transaction. You can also use the card on public transport. Details at www.wherepasslondon.com.

Public Transport The Underground is expensive compared with most European metro systems, but money-saving Travelcards and Oyster cards are available. You can also pay for single journeys with a contactless UK debit card (costing the same fare as Oyster). Children under the age of 11 can travel free on the network, as well as the Docklands Light Railway and buses, providing they are accompanied by an adult (see page 259). Buses are cheaper than the Tube and offer a sightseeing tour along the way, especially if it's a double-decker bus. Alternatively walk – many places, especially in the West End, are closer than you might think.

Tower Bridge at night.

Rush hour at Oxford Circus.

Walking in Green Park in autumn.

LONDON'S ALLURE

What attracts millions of visitors is a potent mixture of continuity and tradition, plus the excitement of never quite knowing what's around the next corner.

enry James described the capital as a 'giant animated encyclopaedia with people for pages.' With all its variety and history, it's hard to know where to start as a tourist, but James's emphasis is a good one. Even though the immensity of London makes it hard to embrace as a whole, and you don't find long-time residents proclaiming their feelings through 'I Heart London' stickers, the people and the culture matter as much as the buildings. To most residents, the city is a collection of communities or villages, once independent but long since swallowed up, along with much of the surrounding countryside, by the expanding metropolis.

Getting a black cab.

At the centre of this patchwork city is a common area of shared London, a city of work and play. This book deals primarily with shared London, the

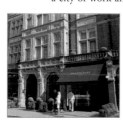

Queen Anne architecture.

essential London of the West End, the City and South Bank, but it also covers some of the interesting local 'villages' such as Hampstead, Islington, Greenwich and Brixton.

London, it is sometimes said, is as unrepresentative of the United Kingdom as New York is of the United States. There's some truth in this. Both cities have astonishingly cosmopolitan populations, they are important centres of international finance, their restaurants are almost as diverse as their immigrants, they pioneer the latest fashions, and their range of shops and theatres is absurdly disproportionate to their size.

But London is umbilically linked to the rest of Britain in some crucial respects. Unlike New York, it is a capital city, spawning governmental institutions. It is also an ancient city, dating back to Roman times. Foreign forces have not occupied it since the Normans arrived in 1066 and, although it was bombed during World War II, most of its iconic buildings survived.

As a result, it exudes a palpable sense of the nation's history. You can walk in the footsteps of Shakespeare, or Dickens, or Churchill. You can journey along the Thames, as Henry VIII did. You can visit the room in the Tower of London where Sir Francis Drake lived out his last days. You can drink in the pubs where Dr Samuel Johnson drank. You can sit in the reading room where Karl Marx studied. This book will show you how to do all these things, and more.

WHO LIVES IN LONDON

The city has absorbed many waves of immigrants and, with more than a quarter of central London's population born outside the UK, is a truly international metropolis.

Celts, Romans, Saxons, Angles, Jutes, Danes and Normans were the first to tumble into London's melting pot. The first South East Asian immigrants arrived in 1579, followed by Indians, Huguenots, Irish and the dispossessed of Eastern Europe. And always there was the tide of new blood from the rest of Britain, drawn to London by hopes of fame, fortune, anonymity, or simply a new start. Today, nearly one in three of London's 8.6 million residents is from a minority ethnic group, and around 300 languages are spoken.

The Cockney

So is there any such thing as a 'true' Londoner? 'Cockneys' would seem to qualify – the definition of which is a native of East London, someone born within hearing of Bow Bells (St Mary-le-Bow church). Being a cockney is as

Girls in Camden.

> Londoners frequently complain about overcrowding. But the population was just as high in 1931 when it reached over 8 million, around the same as it is today.

much a state of mind as it is a turn of phrase, and it is not exclusively genetic. They no longer need to be white and Anglo Saxon; they can also be Italian, West Indian, Jewish and Pakistani. Nor do cockneys necessarily have to live in London; the high cost of property has driven many out, and neighbouring towns such as Stevenage have large cockney populations. So what then makes a cockney? Certain traditions, being a member

of an identifiable urban group, a distinctive language – and a quick sense of humour.

Cockney is a London accent with no use of the aspirant 'h', the 't' in the middle of words such as 'butter', or the final 'g' in words ending 'ing'. Cockneys traditionally spoke in a rhyming slang said to have originated among barrow boys who didn't want their customers to understand their conversations. A 'whistle' is a suit, short for whistle and flute, 'trouble and strife' means wife; new slang terms are continually being invented. True cockneys are traditionally perceived to be shrewd, street-wise people, who prefer to work for themselves and who value freedom more than wealth. The aristocracy of the cockneys are the pearly kings and queens, whose suits are embroidered with mother-of-pearl buttons – a marketing gimmick in the 19th century and now only worn at festivals (see www.pearlysociety.co.uk for events).

Century of immigration

In the 19th century the port of London was the largest in the world, and clippers such as the *Cutty Sark* had races to bring the year's first tea crops home from China. The Chinese community was in Limehouse, where Sherlock Holmes went to mull over his latest conundrums in the relaxing atmosphere of the opium dens. Ming Street, Peking Street and Mandarin Street are the sole legacy of the community that was heavily bombed in World War II. Today, Chinatown is around Gerrard Street in Soho. Resident Chinese opened restaurants here after the end of World War II to cater for British and US forces. Although today the streets and annual Chinese New Year's festivities mark this out as the centre of London's Chinese population of 80,000, they live in all parts of the capital.

Catching up on Paternoster Square.

Street performers on the South Bank.

The traumas of 19th-century Europe led to the mass exodus of Jews, and East London became England's 'Staten Island', with half a dozen refugee ships arriving every day. The Jews settled around the East End, giving it a dominant character. Since then the community, once around 250,000, has dispersed mainly to the North London districts of Stamford Hill, Golders Green and Finchley.

The Irish had been coming to Britain since the Anglo-Norman invasion of Ireland in the late 12th century. Mainly Catholic, they suffered for their faith in the Gordon Riots of 1780. A dozen years later St Patrick's Catholic Church was built in Soho in a former bordello, and is popular with London's migrant community – today it holds services in Spanish, Portuguese and Cantonese.

Irish immigration during the 19th century was brought about largely through the Great Famine of 1846–52, when around million people died of starvation. The Irish were a significant force in the 19th-century building boom, especially on the railways, and many settled in Camden and Kilburn. Today's population, around three percent of Londoners, is scattered mainly across north and west London.

Playing boules in Clerkenwell.

European settlers

Following the German invasion of Poland in 1939, the 33,000-strong Polish military in exile settled as a state-within-a-state in Mayfair and Kensington. Their pilots shot down one in seven German planes in the 1940 Battle of Britain. At the end of World War II, 150,000 were settled in London. While that number later dropped, a new wave of immigrants from Poland, after it joined the EU in 2004, meant 124,000 Poles were resident in London in 2013.

THE LONDON CABBIE

Perhaps the closest that most visitors get to meeting a true Londoner is when they catch a cab. Taxi drivers – or cabbies – are experts on the city and are essential to its life, coursing through its veins in their black cells (not that all the cabs are black any more: advertising has turned some of them into travelling billboards).

Cabbies take pride in their job, knowing that nowhere else in the world does a taxi driver need to know so much in order to qualify for a licence to work. Would-be drivers must spend up to four years learning London in minute detail (called 'doing the Knowledge') by travelling the streets of the metropolis on a moped and working out routes, before passing a special driving test.

About 25,000 drivers work in London, of whom half are owner-drivers. In all, there are more than 15,000 vehicles. The classic cab, known as the FX4, was launched in 1959 and some models are still going strong. The newer Metro-cab, increasingly widespread, is a more spacious vehicle.

In the past, many taxi drivers were white, working class men, a large proportion of whom were Jewish. The demographics are changing. These days there is a small, but growing proportion of women (around 15 percent), and a fifth of new drivers are from overseas, and over half are first-generation immigrants

A new threat to the cab drivers' business is the growth of Uber. The app, which allows the booking of private ride hire (without checks or the need for drivers to acquire 'The Knowledge'), is usually a cheaper option and therefore cabbies are losing potential business. In February 2016, thousands of black-cab drivers took to their vehicles to block traffic in Westminster and Whitehall to protest against Transport for London's licensing of Uber.

Soaking up the sun in Grosvenor Square.

The Italians first settled around the church of St Peter's in Clerkenwell, in an area known to the residents as The Hill and to Londoners as Little Italy. The population was at its height from 1900 to 1930 but, when Italians living in Britain were interned during World War II, their role as restaurateurs began to be eroded by Greek Cypriots, who had been filtering into Britain since the 1920s. Disruptions on Cyprus caused further immigration in the 1950s and 1960s, with Greek and Turkish Cypriots (and Turkish Kurds) amicably settling side by side in North East London, mainly in Haringey. Today they are more dispersed, settling in areas such as Southgate and Enfield.

Seasonal Arabs

In summer, when Middle East temperatures become too hot for comfort, London has traditionally attracted many Gulf Arabs, who spend much of their time enjoying the coolness of the parks and the shopping opportunities. First coming in the wake of the oil price hikes of the 1970s, they funded a mosque in Regent's Park, which can hold 1,800 worshippers.

'Seasonal' Arabs are less common since Iraq War of 2003, but there are resident communities from Egypt, Iraq and Morocco. Most live in Kensington and Bayswater, and they congregate in Edgware Road, north of Marble Arch, where Lebanese restaurants, sheesha cafés and shops shine into the night. London is still one of the largest Arab media centres.

Commonwealth immigrants

The 20th century saw immigration mostly from the Commonwealth, and the resulting ethnic influence extends as far as Heathrow. The

WHERE TO SPOT THE ROYALS

On the second Saturday in June, the Queen's official birthday, she travels by carriage to Horse Guards Parade for the Trooping the Colour ceremony. In November she is transported by state coach for the State Opening of Parliament, escorted along the Mall by the Household Cavalry. Also in November, she attends the service for Remembrance Sunday at the Cenotaph in Whitehall. The engagements of the Royal Family are listed daily in the Court Circular in national newspapers such as *The* Times and the *Daily Telegraph*. If you are more interested in spotting Prince Harry and Princesses Beatrice and Eugenie – and other celebs – try the more exclusive nightclubs, such as Boujis (members only) in Thurloe Street, South Kensington, or Mahiki in Dover Street, Mayfair.

airport itself was largely built by construction workers from India's Punjab. After the Sikhs came the Caribbeans, who found work on London's buses, Underground railway network and in the National Health Service.

But while London likes to think of itself as a multicultural society, it has few black or Asian top administrators or civil servants. You can pass through the City, the Inns of Court or Docklands without meeting many business tycoons, leading lawyers or top editors from the settlers' communities. Until the general election of 1987, there were no black or ethnic-minority Members of Parliament – that situation has since changed and in 2015 there were 42 (6.6 percent of all MPs) elected.

Why there's a welcome

Partly because London's vast number of hotels, bars and restaurants have a great need for cheap but hard-working labour, immigration has been a less contentious issue in the capital than elsewhere in the country. That said, in the current economic climate, there are worries about the pressures migrants place on public services, and the lifting of work restrictions on people coming from Bulgaria and Romania from 2013 is causing concern to some. The call to accept refugees from war-torn Syria in 2015 brought the debate into focus even more sharply.

Happy shoppers at Camden Lock Market.

HOT PROPERTY

Over the past decade or so the dream of living in London has become unattainable for many young people unless they are prepared to rent with friends or strangers, or live with family. London's long overheated property market has pushed the average price of a London home to over £500,000, with properties in the more affluent areas, such as Kensington and Chelsea, averaging £1.5 million. The economic downturn caused prices to drop in the rest of the country, but in London a return to City bonuses and very wealthy international buyers (especially Russian, Arab and Chinese) have meant that prices continue to rise – in some boroughs by as much as 15 percent. Ironically, as more people more to the outskirts of the city where prices are lower, the average annual rise is sharper in areas like Newham and Walthamstow in East London.

Generally, though, London welcomes every type of visitor. Karl Marx, Mahatma Gandhi and Indira Gandhi all studied here. Charles de Gaulle lived in exile here. Writers Paul Theroux, Salman Rushdie and V.S. Naipaul chose to work here. Even Harrods, the quintessentially English store, was owned by an Egyptian, Mohamed Al-Fayed, from 1985 to 2010 and is currently owned by Qatar Holdings. It sells 40 percent of its merchandise to tourists.

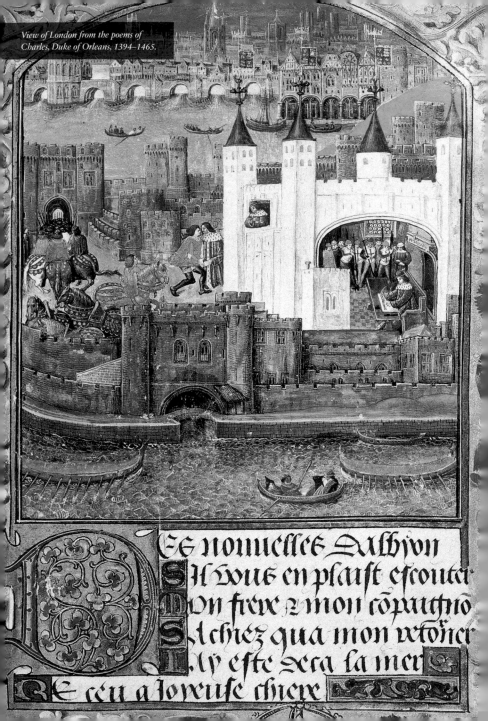

THE MAKING OF LONDON

Fire, plague, population explosions, aerial bombing, economic recessions, urban blight, terrorism... London has survived everything history could throw at it, yet it has remained one of the world's most seductive cities.

In AD 43 the invading Roman army chose gravel banks between what is now Southwark and the City as the site of a strategically important bridge. Roman London, the Celtic 'Llyn-din', ('the fort by the lake'), quickly took shape. However it suffered a setback 17 years later when British guerrillas, led by Queen Boudicca, attacked and burned areas around Lombard Street, Gracechurch Street and Walbrook so completely that archaeologists have identified a change in the colour of the earth.

A rebuilt Londinium, as the Romans called it, had by AD 100 supplanted Colchester as the capital, as well as the trading centre of Britain. But in 410, Rome itself was threatened by the Germanic races from the north and recalled its garrison from England. Culture withered and Londinium crumbled as the Anglo-Saxons allowed the Roman buildings to become derelict.

Recovery and expansion

The city's position made it a natural trading centre and gradually it recovered its importance. In the 8th century the literary monk, the Venerable Bede, called it 'A market for many peoples coming by land and sea'. South of London Bridge, a residential area developed, later known as the Borough.

Two miles (3km) upriver on Thorney Island, the Monastery of St Peter was established, later the great West Minster. Following his accession in 1042, Edward the Confessor moved his court from the City to Westminster, creating the division of royal and mercantile

Aerial view of Roman Londinium from the northwest, c. 2nd century AD.

Roman Londinium had a timber bridge, quays, warehouses, a governor's palace, baths and amphitheatre. Roads radiated to Colchester, York, Chester, Exeter, Bath and Canterbury.

power still in place today. In lieu of making the usual pilgrimage to Rome, he rebuilt the abbey, where most succeeding kings were crowned, married and, until George II (d.1760), buried.

City landmarks

In 1066 William the Conqueror brought the laws of Normandy to England, and gave London privileges that are still honoured today. Self-direction in local affairs was satisfied by the election of a first Mayor (later Lord Mayor) in 1189, with aldermen and a court. A new St Paul's Cathedral was started and the great keep of the White Tower completed in 1097. Westminster Hall was designed as a banqueting hall but, although the largest building of its kind in Europe, fell short of William's dreams – he said it was 'a mere bedchamber' compared to what he had expected. By 1176 work had begun on a stone London Bridge, and the suburb on the south bank was growing.

Union and plague

The city had grown to 50,000 by the time of Geoffrey Chaucer, the 'father of English poetry' – this in spite of the Black Death of 1348, when some 200 bodies a day were taken outside the city and buried in mass graves. This virulent bubonic plague, carried by rats and fleas, ravaged much of Europe but had a particularly

William the Conqueror accompanied by knights and soldiers, by an unknown artist (14th century).

Westminster Hall, c.1460.

devastating effect on London because of the city's narrow streets and insanitary housing.

London stopped growing in the 14th century. The City (now with a capital C) quite simply had no ambitions to get any bigger. Had it wanted to expand, it would have had to change its character, perhaps endangering in the process its hard-won privileges and sacrificing its unique position as a major European market and port. Whatever was happening outside the walls (not completely demolished until the 18th century), the City maintained a blinkered detachment that was not disturbed until Queen Victoria's reign.

The Golden Age

The much married and celebrated divorcé Henry VIII (1491–1547) almost qualifies as the 'father' of modern London, though the changes he brought about were the outcome of a bid for personal freedom from the Church. In 1534, after the Pope refused to annul his marriage to Catherine of Aragon so that he could marry Anne Boleyn, Henry cut all ties with Roman Catholicism. He had already pronounced himself head of the Church of England and

Detail, London from Southwark, c.1630 by an unknown artist.

persuaded Parliament to authorise the dissolution of the monasteries, their property and revenues being granted to the Crown. Cardinal Wolsey's house was added to an expanding palace in Whitehall. Hyde Park and St James's were enclosed as deer parks.

Convent (now Covent) Garden and Clerkenwell, Stepney and Shoreditch, Kennington and Lambeth all expanded during this time, taking London's population to 200,000. A lasting monument to the era is Henry VIII's Hampton Court Palace, southwest of London (see page 224).

Henry's daughter, Elizabeth I, whose mother, Anne Boleyn, had been beheaded for supposed adultery, came to the throne in 1558. She was truly London's queen and the 'Golden Age' began, in commerce, education and the arts. William Shakespeare, a Londoner by adoption, was far from adulated by the authorities. When the Lord Mayor banned theatrical performances from London, he and his fellow playwright Ben Jonson moved outside the Mayor's jurisdiction to new sites on the south bank of the Thames, an area notorious for bear pits, brothels and prisons.

Revolution and style

Being childless, the 'Virgin Queen' Elizabeth chose James VI of Scotland to succeed her as James I of England, thus launching the Stuart dynasty. Religious conflict continued, and a Catholic faction attempted to blow up Parliament in the infamous Gunpowder Plot. On 5 November 1605, Guy (Guido) Fawkes was caught just as he was about to ignite barrels of gunpowder in the cellars. Fawkes was executed but 5 November, Guy Fawkes Day, is still marked with fireworks and the burning of an effigy to represent Fawkes.

Against a background of conflict between the king and Parliament, London responded to a new influence: the Italian architecture of Palladio as seen through the work of Inigo Jones. The purity

Little survives of Tudor London's wood-framed houses with their oversailing upper storeys, but a flavour can be found in the Old Curiosity Shop near Lincoln's Inn (see page 141).

The Great Fire of London 1666, by an anonymous artist, c.1675.

of Jones's style is best seen in the Queen's House at Greenwich, begun in 1616. Three years later came the Banqueting House in Whitehall.

Water, pestilence and fire

Great tragedies lay ahead for London. In 1665 the inadequate water supply and lack of sanitation brought the dreaded plague to the overcrowded city, and before it ran its course some

BUNHILL FIELDS

Local parish burial grounds were unable to cope with the high mortality rate of the 1665 Great Plague. Many victims were buried in plague pits such as the one in Bunhill Fields on City Road (see page 152), where these days city workers eat their lunches. The cemetery was specially built for plague victims, though the site had previously operated as a deposit for old bones from St Paul's churchyard, where space was at a premium. The burial ground was not consecrated and was later associated with Nonconformists, including many notable ones such as Daniel Defoe, John Bunyan, author of *Pilgrim's Progress*, and the poet and artist William Blake.

100,000 inhabitants died. The Great Fire, less than a year later, came as if to cleanse the stricken city. From a baker's shop on Pudding Lane, off Eastcheap Street, the flames raged for five days, watched and recorded by the great 17th-century diarist Samuel Pepys. Miraculously, only half a dozen people were recorded as dead, although the number may well have been higher.

After the fire, 13,000 houses and 87 parish churches lay in ruins, but rebuilding was immediately planned.

Wren's dream

Christopher Wren, Surveyor General to the Crown, was inspired by Paris. London, too, he thought, should have *rond-points* – vistas and streets laid out in a grid pattern. But Wren's best ideas were never realised. Expediency dictated that the new should rise quickly on the sites of the old, with one prudent difference: new buildings were made of brick, not wood.

Wren turned his inventive powers to rebuilding 51 of the City's damaged churches. His achievements lie in the individuality of their soaring towers and steeples that rise above the rooftops. In 1675 work began on his master-piece, a new St Paul's Cathedral.

House building spread through the green fields beyond Soho towards Hyde Park and across the Tyburn road. As the ripple of this 18th-century building ring moved outwards, the older centre was coming to the end of its useful life. The need for better communications brought demands for another river crossing. Westminster Bridge was completed in 1750, but nearly 20 years passed before the City had its own second bridge, at Blackfriars. Whitehall was beginning to take on its 20th-century character, the palace of kings being replaced by the palaces of government.

Splendour and sweatshops

By 1800 London was poised on the brink of a population explosion. In the next 35 years it was to double in size – and the railways were yet to come. While Britain was at war with Napoleonic France, work on public buildings withered, but housing swelled with the increasing numbers of civil servants. Paddington and Marylebone, Camberwell and Kensington, Knightsbridge and Chelsea forged their identities.

Unlike the West End, the East End suffered ribbon building along the roads to Essex.

Queen Elizabeth I, attributed to George Gower.

> *London became increasingly affluent in the early 19th century. Visiting in 1814, the Emperor of Russia asked, 'Where are your poor?' Clearly he had not been east of the Tower of London.*

Whitechapel High Street was "pestered with cot-tages", and Wapping with mean tenements. It was an area vulnerable to the impact of new developments in commerce following the Industrial Revolution. Canals had already linked the Thames with the industrial Midlands. Docks cruelly dismembered the riverside parishes. In 1825, 1,250 houses were swept away for St Katharine's Dock alone. The inhabitants were compressed, sardine-style, into accommodation nearby. The character of the modern East End was in the making. 'Sweatshops' – and the labour to go with them – multiplied in this fertile soil of ruthless competition, poverty and immigration.

By the 1830s the Industrial Revolution was making its impact on the Thames below Wapping. The marshy pools of the Isle of Dogs, long used for duck shooting and hunting, were

Gin Lane, an engraving by William Hogarth, whose works vividly depict 18th-century London life.

deepened to make the West and East India Docks. Wharves and shipyards lined the banks of the river itself in Blackwall, Deptford and Greenwich. With all this activity, London's air was dense with smog – smoke mixed with fog – although this word had not yet been coined.

Congestion and crime

By the early 19th century London was becoming impossibly congested, so bridges were built at Waterloo (1811–17) and Hammersmith (1824–27). London Bridge was rebuilt (1823–31) and foot passengers given a tunnel under the Thames at Wapping.

Courts of law and prisons responded to rising crime, while gentlemen's clubs met the Regency passion for gambling. In Bloomsbury's Gower Street, London University was born, and a fruit and vegetable market came to Covent Garden. Great collections were housed in the British Museum and National Gallery.

Londoners were on the move. In 1829 Mr Shillibeer introduced them to the omnibus (bus), and the first steam train arrived with the London & Greenwich Railway of 1836. Terminal

Covent Garden, by Phoebus Leven, 1864.

By the end of the 19th century, London was throbbing with life and unloading the British Empire's fortunes across its wharves. Its docklands were called the warehouse of the world.

stations followed at Euston, King's Cross and Paddington by 1853, and at Blackfriars, Charing Cross and St Pancras by 1871.

Cleaning up the Thames

At Westminster, the Houses of Parliament burnt down in 1834 when a furnace overheated, but soon Charles Barry and Augustus Pugin's Gothic extravaganza rose phoenix-like from the ashes: the House of Lords by 1847, the House of Commons and clock tower by 1858 and the Victoria Tower by 1860.

By this time, the 'sights' of London had dropped into place. The British Museum gave a home to the Elgin Marbles in 1816, and Trafalgar Square gave a hero's welcome to Nelson's column in 1843. The City Corporation, meanwhile, made efforts to unlock the congested streets, cutting swathes through Holborn's houses and cemeteries for the viaduct to bridge the Fleet valley. Fleet Street, the Strand and Whitehall were by-passed by the grand boulevard of the Victoria Embankment. Tower Bridge opened in 1894, steel dressed up in stone to make it look historic.

By 1859 another problem had arisen, serious enough to cause the adjournment of the House of Commons: the unbearable stench from the

THE GREAT EXHIBITION OF 1851

In 1851 Queen Victoria opened the Great Exhibition of the Works of all Nations in Hyde Park, its magnificent glass building – dubbed 'the Crystal Palace' – displaying Britain's skills and achievements to the world and attracting some 6 million visitors. With the profits of £186,000, Prince Albert, Queen Victoria's German-born husband, realised his great ambition: a centre of learning. Temples to the arts and sciences blossomed in Kensington's gardens, nicknamed 'Albertopolis'. What was later named the Victoria and Albert Museum opened in 1852, moving to its present site in 1857, followed by the Royal Albert Hall in 1871, the Albert Memorial in 1872, and the Natural History Museum in 1881.

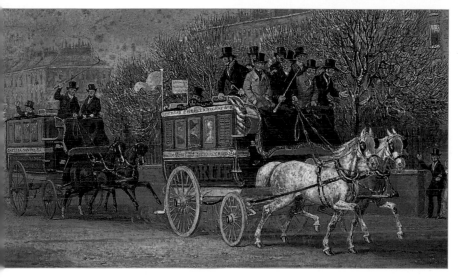

Detail from A Street Scene with Two Omnibuses, by James Pollard, 1845.

Thames. Londoners still depended largely on the river for drinking water, and at the same time disposed of their sewage in it. Cholera was common until the Board of Works' Chief Engineer, Joseph Bazalgette, devised a scheme to take the sewage well downstream to Barking in Essex and release it into the river after treatment. His scheme is still the basis of the modern drainage system.

Dickens and social reforms

But London had become polarised. In the east, there was poverty and overcrowding, and in the west affluence and spacious living. The novelist Charles Dickens described the refuge of down-and-outs and penny-a-nighters in novels such as *Bleak House* (1853). Public conscience was aroused by his writings and those of the social reformer Henry Mayhew. This encouraged both political action and private philanthrophy.

The railways and new roads did some of the reformers' work for them, sweeping away many insanitary dwellings. Soon London's city's edge opened up due to the first suburban railway, the Metropolitan, in 1863.

World War II and the Blitz

Britain's capital has evolved piecemeal over centuries, without any overall plans. Twice in its history, however, it has had to be rebuilt. On the first occasion, after the Great Fire of 1666, and on the second, after World War II and the Blitz, which killed 29,000 London civilians.

World War II left Britain impoverished and without the empire that had provided so much of its wealth. Utilitarian buildings, often of charmless concrete, replaced those destroyed in the Blitz and were condemned by Prince Charles, who said that modern town planners and architects did more damage than the Luftwaffe.

Swinging London

The 1950s were a time of post-war austerity with rationing still in place and efforts concentrated on regeneration in the face of a rapidly disintegrating empire. But there was also a massive baby boom and by the mid-1960s, as the post-war babies became teenagers, times were a-changing. While Paris became the centre of serious political action, London was the place to have fun, where old notions of deference, responsibility and hierarchy were swept away, cultural and sexual attitudes were liberated, and fashion and pop music prevailed. Swinging London centred on Soho's Carnaby Street, the King's Road in Chelsea, where Mary Quant's

Firefighting during the Blitz, World War II.

shop Bazaar epitomised the new fashions, and Barbara Hulanicki's store Biba in Kensington.

Meanwhile, many of the East End's pre-war slums were replaced by new housing estates and tower blocks to meet the growing demand for decent public housing. The deep social problems created by the estates had yet to make an impact.

The roaring eighties

In the 1970s the pendulum swung the other way. Traditional industries collapsed all over Britain. Container ships made London's old wharves and warehouses redundant and the port that had once welcomed 14,000 vessels a year crumbled into dereliction.

By the time the economic boom of the 1980s created a demand for taller office buildings, there was somewhere convenient to put them: the former docklands. The area around Canary Wharf, with its 800ft (244-metre) -high One Canada Square tower, was dubbed Chicago-on-Thames. Meanwhile, for home buyers, the dream of living in London itself faded as the strong economy pushed London house prices and rents well beyond the pockets of the lower paid.

> In 2012 London celebrated the Queen's Diamond Jubilee, marking 60 years since her accession to the throne. The high point was a river pageant, which saw thousands of people line the banks of the Thames to cheer on the royal barge.

The South Bank soars

The next area to be revived was Bankside, the south bank of the Thames where Shakespeare first staged his greatest plays and Dickens mined the material for many of his novels. The London Eye, the giant observation wheel erected to mark the millennium (see page 172) indicates one end of this area, while at the other end towers the Shard, London's iconic landmark and Western Europe's tallest building, and the 'Walkie Talkie' building hosting the Sky Garden.

In between are theatres, restaurants and river walks, recreating the lively hub of activity this area had been 400 years previously. Dominating the South Bank is the Tate Modern, a disused

Office workers in Canary Wharf.

Newly elected mayor Sadiq Khan with Labour Party candidate Rosena Allin-Khan in Tooting.

power station transformed into a fabulous modern art museum. A replica of Shakespeare's Globe Theatre is to the east, and next to it is the new indoor Jacobean theatre, the Sam Wanamaker Playhouse. The Millennium Bridge, the first new river crossing in central London for more than a century, allows you to walk from St Paul's Cathedral to Tate Modern in seven minutes.

LONDON'S MAYOR

In 1997 the UK elected a Labour government led by Tony Blair, ending 17 years of Conservative rule under which the Greater London Council, which had administered London, had been abolished. The new regime decided to restore a measure of self-government to the capital by creating a new post: an elected mayor (distinct from the ceremonial post of Lord Mayor, whose role is confined to the City). The first election was won by Ken Livingstone, who had controversially led the GLC. He was succeeded by the exuberant Tory MP Boris Johnson in 2008, who banned alcohol on public transport and introduced a cycle hire scheme (the Boris Bike). Johnson served two terms as mayor, before being succeeded by Labour MP Sadiq Khan in 2016.

London's Olympic legacy

London's 2012 Olympics were a huge success, with Danny Boyle's opening ceremony, described as 'a love letter to Britain', being particularly memorable. For two weeks in the summer, all eyes were on London as athletes from over 200 countries competed in 300 events, mainly in the Queen Elizabeth Olympic Park. Venues used for Olympic events are now open to the public, including Zaha Hadid's Aquatics Centre and the Lee Valley VeloPark.

'Legacy' was the key to London's successful bid, with a promise of large-scale redevelopment of some of the capital's most deprived areas, located in the east of the city especially around Stratford. At the same time, the hitherto bleak area around King's Cross and St Pancras stations has been turned into a fitting setting for the new Eurostar terminal. The restoration and reopening of the 5-star St Pancras Hotel (now the St Pancras Renaissance Hotel), designed in the 1860s by Sir George Gilbert Scott, seems to symbolise London's capacity for reinvention and renewal.

Continuing the sporting theme, England hosted the prestigious 2015 Rugby World Cup, with several matches held in London, including the final.

DECISIVE DATES

Julius Caesar on an engraving from 1860.

Early times

55 BC
Julius Caesar discovers Britain. He launches an invasion and defeats Cassivellaunus, a British chieftain. However, Roman forces do not stay.

AD 43
Londinium settled during second Roman invasion; a bridge is built over the Thames.

AD 61
Boudicca, Queen of the Iceni tribe in East Anglia, sacks the city before being defeated.

c.200
Three-mile (5km) -long city wall built.

410
Troops are withdrawn to defend Rome.

449–527
Jutes, Angles and Saxons arrive in Britain, dividing it into separate kingdoms.

604
The first St Paul's Cathedral founded by King Ethelbert.

c.750
Monastery of St Peter is founded on Thorney Island, later to become Westminster Abbey.

8th century
Shipping and manufacturing flourish on the river bank near today's Strand.

884
London becomes the capital of Britain under Alfred the Great.

1042
Edward the Confessor moves his court from the city to Westminster and rebuilds the abbey.

After the Conquest

1066
William I, Duke of Normandy and descendant of the Vikings, conquers Britain. He introduces French and the feudal system.

1078
Tower of London's White Tower built.

1154
The Plantagenets, descendants of the French House of Anjou, take over throne.

1176
A new London Bridge is built of stone.

1189
City's first mayor is elected.

1240
First parliament sits in Westminster.

1290
Jews are expelled from the city – a ban not lifted until the 17th century.

Statue of Boudicca on a chariot on the north side of Westminster Bridge.

Richard I, a Plantagenet king.

Henry VIII.

1588
William Shakespeare (1568–1616) begins his dramatic career in London.

1605
Guy Fawkes tries to blow up Parliament.

1620
The Pilgrim Fathers set sail for America.

1642–9
Civil war between the Cavalier Royalists and the Republican Roundheads. Royalists are defeated. Charles I is executed.

1660
After 11 years, monarchy is restored under Charles II.

1660–9
Samuel Pepys writes his famous diary.

1664 6
The Great Plague kills one-fifth of the population.

1300
St Paul's Cathedral, now rebuilt in stone after a fire in 1087, is consecrated.

1381
Much of London is laid waste by the Peasants' Revolt led by Wat Tyler.

1485
The Tudor Age begins. Of Welsh descent, the Tudors preside over the English Renaissance, under Queen Elizabeth I (reigned 1558–1603).

1514
Building of Hampton Court Palace begins.

1532
Henry VIII builds Palace of Whitehall, the largest in Europe. It catches fire in 1698.

1534
Henry VIII declares himself head of the Church of England and dissolves the monasteries.

1536
St James's Palace is built.

1666
The Great Fire destroys 80 percent of London's buildings.

1675
Sir Christopher Wren (1632–1723) begins work on St Paul's Cathedral.

1694
The Bank of England is established.

1714
The House of Hanover is ushered in by George I. The architectural style prevalent

The Gunpowder Plot conspirators.

for the next 20 years is known as Georgian.

1735
George II makes 10 Downing Street available to Sir Robert Walpole, Britain's first prime minister.

1764
The Literary Club is founded by Samuel Johnson, compiler of the first English dictionary.

1783
Last public execution held at Tyburn (Marble Arch).

1811–20
The Prince Regent, later George IV, gives his name to the Regency style.

1820
Regent's Canal completed.

1824
The National Gallery is established.

1829
Prime Minister Robert Peel establishes a police force

(nicknamed 'peelers' and later 'bobbies').

1834
Rebuilding of the current Houses of Parliament, after the old palace of Westminster is destroyed by fire.

The Age of Empire

1837
Queen Victoria comes to the throne at 18.

1840s
Trafalgar Square laid out on the site of royal stables to commemorate Nelson's victory.

1849
Tea merchant Henry Charles Harrod takes over a small grocer's shop in Knightsbridge.

1851
The Great Exhibition is held in Hyde Park.

1857
The Victoria and Albert Museum opens.

Queen Victoria and her family.

1859
A 13.5-tonne bell, nicknamed Big Ben, is hung in the clock tower of the Houses of Parliament.

1863
The first section of the Underground railway is built between Paddington and Farringdon Street.

1888
Jack the Ripper strikes in Whitechapel.

1890
First electric railway is built in deep-level tunnels, between the City and Stockwell.

1894
Tower Bridge is built.

1903
Westminster Cathedral is built. Marks & Spencer's first penny bazaar opens in Brixton.

1904
The first London motor taxi is licensed.

1914
World War I begins.

Trafalgar Square, 19th century.

1915
Zeppelins and, later, Gotha airplanes begin dropping incendiary and explosive bombs on the city.

1922
British Broadcasting Company transmits its first programmes from Savoy Hill.

1923
The first FA Cup Final is held at Wembley Stadium.

1939–45
World War II. Children are evacuated, and London is heavily bombed.

Modern London
1951
Festival of Britain; new concert halls built on South Bank near Waterloo.

1956
The Clean Air Act, introducing smokeless fuel, ends the asphyxiating smogs.

1976
National Theatre opens.

1982
Flood-preventing Thames Barrier, begun after a tidal surge killed hundreds of people in 1953, is finished.

1986
The Greater London Council is abolished.

1991
The first Canary Wharf tower is completed in Docklands.

1994
The first trains run through the Channel Tunnel to Paris and Brussels.

1997
Shakespeare's Globe opens on Bankside.

2000
Tate Modern opens on Bankside. The London Eye opens at County Hall.

2001
Greater London Authority is set up under Mayor Ken Livingstone.

2002
The Millennium Bridge opens again after its unsettling wobble is cured.

2003
A £5 congestion charge is imposed on cars entering central areas.

2005
On 6 July London is chosen to stage 2012 Olympic Games. The following day bombs explode on three Tube trains and a bus, killing 52 people.

2007
The new Wembley Stadium opens. Eurostar terminal opens at St Pancras.

Sebastian Coe at London 2012.

2008
The 'credit crunch' – house prices crash and Northern Rock bank is nationalised.

2009
MPs' expenses scandal rocks Parliament.

2010
The first coalition government is formed since World War II.

2011
Phone hacking scandal – the *News of the World* closes after 168 years.

2012
The nation celebrates Queen Elizabeth II's Diamond Jubilee – 60 years on the throne. London Olympics are held and are a resounding success.

2013
A viewing platform called The View from the Shard opens. The Duchess of Cambridge gives birth to Prince George on 22 July.

2014
A field of ceramic poppies is laid at the Tower of London as a memorial art installation commemorating the centenary of World War I.

2015
The Duchess of Cambridge gives birth to Princess Charlotte on 2 May. London hosts the Rugby World Cup Final at Twickenham.

2016
Labour MP Sadiq Khan succeeds Boris Johnson as Mayor of London.

Hackney Empire Theatre, which opened
in 1901 as a music hall.

THEATRELAND

Shakespeare, Sondheim, ABBA and a host of stars – the great (and the not-so-great) plays and musicals turn up in the West End, and all kinds of innovative shows take place in fringe venues around the city.

On stage at the Globe.

simply to savour the experience. The brainchild of American actor-director Sam Wanamaker, who didn't live to see it completed, the theatre is a replica of the 1599 auditorium in which William Shakespeare staged many of his plays. Like many theatres over the years, the original Globe was destroyed by fire. A new indoor theatre, the Sam Wanamaker Playhouse, was completed in 2014; it stages period plays and live music in an intimate setting lit by beeswax candles from grand chandeliers.

> It is with good reason that London is famous for its amazing variety of theatre; here you can see everything from Shakespeare to new British playwrights, from cutting-edge fringe to long-running musicals.

The opening of Shakespeare's Globe on Bankside in 1997 was seen by some as a triumph of culture over commercialism. Here, for the price of a ticket, you can sit on rock-hard benches (or stand in the yard), squint through the sun streaming in through the opening in the thatch roof, and peer around pillars to try to catch lines from the acoustically challenged stage. You may even be disturbed by a noisy overhead helicopter, but it's all part of the unique experience.

This is theatre heritage to appeal to the tourist and purists alike, an Elizabethan playhouse risen from the rubble of time; many head there

That's show business

London's theatrical history goes back to a playhouse opened at Shoreditch in 1576 by James Burbage, the son of a carpenter and travelling player, and its development encompasses a strong tradition of taking sideswipes at social issues. In the *Roaring Girl* of 1611, for example, playwright Thomas Dekker dwelt at some length on London's traffic jams.

In modern times, live theatre was expected to succumb first to films, and then to TV. However, theatre is still one of those essential attractions every visitor to London should experience – even if many opt for a blockbuster musical rather than anything more adventurous.

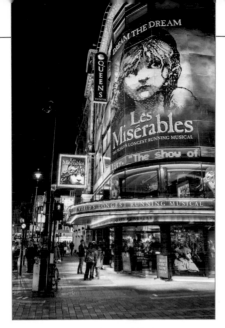

Les Mis at the Queen's Theatre, Shaftesbury Avenue.

In the days when *South Pacific* and *Camelot* dominated musical theatre, no one would have guessed the West End would hijack the genre from Broadway. Yet in the 1970s, Tim Rice and Andrew Lloyd Webber first demonstrated the possibilities of rock-musicals with *Jesus Christ Superstar* and *Evita*, before Lloyd Webber moved on to dominate the stage musical with *Cats* (a collaboration with the late T.S. Eliot) and *Phantom of the Opera*.

Critics might scoff, but shrewd theatre brains saw that income from musicals could underwrite

WHERE TO SIT

It's useful to know the terminology of English theatre layout. What in America is called the 'Orchestra' (the seats at the lowest level) is in England called the 'Stalls'; then, in ascending order, come the 'Dress Circle' (or 'Royal Circle'), and the 'Upper Circle' (or 'Grand Circle' or 'Balcony'). The very top balconies, once known as 'The Gods', are not recommended to anyone with vertigo or a hearing impediment. If in a party, consider asking for a box, which can sometimes work out cheaper than seats in the stalls. You'll have more leg room, too. As they tend to be at the sides of the theatre, however, boxes sometimes have a restricted view of the stage.

other work. Trevor Nunn masterminded the Royal Shakespeare Company's 1985 production of *Les Misérables*, which went on to conquer the world, and is still running in London. More recently the National Theatre's epic production of *War Horse* is still going strong, now on stage in Drury Lane, after opening in 2007.

Musicals dominate the modern West End and are its biggest money-spinners: Roald Dahl's much loved story *Matilda* burst into life as an award-winning musical and another of his books, *Charlie and the Chocolate Factory*, was recreated for the stage by Sam Mendes; *Billy Elliot the Musical* has been another successful screen-to-stage production.

Broadway has reasserted its clout, whether in revivals of musical classics like *Guys and Dolls* and *Chicago* or recent successes such as *The Producers*, *Wicked* and *Monty Python's Spamalot*. The trend that gets critics tearing their hair out, though, is for the pop-music musical, known as 'jukebox musicals', reprising the song catalogue of favourite artists. Begun by ABBA-based *Mamma Mia!*, this has continued with *The Commitments* (Motown) and *Jersey Boys* (The Four Seasons).

Nicole Kidman and Stephen Campbell-Moore at the Noel Coward Theatre.

High visitor numbers to London in 2012 during the Olympics and Diamond Jubilee, leading to an increased number to London's Theatreland, showed no let up in the following years. 2014 saw ticket sales up yet again, with a 1 percent increase on the previous year to 14.7 million attendances, and sales up to £624 million, a 6.5 percent growth.

The plots woven around the songs are wafer-thin, but the crowds keep coming in.

Some claim musical-mania has squeezed out new drama, but the theatre pages in national newspapers don't really bear this out. New productions of classics still appear each year, new writing still gets aired in fringe and mainstream venues, and writers such as Tom Stoppard, Alan Bennett or Mark Ravenhill do not lack audiences. Well-known stage actors, now better known on screen, often return to the stage – most recently Dame Judy Dench, Glenn Close and Sir Kenneth Branagh.

A Royal Shakespeare Company production of Hecuba.

Hollywood-on-Thames

As well as locally grown stars such as Michael Gambon, Ian McKellen, Maggie Smith and Diana Rigg, American actors have never been strangers to the West End – Dustin Hoffman played Shylock in *The Merchant of Venice* here in 1989. Lately, however, this flow has become a flood, as nearly every Hollywood name has seemed to feel a need to add a London stage appearance to their résumé.

Nicole Kidman, Val Kilmer, Woody Harrelson and Christian Slater have all graced hopped over the pond to grace London's stages. Kathleen Turner won huge praise in a production of *Who's Afraid of Virginia Woolf*, but London's favourite American actor is Kevin Spacey. After scoring a massive hit in *The Iceman Cometh* in 1998, he was artistic director of the venerable Old Vic theatre from 2003 to 2015, where he brought in a string of high-profile names and won critical acclaim.

National companies

London has two major state-subsidised companies: the National Theatre and the Royal Shakespeare Company. The National has the advantage of its own huge building on the South Bank, with three auditoria. Not everyone was impressed with the stark concrete exterior when it opened in 1976, but today it is a firm favourite with the British public. By contrast, the RSC gave up its London home at the Barbican Centre in 2001 (its main base is in Shakespeare's home town, Stratford-upon-Avon) and now rotates between a number of theatres.

The previous director of the National Theatre, Nicholas Hytner, who stepped down in 2015, introduced variety and innovation into the programme, and aided by business sponsorship, has made many seats available for just £15. *War Horse*, with its stunning life-sized puppets, is just one example of the National's work, now very profitably transferred to the West End. One of Hytner's final innovations was a massive project called NT Future, a £70-million scheme to open up the National's buildings and to contribute to the regeneration of the South Bank.

Off-West End to the fringe

There are many smaller or 'fringe' venues around London, from substantial theatres to tiny rooms above pubs. Their productions range

War Horse at the National Theatre.

from low-budget Shakespeare to political shows and international theatre. Much of new young British writing is dark, funny and well-observed.

The Royal Court, Donmar Warehouse, the Young Vic, Almeida Theatre in Islington and the Tricycle in Kilburn are the main outlets for new writing, which between them have pioneered many of London's most exciting recent productions. Lively pub theatres include the Bush (in Shepherd's Bush), the King's Head (Islington) and the Gate at Notting Hill Gate.

Every summer there is a very enjoyable open-air theatre season in Regent's Park, focusing on Shakespeare's comedies.

WAYS TO BUY YOUR TICKETS

Despite the notion that everything in London is so successful that it sells out fast, most shows do have seats, especially early in the week. It's the more expensive tickets – generally for the top musicals – that are usually hardest to obtain, and those in smaller theatres with famous actors. The best way to get tickets is from the theatre itself, either by calling at the box office or online. This cuts out the sometimes extortionate fees of ticket agencies. Agencies and hotels are most handy for obtaining hard-to-get tickets. A reputable agency should be a member of STAR (Society of Ticket Agents and Retailers), and follow a clear code of conduct.

Many theatres offer unsold tickets for performances the same day at reduced 'standby' prices, although some are only available to students. Tickets for same-day performances, or up to a week in advance, are also available at around half-price from the TKTS ticket booths in Leicester Square (Mon–Sat 10am–7pm, Sun 11am–4.30pm). Matinees can be cheaper, but understudies may replace the stars. The National Theatre puts some same-day tickets on sale at 9.30am at its box office.

Tickets are offered outside theatres by touts for anything up to 10 times their face value. This isn't illegal, surprisingly, but make sure you check the ticket's face value and the position of the seat before purchasing.

EATING OUT

London's thousands of restaurants and cafés offer some of the world's best culinary experiences. New eateries open as frequently as new movies, so how do you find the good and avoid the bad?

Hipsters out to lunch.

London, once derided for mediocre cuisine, is today straining under a bombardment of Michelin stars and it's considered one of the world's greatest cities for dining. You can eat sushi and ceviche, tapas and tagliatelle, borscht and bhajis; you can try pizza with Japanese toppings and deconstructed desserts; choose from nearly 200 Thai restaurants or dine on world-class contemporary British cuisine.

This culinary revolution began in the 1980s, when the restructuring of London's financial world produced a legion of footloose brokers and traders looking for places to spend skyrocketing salaries. Innovative restaurants, like designer labels, were avidly sought out. At around the same time, the British discovered food. Cookery programmes proliferated on TV, bookshops filled up with lavishly illustrated cookbooks and newspapers covered new restaurant openings with ever more excitement. The phenomenon of the 'celebrity chef' was born, and famous chefs took to running their restaurant chains rather than doing much cooking.

Until then it had been *de rigueur* for chefs to be French, and the country's best-known were Albert and Michel Roux of Le Gavroche. Now local stars emerged: Ruth Rogers and the late Rose Gray opened their River Café in Fulham, West London, presenting Tuscan cooking with a metropolitan twist. Terence Conran, the style-maker whose Habitat stores had brought the earthy kitchenware of Provence to Britain, opened Bibendum restaurant in the Art Deco Michelin tyre company building in Fulham Road, the first of a string of Conran venues in striking locations. The epitome of the style is Quaglino's, near Green Park, with a look that deliberately recalls a 1930s ocean liner. This was food as entertainment, out-to-impress dining that symbolised the early 1990s, but – though some have maintained high standards – these are not restaurants where you can generally expect much individuality or charm.

Current movers and shakers

Nowadays, London's food scene has settled down a little: it's still devoted to fads – Peruvian one year, Argentinian the next – but

English cuisine at St John Bread and Wine.

alongside them there's also a more consistent idea of quality, as the city has got used being one of the world's dining capitals. There is more emphasis now on good quality, seasonal local ingredients.

Some stalwarts have absorbed new trends while sticking to what they know their clients want: the River Café remains inviolate, The Ivy and Le Caprice are ever-popular with the rich and famous, the Savoy Grill with businessmen, and Le Gavroche with traditionalist gourmands. The fashion for 'mega restaurants' has faded – the style has moved onto 'industrial chic' – all exposed beams and heavy wooden tables in an informal setting.

Attention has shifted back from restaurant entrepreneurs to cooks, although London's best-known chef, Gordon Ramsay, manages to be both. A former footballer whose cooking skills won Michelin recognition and whose

Dinner by Heston at the Mandarin Oriental.

short temper made him a TV star, Ramsay still cooks himself (sometimes), installs talented young chefs in his restaurant stable and is an inescapable media face. London's grand hotels, traditional bastions of good cookery, have spruced up their restaurants to keep up with the dining boom, and Ramsay has taken astute advantage of this, taking over Claridge's restaurant but also opening less formal restaurants like Union Street Café. His protégée Angela Hartnett now has her own restaurant, Murano. There are many other inventive British chefs around town, notably Heston Blumenthal, whose classical, French-based training has developed into an eclectic, adventurous approach. Other stars include Chris Galvin, in charge of the top-floor restaurant at the Hilton on Park Lane (as Galvin at Windows), Tom Aikens, with his eponymous restaurant in Kensington, and Jason Atherton, who trained with Ramsay and now runs 15 of his own restaurants including the Michelin-starred Pollen Street Social.

Italian antipasti.

Chefs hard at work at St John.

Around the world, and back again

Many fans of eating out in London, however, say that what they enjoy most is the incredible variety of cuisines on offer. Its status as an international city attracts fine cooks from every part of the world to work here. French chefs are still prominent, such as Hélène Darroze (The Connaught) or Alain

WHERE TO EAT

The biggest concentration of restaurants is in the West End, with Soho providing the most interesting choice. Chinatown, north of Leicester Square, has a bewildering array of Asian eateries, and Covent Garden good-value pre-theatre suppers. Kensington and Chelsea, with their abundance of wealthy residents, contain many expensive restaurants but also a good sprinkling of reasonably priced bistros. Islington and Notting Hill also offer a good choice, and Clerkenwell and Shoreditch house some of the most interesting new restaurants. The City, whose oyster bars and restaurants cater to business lunchers, tends to be a ghost town in the evenings and at weekends.

Vietnamese food in Hoxton.

Since its appearance in the 1990s, the local gastropub has started to become London's equivalent of the Parisian street corner bistro – essentially a restaurant serving good food in an informal setting.

have limitless wallets or full mastery of the strategems used to get a table in restaurants such as Gordon Ramsay's, these are places that are only visited for a special occasion. Among more regularly accessible eating places, London's fad-chasing can be a source of disappointment, as time and again restaurant promoters have placed 'concept' – decor, style, general trendiness – above quality of food, or value for money. This being so, it's pleasing to report that one of the best current trends has been for the new culinary flair at last to filter down into a wider range of restaurants at mid-range prices. Many 'new-British' restaurants, especially, are decently

Ducasse (The Dorchester), and even France's grandest current chef has a London operation, L'Atelier de Joël Robuchon. Asian restaurants are no longer just cheap options either: London has some of the finest Indian (Amaya, Trishna), Japanese (Nobu, Araki) and Chinese (Hakkasan, Kai) restaurants in the world. You can find regional variations, such as the superb south Indian vegetarian food of Rasa Samudra, and Cantonese dim sum at Royal China.

There has also been a re-evaluation of traditional British dishes, long dismissed as dreary. Pioneer of this new British style was Alastair Little in his Soho restaurant, but it was extended with still more zest by Fergus Henderson at St John. He has been hugely influential in showing that British favourites such as oxtail, smoked herrings and farm-reared pork, can be delicacies if prepared with care and flair.

The middle ground

The ever-rising standard of fine dining in London may grab the headlines, but it has to be said that for most people who do not

Table at The Old Shoreditch Station café-bar.

priced: even the prestigious St John is not expensive, particularly for lunch, and places such as Shoreditch's Canteen or Roast in Borough Market similarly offer flavour-rich, modern food in stylish settings. Eating out in London may still be more expensive than in many cities, but at least the difference is getting a little less.

The trend for big institutions to re-examine their food has thrown up attractive novelties too: major museums such as the National Gallery, Tate Britain and Tate Modern all now have imaginative, good-value restaurants, and even the Royal Institute of British Architects has opened up its elegant Art Deco 'canteen' as a smart modern brasserie, the RIBA Café.

The great pub renaissance

Another vital element in making good food more accessible – as well as the unstoppable growth of 'ethnic' restaurants – has been the revolution in pub food. Realising there was more money to be made from food and wine than just beer and crisps – and more appealing since the smoking ban – pub after pub has become a 'gastropub', throwing out the limp sandwiches and plastic 'ploughman's lunches' of old-style pub fare in favour of chalkboard menus that mix traditional British favourites with French, Italian or Oriental influences.

Old standards like sausage and mash have been given new life by the use of Toulouse sausages and mustard sauces, and imaginative salads and sides have become a hallmark. This

The classic fish and chips.

combination of good food and a relaxed feel that preserves a fair bit of the atmosphere of a London pub has been a real winner with both Londoners and visitors; these are typified by The Eagle (159 Farringdon Road, EC1), the first of the breed, The Cow (89 Westbourne Park Road, W2) or trendier variants like the Lots Road Pub & Dining Rooms (114 Lots

FISH AND CHIP SHOPS

A classic British dish, fish and chips originated in the 1850s. Today, fewer than 10,000 fish and chip shops remain in Britain, compared with over 30,000 in the 1930s. Many of the best were started by immigrants, especially Italians (Rock & Sole Plaice in Covent Garden, and the Fryer's Delight in Theobalds Road, Holborn) and Greek Cypriots (the Golden Hind, Marylebone). Nautilus in Fortune Green Road, West Hampstead, is Jewish and coats its fish in matzo flour.

Other notable fish and chip establishments are the long-standing favourites the Sea Shell in Lisson Grove, and Geales in Notting Hill. Fish Central is a blessing to concert- and theatre-goers near the Barbican Centre, Seafresh in Wilton Road is handy for Victoria Station, and

Masters Super Fish is convenient for Waterloo. These days you'll find more contemporary spins on the classic fish and chips, such as at the laid-back Fish Club in Clapham, and Poppies in Camden and Spitalfields Market, a retro take on 1940s East End fish and chip restaurants.

You generally get better value in a real fish and chip restaurant (attached to a takeaway shop) than in pubs or restaurants that offer fish and chips on their menus. One test, apart from truly fresh, sustainably sourced fish and crisp batter, is that they offer fresh lemon instead of just malt vinegar, and tartar sauce.

Although you'll find plenty of 'greasy spoon' cafés with fried, full English breakfast, there's also a slightly more upmarket take in plenty of all-day outlets.

AFTERNOON TEA

Throughout the world there are people still convinced that everyone in England sits down for 'afternoon tea' around 4pm every day, using best-quality porcelain. Sadly, this is a myth, and a full-scale, formal tea – with thin-cut sandwiches, cakes, scones and a choice of fine teas – is nowadays a luxury (when at home). However it's easy to find then in London. The venues that keep up the tradition are the grand hotels, most typically Brown's, The Ritz, the Langham and the Dorchester, which offer tea with all the trimmings in luxurious settings (reservations and smart dress are often required). Several upscale restaurants also offer set afternoon teas, such as The Wolseley, as do smart stores like Fortnum & Mason and Selfridges. There are often seasonal and event 'themed' teas in mid-range hotels and restaurants.

Road, SW10), or the Jugged Hare (49 Chiswell Street, EC1). The London gastropub can sometimes seem to have become a new cliché – every one has to have stripped floorboards

A Shepherd Market restaurant

and stressed furniture – but they're ideal for anyone looking for interesting food in relaxed surroundings.

The chain gang

As in every part of the world, in London plenty of restaurants, cafés, bars and pubs belong to chains.

They have their uses and some are worth looking out for. For Italian standbys (pasta, pizza), ASK and Pizza Express are good bets, with Carluccio's Caffè a more creative, deli feel. Sofra provides enjoyable Turkish fare. If you want burgers, try Byron (upmarket but traditional) in several locations around town, or Honest Burger (quality British beef at good prices) in Brixton and Soho. The Wagamama outlets are excellent Japanese-style noodle houses, or if you prefer sushi, try Itsu, a chain of Asian-inspired eat in and takeaway restaurants. For tasty Mexican market food, head for Wahaca. Branches of Giraffe (South Bank and many more) are bright, family-friendly brasseries with 'global fusion food'.

RETAIL THERAPY

London's innovative department stores are redesigning the one-stop shopping experience.

The past decade has seen dramatic changes in that most traditional of London shops: the department store. The stuffy image has gone and stores are now imaginatively designed spaces stocking everything from freshly cut flowers and organic food to cutting-edge designer clothes and bespoke jewellery. Their hairdressers have become on-site spas, and they offer a host of bars and restaurants.

Oxford Street has the greatest concentration of department stores, headed by Selfridges. Marks & Spencer and John Lewis provide a more traditional shopping experience, while round the corner on Regent Street, Liberty is both eccentric and chic. Head to Knightsbridge for Harvey Nichols, the fashionista's choice, and Harrods.

Liberty was started by Arthur Liberty in 1875 and was originally known for its homewares and fabrics, both of which are still going strong today. Past collaborations with British designer Luella Bartley and Ronnie Wood of the Rolling Stones have made this Regent Street institution more fashionable.

Liberty's eye-catching 1920s mock-Tudor building was created using the timbers of two ships, HMS Impregnable and HMS Hindustan. The home interiors floor feels more like an exhibition of contemporary furniture. In the accessories department, the iconic William Morris Libertyprint adorns everything from notebooks to bikinis.

Opened as a grocer's shop in 1849, today Harrods is a tourist destination in its own right. Harrods sells pretty much everything you can think of in surroundings that range from the sublime to the ridiculous. But whatever you think of Harrods, no trip to London would be complete without a visit to its wonderfully extravagant food halls.

BRITISH DESIGNERS

Carnaby Street storefront.

Creativity and eccentricity mark out British designers from the international fashion pack.

Many British designers have made their mark on the world stage. Stella McCartney's designs mix strong tailoring with feminine fabrics. Her popularity has sparked collaborations with Adidas and high street chain H&M. Punk diva Vivienne Westwood's theatrical clothes never fail to cause a stir. She has shops at 430 King's Road, SW10, and in Conduit Street, W1. For exquisite tailoring, silk ties and signature striped accessories, try Paul Smith, and for edgy, colourful suits head to Ozwald Boateng.

British milliners have long been respected worldwide, and perhaps the most famous is Philip Treacy, whose sculptural headgear can be found in the top department stores, including Harrods. Mulberry is famous for its leather accessories – from personal organisers to weekend bags, all embossed with the classic tree logo. Another distinctive British designer is Cath Kidston; her floral and polka dot designs are used for everything from gifts, clothes and camping accessories.

Designer necklaces at the Lesley Craze Gallery in Clerkenwell.

Selfridges has become the ultimate London department store. Combining luxury brands with high-street concessions, it manages to be both accessible and cool. The store has a changing programme of themed events, as well as services ranging from leather repairs to ear piercing.

For a department store specialising in fine food and beverages visit Fortnum & Mason at 181 Piccadilly.

MARKETS

There are few better introductions to London's rich mix of cultures and tastes than a visit to one of its markets, where you can buy almost anything.

Many of the capital's markets have been in operation for centuries and a visit can conjure up images of an old London now largely lost to supermarket chains and developers. At the same time, London's markets have experienced a revival, and alongside the traditional stalls selling fruit and veg you'll find organic meat and fish and specialist produce from all over the world.

The resurgence of markets has encouraged the renovation of surrounding areas and all kinds of independent shops and restaurants are popping up. For some this has gone a step too far – for example, there is little doubt that the creation of a restaurant and boutique precinct at Spitalfields has damaged something of its original haphazard appeal – and the high prices charged for goods have taken the edge off bargain-hunting.

Despite this, a wander around places like Borough Market, Broadway Market and Spitalfields continues to be a treat for all the senses – you just have to be prepared to brave the crowds especially on Saturdays.

Handmade soaps, Spitalfields Market.

On Sunday mornings Londoners flood to Columbia Road Market in Hoxton (see page 232) for cut flowers, bulbs, shrubs, trees and garden ornaments. The old-fashioned streets around the market offer funky shops and cafés too.

Leadenhall Market (see page 159) is a fine example of one of London's great 19th-century covered markets. It was used as a setting for Diagon Alley in the film Harry Potter and the Philosopher's Stone.

MARKET TREASURES

Directional vests at Camden Market.

A wide range of offbeat clothing, crafts and trinkets are available at Camden's various markets.

The covered market at Greenwich is the place for handmade jewellery and accessories. Quality varies and it's very crowded, but if it gets too much adjourn to the calmer antiques market a short walk away.

Portobello Road in Notting Hill is one of London's best-loved markets. For antiques explore the northern end of the street; for junk, offbeat fashions and arts and crafts (market Sat, shops Mon–Sat) head further north, towards the Westway flyover.

Trendy shoppers on Portobello Road.

The variety and quality of fresh produce at Borough Market is unrivalled in London, and some of the prices certainly reflect this. If you're happy to brave the lunchtime crowds, many of the stalls offer takeaway snacks – a favourite are the hot chorizo and rocket rolls from Spanish store Brindisa.

The Sunday UpMarket at Ely's Yard (Brick Lane) is a treasure trove of second-hand clothing and one-off designs.

THE ARCHITECTURAL LEGACY

London's haphazard development, together with the contribution of men of genius such as Christopher Wren, John Nash and Inigo Jones, has given the capital its principal allure: infinite variety.

Tudor building on Fleet Street.

Little remains of Roman Londinium, and even less of Saxon Lundenwic. Glimpses of the Roman city wall can be had at Tower Hill, and foundations of a Temple of Mithras have been exposed in Queen Victoria Street. The Saxons built mostly in timber, but were grateful for Roman stones. All Hallows-by-the-Tower has a Saxon arch, built with Roman tiles. Otherwise, they left little trace.

Norman to Gothic

The Norman Conquest of 1066 brought firmer resolution to the city, in the White Tower in the Tower of London, a sturdy box that showed the natives who was in control. Within it is St John's Chapel, with the squat pillars and round arches of Norman Romanesque architecture architecture.

Medieval London grew out of the Gothic style, imported from France in the 13th century and in vogue until the 1550s. Far more delicate than Norman, it made outer walls thinner by supporting them with exterior buttresses, allowing larger windows. Southwark Cathedral is a fine example of simple, unadorned early English Gothic; Westminster Abbey, begun in 1245, was enhanced by royal mason Henry Yevele (1320–1400), London's first known architect. He also built the Jewel Tower and Westminster Hall in the Houses of Parliament, a vauntingly ambitious space with a timber roof by carpenter Hugh Herland.

The Tudor monarchs were great builders and brought the first real touches of grandeur and extravagance to London's buildings – fitting for what was by now the largest city in Western Europe.

Tudor London

The finest work of Gothic architecture in London is the lavish Henry VII's Chapel in Westminster Abbey, completed by his son, Henry VIII. The Tudor monarchs oversaw constant expansion and building in London. Hallmarks of Tudor buildings – also called 'Elizabethan', after Queen Elizabeth I – are the use of half-timbering and red brick. Staple

Banqueting Hall, Whitehall.

style (from King James I): Prince Henry's Room (1610–11) above 17 Fleet Street. Its original ceiling, with geometric patterns, is still in place.

Inigo Jones and the Italian style

James I and his son Charles I brought a new elegance to London in the work of Inigo Jones (1573–1652). The court architect had studied in Italy, and was full of Italian Renaissance ideas. He introduced classical proportions in his Banqueting Hall in Whitehall and the Queen's House in Greenwich, and his original Palladian layout for Covent Garden, set out, with the neoclassical St Paul's church, London's first true square.

Wren and the Great Fire

Sir Christopher Wren (1632–1723) is undoubtedly London's greatest architect, but if there had been no Great Fire in 1666 his name would not be so well known. In three days 80 percent of London's buildings were destroyed: among the losses were the Guildhall and Old St Paul's, as well as 87 churches.

Inn in High Holborn is the sole survivor from this time, but the era also saw the building of London's first theatres such as Shakespeare's Globe, now reconstructed near its original Southwark site.

Brickwork was confined to the rich, used to produce octagonal towers, fancy chimneys and patterns of colours and shapes. Royal palaces were built like this at Greenwich, Hampton Court, St James's, Lambeth and Westminster. London has only one example of the Jacobean

Hampton Court.

OPEN HOUSE

During Open House London weekends, more than 600 buildings of architectural and historical interest that are usually closed to the public open their doors, free of charge. The range of buildings participating is huge, from modern private residences to ancient sites – Billingsgate Roman House and Baths – to towering modern office blocks like Lloyd's of London and the 'Gherkin'. The main weekend is usually in mid-September, but more limited Open House tours are run all year. See www.londonopenhouse.org for details. Queues can be long at the more popular attractions, such as the Bank of England or Horse Guards, and at some venues you will need to book.

Wren was a scientist and self-taught architect. His plans for the rebuilding of London were rejected, but he managed 53 churches in the City and Westminster (26 remain) as well as St Paul's. These very English classical-baroque monuments eschewed earlier styles, their windows bathing white and gold interiors with light. His mastery of design is also displayed in the superb Greenwich and Chelsea hospitals, and several royal palaces.

John Nash and Georgian London

John Nash (1752–1835) is the man who gave the West End its style. He gained his reputation designing country houses, and in 1811 was commissioned by the Prince Regent, later George IV, to turn his 'Marylebone Farm' into Regent's Park, ringed by elegant neoclassical villas. Nash added theatrical terraces, colonnades and sculpted pediments, and his master plan included connecting the park with the Prince's residence – Carlton House Terrace, by The Mall – via Portland Place and Regent Street, London's first refined boulevards.s

Nash's supremely elegant Regency style was the summit of Georgian architecture. The houses of Bedford Square are typically Georgian,

The Natural History Museum is another example of Gothic Revival.

St Pancras Station typifies Gothic Revival, a favourite of Victorian architects.

with brick facades, sash windows and elaborate porticoes. As Italian influence waned, all things Greek became the vogue: Sir Robert Smirke (1780–1867) accordingly built the British Museum as a giant temple, to house Lord Elgin's plunder from the Parthenon.

Victorian revivals

Against this pagan Greek influence, Augustus Pugin (1812–52) contended it was time to return to 'true Christian architecture', the Gothic. His chance to lead the revival came on 16 October 1834, when the old Palace of Westminster burnt down. His design for the new Houses of Parliament, carried out with Charles Barry (1795–1860), took as inspiration the Henry VII chapel in Westminster Abbey.

Gothic Revival was the cornerstone of Victorian architecture. It produced a distinctive Tower Bridge, while Sir George Gilbert Scott (1811–78) built St Pancras Station as a romantic castle. Victorian eclecticism even allowed a Tudor Revival, as in New Hall at Lincoln's Inn.

Modern architecture

Britain was virtually bankrupted by World War II, which accounts for the number of utilitarian

The Sky Garden.

blocks that had to be built quickly and cheaply in the 1950s and 60s, which have not worn well. Buildings from the 1951 Festival of Britain such as the Royal Festival Hall, though, stand out beside more brutalist Modernist projects such as the all-concrete National Theatre (1967–77).

London's economic boom in the 1980s and the redevelopment of vast areas like Docklands have launched a whole new wave of construction, begun by Richard Rogers' futuristic Lloyd's Building in 1986. A city that resisted tall buildings has acquired scene-stealing skyscrapers like

The Shard at London Bridge, the 'Gherkin' (30 St Mary Axe), the 'Cheesegrater' (the Leadenhall Building) and the 'Walkie-Talkie' (20 Fenchurch Street) in the City. London's nicknames for its new tall buildings reveal the (sometime) affection in which they are held.

The site of the 2012 Olympic Games has now been transformed into the Queen Elizabeth Olympic Park, incorporating the Olympic sporting venues (most of which are now open to the public), thousands of new homes and acres of parkland and recreational space.

THE SKY'S THE LIMIT

Until the 1950s no new building in London was allowed to exceed the height of St Paul's Cathedral (355ft/108 metres). However, this has changed over the past few years with a wave of giant-scale building that is altering London's skyline dramatically.

The Leadenhall Building, a 740ft (225-metre) glass-and-steel wedge that soars up from the streets of the City, is the latest arrival in an ever-growing collection of novelty silhouettes. Completed in 2014, the slanting, wedge-shaped design – hence its nickname, the Cheesegrater – means the view from Fleet Street to St Paul's will not be ruined as it would have been had the building not sloped off at the top. It has the characteristic inside-out design of architect Richard Rogers, just

like his Lloyd's Building which stands opposite, a symphony of pipes and ducts finished 30 years earlier.

Alongside the Cheesegrater stands Norman Foster's curvaceous Gherkin. To the south is the Walkie-Talkie (590ft/180 metres), also completed in 2014. The top-heavy design gives the building its nickname, and houses the Sky Garden, an enlarged glass dome, which houses landscaped public gardens, an open-air terrace and restaurants. At 1,016ft (310 metres), The Shard at London Bridge is the tallest building in Western Europe. This striking skyscraper, resembling a shard of glass, comprises exclusive apartments, offices, a hotel, restaurants and stunning 360-degree views from the 72nd floor.

King's Cross station.

St Paul's Cathedral.

The O2 arena and Canary Wharf skyline viewed from the Emirates Air Line cable car.

ORIENTATION

The Places section details all the attractions worth seeing, arranged by area. Main sights are cross-referenced by number to the maps.

For a cosmopolitan city of 8.2 million people, London is quite parochial. Each neighbourhood, each street corner, is proud of its own identity. Central London is the shared London of all these groups and of nearly 20 million visitors a year as well. Symbols of London – the Beefeaters, the bobbies, the cabbies, the red buses, the pageantry, the Royal Family, the Houses of Parliament – all are here, along with the stock market, motorcycle messengers, dirty air and crawling traffic.

After an initial tour on an open-top bus, the top deck of a regular double-decker bus or a spin on the London Eye, to orientate yourself, the best way to see Central London is on foot. Although Greater London sprawls for 610 sq miles (1,580 sq km), the central area is surprisingly compact. Walkers have time to appreciate the infinite variety of architectural detail that traces the city's long development. What's more, they will be treading in the footsteps of some of history's most celebrated citizens – to aid the imagination, blue plaques (see page 132) show where the great, the good and the notorious once lived.

We begin the Places section by focusing on the royal and ruling heart of the city: Parliament and Buckingham Palace. The ensuing chapters cover the remainder of the central area, from Piccadilly to Chelsea, and cross the river to explore the vibrancy of Southwark and the South Bank. Village London (see page 215) tours some of the most interesting local communities outside the central area, usually reached by bus or Underground. Day Trips (see page 247) suggests a range of convenient excursions from London.

Tower Bridge.

All the sites of special interest are numbered on specially drawn maps to help you find your way around, and there is a street atlas towards the back of the guide.

As a visitor, you may be one of the 72 percent who visit the Tower of London, or the 92 percent who make their way to Piccadilly Circus. But you will probably also be one of the millions who find some small, distinctive corner of this remarkable city to be enthusiastic about.

Central London

Open Air Theatre
QUEEN MARY'S GARDENS
London Zoo
REGENT'S PARK
THE REGENT'S PARK
Camden
ST JAMES'S GARDENS
British Library
Shaw Theatre
ST PANCRAS
King's Cross Rd
Swinton
Grays
Euston Station
Euston
Albany
Hampstead Road
Eversholt Street
Euston
Judd St
Hunter St
ST ANDREW'S GARDENS
Foundling Museum
CORAM'S FIELDS
Charles Dickens Museum
Madame Tussauds
Regent's Park
Euston Road
Warren Street
Euston Square
Tavistock Square
Woburn Pl
Bernard St
Brunswick Sq
Guildford
Street
Theobald's Road
Marylebone Road
Park Cres.
Gt Portland Street
Cleveland
Warren Street
Gower Street
University College
University of London
Russell Square
Russell Square
Southampton
GRAYS INN GARDEN
St Marylebone
MARYLEBONE
Marylebone High St
Portland Place
Great
Portland Street
BT Tower
Goodge Street
Goodge St
BLOOMSBURY
Montague Pl.
Bloomsbury
Drake St
Gray's Inn
Wallace Collection
Wigmore Hall
Harley Street
Mortimer St
Tottenham Court Road
Bedford Square
British Museum
Gt. Russell St
High Holborn
Holborn
Sir John Soane's Museum
Lincoln's Inn Hall
Wigmore Street
Cavendish Square
Portland Street
Oxford Circus
Oxford Street
New Oxford St
Holborn
High
Kingsway
LINCOLN'S INN FIELDS
HOLBORN
Royal Court of Justi
Selfridges
Oxford Street
Bond Street
Hanover Square
Palladium Theatre
Liberty
Soho Square
Drury
Endell
Covent Garden Acre
Royal Opera House
Theatre Royal Drury Lane
Aldwych
Handel & Hendrix in London
New Bond St
Conduit St
Carnaby St
Wardour Street
SOHO
Charing Cross Road
St Martin's
Long Acre
Covent Garden Market
Covent Garden
London Transport Museum
Somerset House
Temple
American Embassy
Grosvenor Square
Berkeley Street
Regent Street
Hamleys
Piccadilly Circus
Shaftesbury Avenue
Cambridge Circus
Chinatown
Leicester Square
Leicester Square
St Martin's La
STRAND
Strand
MAYFAIR
MOUNT ST GARDENS
Faraday Museum
Royal Academy of Arts
Old Bond St
Piccadilly
Piccadilly Circus
Eros
Haymarket
National Gallery
St Martin-in-the-Fields
Charing Cross
Charing Cross Station
Cleopatra's Needle
BFI (British Fil Institute
Grosvenor Chapel
St James
Fortnum & Mason
Regent St
Trafalgar Square
Nelson's Column
Northumberland Ave
Embankment
Natio Thea
The Ritz
St James's St
Cockspur St
Southbank Centre
Curzon
Institute of Contemporary Arts
Admiralty Arch
Banqueting House
HYDE PARK
Green Park
Pall Mall
Duke of York Memorial
Horse Guards Parade
Whitehall
Royal Festival Hall
SOUTH BANK
Wellington Museum, Apsley House
GREEN PARK
St James's Palace
The Mall
ST JAMES'S
PARK
Downing Street
Foreign Office
London Eye
JUBILEE GDNS
Water
Hyde Park Corner
Wellington Monument
Constitution Hill
Clarence House
Churchill War Rooms
London Aquarium
London Dungeon
County Hall
Water Stati
Belgrave Square
Buckingham Palace
Queen Victoria Memorial
Birdcage Walk
St James's Park
Parliament St
Westminster
Westminster Bridge
York Rd
Nightingale Museum
Belgrave Pl.
Grosvenor Place
Queen's Gallery
Royal Mews
Palace Road
Buckingham Gate
Victoria Street
Parliament Square
Big Ben
Houses of Parliament
Palace
ARCHBISHOP'S PARK
Hobart Pl.
Eaton
Eccleston
Westminster Chapel
Westminster Roman Catholic Cathedral
Victoria Street
Victoria
Westminster Abbey
WESTMINSTER
VICTORIA TOWER GARDENS
Thames
Lambeth Palace
Lambeth
Victoria Station
Buckingham
Rochester Row
St John's Concert Hall
Marsham Street
Horseferry Road
Lambeth Bridge
Victoria Coach Station
BELGRAVIA
Vauxhall Bridge Rd
Millbank
Tate Britain

Sadler's Wells Theatre
FINSBURY
Anwell St
Rosebery Avenue
St John St
City Road
SHOREDITCH
HOXTON
Pifield Street
Vestry Rd
East Rd
Shoreditch High Street
Calvert Ave
Club Row
Sclater St
Bethnal Green Road
Skinner St
Percival St
Lever
Street
Old
Street
City
Road
Great Western Street
Curtain Rd
SPITALFIELDS
Commercial St
Brick Lane
CLERKENWELL
Goswell Road
St John Street
Old
Street
Bunhill Row
Finsbury
Worship Street
Commercial St
Brushfield St
Whitechapel Art Gallery
Farringdon Road
Charterhouse
Road
Aldersgate
Beech St
Chiswell St
Dennis Servers' House
Liverpool Street Station
Spitalfields Market
Clerkenwell
Farringdon Station
Farringdon
Barbican
Arts Centre
BARBICAN
Museum of London
Moorgate
Finsbury Circus
Liverpool Street
Petticoat Lane Market
Middlesex St
Wentworth Street
Aldgate East
Chancery Lane
Holborn
Holborn Circus
Farringdon Rd
Smithfield Market
St Martin's le Grand
London Wall
London Wall
Houndsditch
Aldgate
Aldgate High St
Mansell St
New Fetter Lane
Holborn Viaduct
Newgate St
Gresham
Guildhall
Street
Bishopsgate
30 St Mary Axe (The Gherkin)
City Thameslink Station
Stock Exchange
St Paul's
Bank of England
Threadneedle St
Royal Exchange
Leadenhall Street
Lloyd's of London
Minories
St Andrew's
Fleet Street
Dr Johnson's House
Ludgate Hill
St Paul's Cathedral
CITY
Mansion House
Mansion House
Bank
Gracechurch St
Leadenhall Market
Fenchurch Street Station
Tower Gateway
Strand
Temple Church
St Bride's
New Br St
Cannon Street
Cannon Street Station
Monument
Corn Exchange
Trinity House
Tower Hill
Middle Temple Hall
Inner Temple
Blackfriars
Blackfriars Station
Blackfriars Bridge
Upper Thames Street
Cannon Street
Monument
Lower Thames St
Byward St
Tower Hill
Victoria Embankment
Millennium Bridge
Southwark Bridge
London Bridge
Thames
Tower Pier
Tower of London
Canary Wharf
Gabriel's Wharf
OXO Tower
Tate Modern
Shakespeare's Globe
Southwark Cathedral
London Bridge City Pier
Hay's Galleria
HMS Belfast
Tower Br App
St Katherine's Dock
Upper Ground
Stamford Street
SOUTHWARK
Southwark St
Borough Market
Duke St Hill
City Hall
Tower Bridge
Tower Bridge Experience
Waterloo East Station
Southwark St
Union Street
London Bridge
The Shard
London Bridge Station
St Thomas St
Tooley Street
Butler's Wharf
Greenwich
The Cut
Blackfriars Road
Union St
High Street
Crucifix Lane
Tooley St
Jamaica Rd
Baylis Rd
Waterloo Road
Borough
Marshalsea Rd
Borough
Long Lane
BOROUGH
Bermondsey St
Fashion & Textile Museum
Bermondsey Rd
Abbey Street
Lambeth North
Borough Road
Great Dover St
Long Lane
TABARD GARDENS
Tower Bridge Rd
BERMONDSEY
Westminster Br Rd
Lambeth Rd
St George's Road
London Road
Southwark Bridge Road
Newington C'way
Hamp
Street
Imperial War Museum
Elephant & Castle
Elephant & Castle
New Kent Road
Kennington Rd
Elephant & Castle Station
NEWINGTON

0   500 yds
0   500 m

N

WESTMINSTER AND BUCKINGHAM PALACE

Westminster is the centre of official London. Parliament meets here, the Queen and the prime minister have their London homes here, and state funerals are conducted in Westminster Abbey.

A s the focus of government and the monarchy, Westminster contains within its ancient and easily walked boundaries the headquarters of the nation's policy-making civil servants, the prime minister and the Cabinet, and the Royal Family. Many kings and queens are buried in Westminster Abbey, founded by the last Saxon ruler, Edward the Confessor (1042–66).

Whitehall

Official London begins immediately south of **Trafalgar Square** (see page 97), where the broad and unmistakably official thoroughfare of **Whitehall** ❶ stretches imperiously southwards towards the Houses of Parliament. Most buildings along here are government offices, built from Portland stone in an imposing classical style.

On the right, beyond the Trafalgar Studios, are the former offices of the Admiralty (for centuries the headquarters of the Royal Navy until the Ministry of Defence took over in 1964), and the offices of the Household Cavalry's headquarters, known as the **Horse Guards** ❷. Outside this colonnaded building are two mounted Life Guards in fancy uniforms, white gloves, plumes

and helmets, rigidly oblivious to the throng of camera-toting tourists. Changed every hour from 10am to 4pm, they guard the site of the main gateway to what was the Palace of Whitehall, used by King Henry VIII in the 16th century and burnt to the ground in 1698. Through the archway of Horse Guards and opening out on to St James's Park is the huge **Horse Guards Parade**. Here in June the Queen's birthday is honoured by a splendid pageant called **Trooping the Colour**; the name is derived

Buckingham Palace.

from the regimental colours which are paraded.

Banqueting House ❸

Address: Whitehall, www.hrp.org.uk
Tel: 020-3166 6000
Opening Hrs: Mon–Sat 10am–5pm
Transport: Embankment

Opposite Horse Guards, on the other side of Whitehall, is the Renaissance-style **Banqueting House**, built in 1620 by Inigo Jones, the man responsible for bringing this Italian style of architecture to England. It is the only surviving fragment of the palace destroyed by fire in 1698. Inside the huge hall upstairs, the ceiling is divided into nine large panels filled with rich baroque paintings by Rubens. They were commissioned by Charles I to glorify (or deify) the House of Stuart (Rubens was paid £3,000 and knighted for his work), but the Civil War followed and Charles I was beheaded on a scaffold outside the building. The hall is still used for official state banquets.

The prime minister's home

London's most famous address, **Downing Street** ❹, just off White-hall, is little more than a terrace of

Downing Street gates.

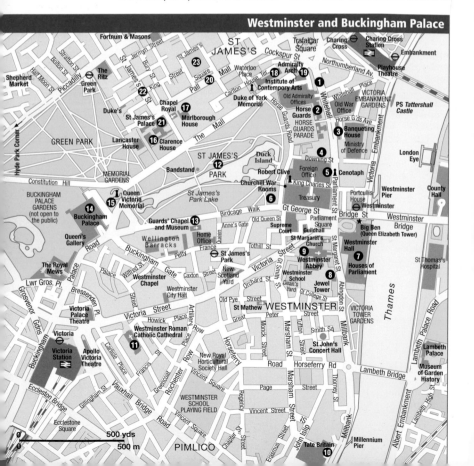

Westminster and Buckingham Palace

four 18th-century houses, sealed off behind a heavy gate. The street is named after the diplomat Sir George Downing, who went to America with his parents in 1638 and became the second student to graduate from Harvard University. No. 10 is the official residence of the prime minister, and the venue for Cabinet meetings.

The plain black door and net-curtained windows suggest nothing of stylish rooms or of the state business conducted inside. Successive prime ministers have lived here since 1735. The chancellor of the exchequer has his (or her) official residence at No. 11.

Across Whitehall from Downing Street are the offices of the Ministry of Defence. Just south of here, the **Cenotaph** ❺, the national war memorial designed by Sir Edwin Lutyens, breaks Whitehall's monotony. On Remembrance Sunday in November it is the focal point of a service attended by the Queen and political leaders to remember the dead of two world wars, as well as other conflicts.

Beyond the Cenotaph, Whitehall becomes **Parliament Street**. The stolid buildings on the same side as the Horse Guards house the Foreign and Commonwealth offices; its designer, Sir George Gilbert Scott, described it as 'a kind of national palace'.

Turn right into King Charles Street, which runs between the **Foreign Office** and the **Treasury** and **Cabinet offices** before reaching **Clive Steps** and a statue of Robert Clive (1725–74), a key figure in the establishment of British power in India. Beside the steps is a small wall of sandbags, the only above-ground sign of the Churchill War Rooms, one of London's best small museums.

Churchill War Rooms ❻

Address: Clive Steps, King Charles Street, www.iwm.org.uk
Tel: 020-7930 6961
Opening Hrs: daily 9.30am–6pm
Transport: Westminster

This was the wartime bunker from which Sir Winston Churchill conducted World War II. Many of the 21 rooms were abandoned in 1945 and

The statue of Robert Clive, who rose from being a humble scribe in the East India Company to become governor of the Bengal Presidency, laying the foundations for British rule in India. His suicide at the age of 49 was linked to opium use and depression.

Horse Guards.

Churchill War Rooms.

David Lloyd George statue.

left untouched until the museum opened in 1984; others have been meticulously restored to their wartime condition, 'down to the last paper clip'. The Central Map Room and the rooms that served as a round-the-clock typing pool illustrate the problems of communications in the 1940s. A converted broom cupboard housed a pioneering hotline to the White House, enabling Churchill to have confidential talks with President Roosevelt, despite air raids.

The **Churchill Museum** within includes a selection of letters and other memorabilia, as well as an interactive table on which visitors can find information about Churchill's life.

PARLIAMENT SQUARE

Parliament Street empties out into **Parliament Square**, with its tall trees and lawns lined with statues of illustrious statesmen. This, the country's first official roundabout, is surrounded by national landmarks.

The Houses of Parliament ❼

Address: www.parliament.uk
Tel: 020-7219 4114
Opening Hrs: see page 77
Entrance Fee: charge for tours; free for UK residents if arranged through their MP
Transport: Westminster

The clock tower of the **Houses of Parliament** has become a symbol of London. Its elaborately fretted stone sides rise up nearly 330ft (100 metres) to a richly gilded spire and a 13.5-tonne hour bell, nicknamed **Big Ben** supposedly after a rather fat government official called Sir Benjamin Hall who was commissioner of works when the bell was installed. Its chimes first rang out across Westminster in 1859, after an earlier bell was damaged while being tested three years previously.

Facing Big Ben is the unusual-looking **Portcullis House**, a £250 million office block for members of Parliament; its prominent and much criticised 'chimneys' form part of the air-conditioning system.

The oldest part of the Houses of Parliament and one of the oldest buildings in London is **Westminster Hall**, begun in 1097. The thick buttressed walls are spanned with a magnificent hammer-beamed oak roof. This hall has witnessed many seminal events in British history: coronation celebrations, lyings-in-state and treason trials. Among those condemned to death were Sir Thomas More, who fell foul of King Henry VIII; King Charles I, accused of treason against Parliament; and the 17th-century revolutionary Guy Fawkes, who tried to blow up the buildings (see page 29).

Fire and reconstruction

In 1834 a fire achieved what Guy Fawkes had failed to do and most of the ancient Palace of Westminster was destroyed. Westminster Hall, a small crypt chapel and the Jewel Tower (see page 77) survived. Following this conflagration, the current purpose-built structure was created in exuberant Gothic style by Sir Charles Barry and Augustus Pugin.

The houses are embellished with gilded spires and towers, mullioned windows and intricate stone carving and statues. The complex, which took some 30 years to complete, covers 8 acres (3.2 hectares); there are 100 staircases and more than 1,100 rooms. Apart from the ceremonial state rooms and the two main debating chambers, the House of Lords and the House of Commons, there are libraries, dining rooms, offices and secretarial facilities for government ministers, opposition leaders and ordinary Members of Parliament.

Main points of interest

St Stephen's, on the western side of the building, is the main entrance to the House of Commons, and anyone can watch debates from the visitors' gallery, though there may be queues (see box). Beneath **St Stephen's Hall** is the ancient crypt chapel that survived the 1834 fire. Members can

TIP

The name Big Ben, commonly used for the clock tower of the Houses of Parliament, properly refers only to the bell. The tower itself was renamed Queen Elizabeth Tower in honour of the Queen on her 2012 Diamond Jubilee. If you want to climb the 334 spiral steps to see the bell, and enjoy a fantastic view, you will need to be a UK resident and contact your MP to arrange a tour (allow several months for confirmation). Children under the age of 11 are not admitted. Tours last around 75 minutes.

The opulent House of Lords.

How Parliament Works

England is known as the mother of parliaments, and the Westminster Parliament has been a model for democracies all over the world.

The Houses of Parliament consist of the House of Commons and the House of Lords. The Commons, the House of locally elected Members of Parliament (MPs), known as the Lower House, wields virtually all the power but inhabits only half the building. Jutting out towards is Westminster Hall, with the offices, dining rooms and libraries of the Commons; in the centre is the Commons' debating chamber. To the right of Westminster Hall is the domain of the Lords, whose role is to examine and sometimes block bills proposed by the Lower House, although a bill can be reintroduced. Until recently, most lords governed by birthright, as descendants of the previous ruling classes, but the voting rights of many hereditary peers

The Queen's speech at the State Opening of Parliament.

have been abolished and the make-up of the Lords has changed. Most members are now life peers, ennobled for services to the nation, and their titles cannot be passed to their children. Former MPs are often made peers in recognition of years of public service.

There are 650 elected MPs, yet the Commons seats only about 450. This is not usually a problem since MPs attend sessions when they wish. The governing party sits on one side, facing the opposition. Cabinet ministers sit on the front bench, opposite the 'Shadow Cabinet' (the leading members of the opposition). The Cabinet, consisting of up to two dozen ministers and chaired by the prime minister, meets at 10 Downing Street weekly to review major issues.

The General Election

Major parties represented are the Conservatives, Labour and the Liberal Democrats. General elections are run on the basis of local rather than proportional representation. Therefore, a party's presence in the house may not reflect its overall national standing. A party, however, needs an overall majority in the house to push through its bills, hence the need for the coalition after the 2010 election. The procedure of law making is so complex that a bill usually takes more than six months to be enacted. If it is still incomplete at the end of the parliamentary year, it is dropped. Various techniques are employed by the opposition to delay a bill.

The press can report on Parliament and the business of both houses is televised. A select group of journalists ('lobby correspondents') have daily informal 'background' briefings with ministers.

Parliament meets from October to July. In November, the government's plans for the year are announced in the Queen's Speech at the State Opening of Parliament. From the Visitors' Gallery, the public can watch the House of Commons at work, though seats are limited and security precautions tight. The weekly Prime Minister's Question Time every Wednesday – an unruly affair – usually attracts a full house.

take their marriage vows and have their children baptised here. The **Commons chamber** was bombed in 1941; the current chamber only opened in 1950.

The immense **Victoria Tower** marks the grand entrance to the House of Lords. It is also the entrance used by the Queen when opening a new session of government.

Opposite Parliament is the moated **Jewel Tower** ❽, a relic of the Palace of Westminster dating from 1365. Its small museum of Parliament Past and Present (Apr–Sept daily 10am–6pm, Oct daily 10am–5pm, Nov–Mar Sat–Sun 10am–4pm) has more information panels than artefacts.

Opposite Parliament at the other end is the Supreme Court (Parliament Square, www.supremecourt.uk; Mon–Fri 9.30am–4.30pm), the UK's highest court of appeal. Guided tours are available on Fridays (except public holidays) at 11.30am, 1.30pm and 3pm. Booking is advised.

Westminster Abbey ❾

Tel: 020-7222 5152, www.westminster-abbey.org
Opening Hrs: Mon–Tue, Thu–Fri 9.30am–4.30pm; Wed 9.30am–7pm; Sat 9am–2.30pm; last admission one hour before closing
Transport: Westminster

The most historic religious building in Britain is **Westminster Abbey**. It is also an outstanding piece of Gothic architecture, which is probably more striking from the detail on the inside than from its outward aspects. So many eminent figures are honoured in this national shrine that large areas of the interior have the cluttered appearance of an overcrowded sculpture museum. For full coverage of the abbey, see page 86.

ST MARGARET'S CHURCH

On the northeast side of Westminster Abbey facing the Houses of Parliament is **St Margaret's Church**, used by MPs for official services and for high-society weddings. Sir Walter Raleigh (1552–1618), the sea captain, poet and favourite of Queen Elizabeth I, who established the first British colony in Virginia and introduced tobacco and potatoes to Britain, was interred here after his execution. William Caxton (c.1421–92), who ran the first English printing presses nearby, is also buried here.

Beyond Westminster Abbey and Victoria Gardens a short street leads to one of London's most unobtrusive but notable concert halls, **St John's, Smith Square**. This former 18th-century church has fine acoustics and a reputation for a varied programme of classical music. In the crypt is a good restaurant.

Tate Britain ❿

Address: Millbank, www.tate.org.uk/britain
Tel: 020-7887 8888
Opening Hrs: daily 10am–6pm
Entrance Fee: free except for feature exhibitions. Donation welcome.
Transport: Pimlico

The Jewel Tower has had several functions over the centuries. It was used to test official standards of weights and measures from 1869 until the 1930s, and its moat once supplied fish for the sovereign's table.

VISITING THE HOUSES OF PARLIAMENT

Tours of the Houses of Parliament are available on Saturdays throughout the year, and on most weekdays during parliamentary recesses including February, Easter, August, late September/early October and Christmas. A choice of guided tour (90 minutes) or self-guided audio tour (75 minutes) is offered in a range of languages. There is a charge for these tours and advanced booking is recommended particularly in the summer. If you are a permanent UK resident, you can contact your MP to arrange a free Member's tour up to six months in advance. To watch parliamentary debates from the public galleries when the House of Commons and House of Lords are sitting, queue outside the Cromwell Green visitor entrance. For further information visit www.parliament.uk/visiting.

Entry times vary depending on when Parliament is in session, but normal sitting times for the Commons are Mon 2.30–10.30pm; Tue–Wed 11.30am–7.30pm; Thu 9.30am–5.30pm. The Commons does not normally sit on Friday, but when it does the hours are 9.30am–3pm. Expect to queue for 1–1.5 hours, less in the evenings. The longest queues are for Prime Minister's Question Time (Wed noon–12.30pm); UK residents should contact their MP for an advance ticket, as ticket-holders have priority.

TIP

For art lovers in a hurry, a 220-seat catamaran runs every 40 minutes between Tate Britain on the Thames' north bank and Tate Modern on the south bank. It stops at the London Eye. Tel: 020-7887 8888; www.tate.org.uk/visit/tate-boat

A 10- to 15-minute walk along Millbank from the Houses of Parliament is **Tate Britain**, founded in 1897 by Henry Tate, of the Tate & Lyle sugar empire, and today the storehouse for the Tate's collection of British art from 1500 to the present. It is complemented by Tate Modern, further down the river on Bankside, which houses most of the Tate's modern and contemporary international collection (see page 182).

The galleries within Tate Britain are arranged by date and theme. The only criticism is that there isn't enough space: the majority of the collection has to be kept in storage out of the public view. A much-needed extension is being considered.

Among the British paintings are portraits by William Hogarth (1697–1764) and Thomas Gainsborough (1727–88), views of the English countryside by John Constable (1776–1837) and, in the Clore Gallery, seascapes and landscapes by J.M.W. Turner (1775–1851). Turner bequeathed the paintings to the nation on his death, with the stipulation that they should all be hung in

The Union flag on top of Victoria Tower indicates that Parliament is in session. Night sessions are indicated by a light shining over the clock tower.

one place, and should be available for the public to see without charge.

The most popular 19th-century painters represented are the Pre-Raphaelites, including Millais,

The Cholmondeley Ladies, artist unknown, in Tate Britain.

Holman Hunt, Rossetti and Burne-Jones. Modern British artists represented include Stanley Spencer, Francis Bacon and David Hockney. Sculptures include works by Jacob Epstein, Barbara Hepworth and Henry Moore. The Tate also stages free lectures and film shows, and has a reputation for the avant-garde, with the award of an annual Turner Prize. Its Rex Whistler-designed restaurant is a great place to have lunch, dominated by an attractive food-themed mural.

Across the river from Millbank, to the right, the modern green-and-cream building is **Vauxhall Cross**, headquarters of MI6's spymasters; this secret services building, designed by Terry Farrell, is built in a 'Faraday Cage' which stops electro-magnetic information passing in or out.

VICTORIA STREET

The west door of Westminster Abbey opens on to **Victoria Street**, important commercially but, since its rebuilding, a long grey canyon of undistinguished office blocks. Down this street, close to the Victoria Station end, is **Westminster Cathedral**.

Westminster Cathedral ⓫

Address: www.westminstercathedral.org.uk
Tel: 020-7798 9055
Opening Hrs: cathedral daily 7am–7pm; tower Mon–Fri 9.30am–5pm, Sat–Sun 9.30am–6pm
Entrance Fee: free except for tower
Transport: Victoria

This is the most important Catholic church in London. Its bold red-and-white brickwork makes it look like a gigantic layer cake. Built at the end of the 19th century in an outlandish Italian-Byzantine style not seen elsewhere in London, it has a 273ft (83-metre) tower incorporating a lift – the views from the top are superb. Inside, many of its chapels are clad in coloured marble, but the decor was never finished; the numerous mosaics included in the original designs are absent, and the ceiling is largely bereft of decoration.

On the north side of Victoria Street behind St James's Park Underground station is **Queen Anne's Gate**, a small, quiet street which has retained much of its 18th-century atmosphere. Lord Palmerston, who became prime minister in 1855, was born at No. 20.

The Italian-Byzantine-style facade of Westminster Cathedral.

Westminster Cathedral.

ST JAMES'S PARK AND BUCKINGHAM PALACE

The formal arrangement of lakes and flora at **St James's Park** ⑫ is one of the most delightful in London. Formerly the grounds of St James's Palace acquired by Henry VIII in 1531, it was laid out in 1603, then re-landscaped in formal style by John Nash in 1827. It has always had a collection of ducks and water fowl, the highlight being the pelicans, fed every day between 2.30 and 3pm by the lake. Pelicans have been a feature in the park for nearly 400 years.

Continuing the ornithological theme is **Birdcage Walk**, which takes its name from an 18th-century aviary, running along the south side of the park from Parliament Square to Buckingham Palace and dividing the park from the drilling ground of the **Wellington Barracks**, the home of the Royal Grenadier Guards and the Coldstream Guards. Here the **Guards' Chapel and Museum** ⑬ (tel: 020-7414 3271; www.theguardsmuseum.com; daily 10am–4pm) are on the site of a former chapel which was

Longcase equation clock next to a portrait of King George III.

hit by a bomb in 1944, killing 121 members of the congregation.

There are five of these aristocratic infantry regiments of Guards, first formed during the English Civil War (1642–9), and the museum provides a social history in uniform (including a uniform worn by the Duke of Wellington), as well as a large collection of toy soldiers.

Buckingham Palace ⑭

Address: Buckingham Palace Road, www.royalcollection.org.uk
Tel: 020-7766 7300
Opening Hrs: State Rooms daily late July–late Aug 9.15am–7.45pm, last admission 5.15pm; Sept 9.15am–6.45pm, last admission 4.15pm; tickets are timed, and a visit lasts 2–2.5 hours (check for other special tours during winter months)
Transport: Green Park, Hyde Park Corner, Victoria

St James's Park.

Buckingham Palace has been the main London home of the royal family since Queen Victoria acceded to the throne in 1837. George IV had earlier employed John Nash (responsible for many of the grander parts of central London) to enlarge the building which had been built in the 17th century for the Duke of Buckingham (it originally became the property of the Crown when George III bought it for his wife in 1761). Nash added two wings that were later enclosed in a quadrangle, while the main facade came later still, being designed by Aston Webb in 1913.

A tour of the palace

The sumptuous **State Rooms** are open to the public for a few weeks in late summer when the Queen is not in residence, with audio guides in many languages. These include the Dining Room, Music Room, White Drawing Room and Throne Room, where there are paintings by Vermeer, Rubens and Rembrandt. You can also take a stroll through part of the 40-acre (16-hectare) Palace Gardens, where the cream of society mingles with the good and the worthy from all walks of life at the celebrated garden parties. The guests are invited because of some commendable contribution made to the nation, although few of the 8,000 people a year get to shake the Queen's hand.

Only the invited get further into the 775-room palace, although one enterprising intruder penetrated

Buckingham Palace.

State Banquet table.

ICA gallery.

as far as the Queen's bedroom one night in 1982. She talked to him quietly while managing to summon palace security. The Queen and the Duke of Edinburgh occupy about 12 of the rooms, on the first floor of the north wing, overlooking Green Park. If the Queen is in residence, the royal standard flies from the flagpole.

Next to the Royal Mews on Buckingham Palace Road, the **Queen's Gallery** (tel: 020-7766 7300; daily 10am–5.30pm; combined tickets with admission to Buckingham Palace and the Royal Mews are available late July–late Sept) holds one of the top private art collections in the world, including an exceptional collection of Leonardo da Vinci drawings, portraits by Holbein and Rubens, and watercolour views of Windsor by Paul Sandby. A significant new addition to the gallery is a gift of 97 works by the Royal Academy of Arts to celebrate the Queen's Diamond Jubilee in 2012. The portfolio includes prints, drawings, photographs and works in oil, watercolour and mixed media by 93 Academicians, among

them Tracey Emin, David Hockney, Anish Kapoor, Grayson Perry and Tom Phillips.

The adjoining **Royal Mews** (tel: 020-7766 7300; Nov and Feb–late Mar Mon–Sat 10am–4pm, late Mar–Oct daily 10am–5pm, closed Dec–Jan) contain royal vehicles, ranging from coaches to Rolls-Royces. The Gold State Coach, built for George III in 1762, is still used by the Queen on major state occasions.

Most of the everyday crowds come to see the **Changing the Guard** ceremony which takes place outside the palace on alternate mornings at 11.30am, and daily in May, June and July. The New Guard, which marches up from Wellington Barracks, meets the Old Guard in the forecourt of the palace and they exchange symbolic keys to the accompaniment of regimental music. The Foot Guards are distinctive for their bearskin hats.

The **Queen Victoria Memorial** ⓭ in front of the palace was built in 1901. It encompasses symbolic figures glorifying the achievements of the British Empire and its builders.

The Mall

The Mall, the wide thoroughfare leading from Buckingham Palace to Trafalgar Square, was laid out by Charles II as a second course for the game of *paille maille* (a kind of croquet which spread from Italy to France, and then to Britain), when the one in Pall Mall (see page 84) became too rowdy. The Mall is the venue for the autumn **State Opening of Parliament**, when the Queen rides in a gold stagecoach surrounded by more than 100 troopers of the Household Cavalry wearing armorial breastplates. A further eccentricity are two farriers who accompany the procession, bearing spiked axes that would once have been used to kill any horse lamed in the parade and chop off its hooves to prevent the horse flesh being sold to a butcher.

The Mall is lined with a succession of grand buildings and historic houses reflecting different styles and periods. The ducal palaces have been used as royal residences: **Clarence House** ⓰ is home to Prince Charles; at **Lancaster House** Chopin gave a recital for Queen Victoria; **Marlborough House** ⓱, designed by Sir Christopher Wren, was the home of Queen Mary, consort of George V (1865–1936) until her death in 1953. Now it is a Commonwealth conference and research centre. The brick Tudor **St James's Palace** faces onto Pall Mall (see page 84).

Near the end of the Mall is **Carlton House Terrace**, built by John Nash, part of which houses the headquarters of **The Royal Society**, a learned body for the promotion of natural sciences. The oldest society of its kind, it was founded in 1660.

At the Trafalgar Square end, the terrace incorporates the **Mall Gallery** and the **Institute of Contemporary Arts** ⓲, a venue for avant garde exhibitions, cinema and theatre, held in the restored Nash House.

The reinforced concrete structure across the Mall on the corner of the park is a bomb-proof shelter built for the Admiralty and nicknamed the Citadel, or Lenin's Tomb.

Admiralty Arch ⓳, leading from The Mall to Trafalgar Square, is a five-arched gateway commissioned by

The bronze statue of Frederick, the Duke of York, at the top of the Duke of York Steps.

Admiralty Arch.

Lobb's, the bootmaker.

St James's Palace.

King Edward VII in memory of his mother, Queen Victoria, and completed in 1911. Traffic passes through the two outer arches: the central arch is opened only for state occasions, letting royalty in and out of the city.

PALL MALL AND ST JAMES'S

Along elegant **Pall Mall** ⑳ exclusive gentlemen's clubs mingle with the grand homes of royalty. Their lofty book-lined rooms, picture-lined dining rooms and chandeliered lounges can be seen from the street. The area has been the haunt of men of influence since the 17th century.

In **Waterloo Place**, at the east end of Pall Mall and the bottom end of Regent Street, the statue of Frederick, the 'grand old' Duke of York (whose 10,000 men are fruitlessly marched up and down hill in a popular nursery rhyme), overlooks the Mall and St James's Park from its 124ft (37-metre) column. His monument's cost was met by extracting a day's wages from every man in the armed services.

One building that is unmistakable in Pall Mall is the red-brick **St James's Palace** ㉑ at the western end, built by Henry VIII in 1540 in a style that echoes his palace at Hampton Court. The state apartments are not open to the public and the chief relic of the original Tudor palace, the Gatehouse or **Clock Tower**, one of the finest examples of Tudor architecture in the city, is best viewed from the street. Clarence House is part of the complex, (open for tours in August).

North of St James's Palace **St James's Street** ㉒ leads into an area traditionally associated with gentlemen's tailors and shoemakers. The characterful shop frontages include **Berry Bros and Rudd**, at No. 3, a wine and spirits merchant which could be straight out of a Dickens novel. **James Lock and Co**, at No. 6, is the birthplace of the bowler hat. A few doors up is **Lobb's**, shoemakers to Queen Victoria, and now to the Duke of Edinburgh.

St James's Square

Also off the north side of Pall Mall is **St James's Square** ㉓ laid out by Henry Jermyn, 1st Earl of St Albans, in about 1660. The Dukes of Norfolk had a town house in the square from 1723 until 1938. The building was used by General Eisenhower when he was preparing to launch the invasions of North Africa and northwest Europe in World War II. Also here is the London Library, an independent subscription library whose past members have included Charles Dickens and George Eliot.

WESTMINSTER ABBEY

More than 3,000 notable people are buried here – it's an awe-inspiring collection of stone monuments dedicated to ecclesiastic greats.

Monarchs were interred here until George II in 1760, and they are still crowned here. Among the royal tombs, look out for those of Elizabeth I and her half-sister Queen Mary, both in the Lady Chapel. Poets lie close by, beginning with Geoffrey Chaucer in 1400, who had been Clerk of the King's Works to the Palace of Westminster.

Other tombs include those of the naturalist Charles Darwin, the explorer David Livingstone and the scientist Sir Isaac Newton.

The Tomb of the Unknown Warrior houses a body brought back from France at the end of World War I. As the national shrine, Westminster Abbey was the natural resting place for this anonymous representative of the war dead.

Royal weddings also take place in the Abbey, the most recent of which was Prince William and Kate Middleton in 2011.

Much of the present abbey, the third on the site, was built in the 13th century in early English Gothic style by Henry III. In the 16th century, Henry VII added the chapel in the late Gothic Perpendicular style. During the 18th century, Nicholas Hawksmoor designed the towers at the main west entrance.

The Essentials

Address: www.west minster-abbey.org
Tel: 020-7222 5152
Opening Hrs: Mon–Fri 9.30am–4.30pm, Wed until 7pm, Sat 9.30am–2.30pm; last admission one hour before closing. Free audio guide included in ticket price.
Transport: Westminster

The Tomb of the Unknown Warrior.

The Lady Chapel where King Henry VII is buried.

SOME HIGHLIGHTS

The south rose window and lancets.

Poets' Corner. The remains of Chaucer, Edmund Spenser, Samuel Johnson, Dryden, Sheridan, Browning, Tennyson, Dickens and Kipling lie here. Ben Jonson is buried standing up because he didn't wish to occupy too much space.

Coronation Chair. This has been used for every coronation in the Abbey since 1308.

Henry VII's Chapel. Contains exquisite fan-vaulting and the statues of nearly 100 saints.

Chapter House. Parliament met here in the 14th century. It has a fine tiled floor from 1259 and some lurid wall paintings based on the Apocalypse.

Undercroft Museum. This 11th-century room contains many of the Abbey's treasures as well as waxworks and death masks of various monarchs.

Sculptures. There are superbly carved angels in the south transept, and the chapels of Henry V and Henry VII are packed with saints and philosophers.

Organ recitals. Weekly, 30-minute organ recitals take place every Sunday at 5.45pm, free of charge.

Brass band concerts are often held in a garden off the Cloisters in July and August.

Poets' Corner consists of a mixture of burials and commemorations of playwrights, poets and writers. Shakespeare's memorial comprises the central feature of this group memorial.

The choir is the part of the abbey where the monks worshipped. This area includes the abbey organ; famous organists who played here include Henry Purcell, who is also buried in the abbey.

The marble effigy of Queen Elizabeth I sits over her tomb and that of her half-sister, Queen Mary Tudor, in the Lady Chapel. Originally buried in the vault of King Henry VII, Elizabeth's tomb was moved here in 1606. Her crown, collar, orb and sceptre are replacements, the originals having been stolen.

Gateway to Chinatown.

SOHO AND CHINATOWN

Soho, Chinatown and Leicester Square form London's main entertainment centre, where you'll find abundant clubs, pubs, cinemas and theatres, and cuisines from all over the globe.

The West End has long been seen as the place to head for a night out in London. Piccadilly Circus is a springboard for London's theatreland, while Leicester Square is the gateway to Chinatown and the location of the Empire cinema, the venue for UK film premieres. Over the past few decades, however, as tacky shops and chain restaurants have muscled in on these famous squares, their glamour has begun to look a little tarnished. Neighbouring Soho, on the other hand, has largely shed its once-dubious image as London's dark underbelly to become one of the capital's foremost destinations for drinking and dining.

PICCADILLY CIRCUS

At the heart of the West End is **Piccadilly Circus ❶**, star of millions of postcards. The first illuminated advertising signs appeared here in 1890, offering lucrative rental income to shopkeepers but contrasting harshly with the elegant architecture of neighbouring Regent Street. The statue of Eros, Greek god of love, was erected in 1893 as the Angel of Charity in honour of the philanthropic seventh Earl of Shaftesbury (1801–85), who drove the broad thoroughfare bearing his name through the squalid slums

that had grown up to the northeast. It's a popular meeting and photo spot for tourists, day and night.

Adding to Piccadilly's bright lights are the refurbished Victorian Criterion Theatre on the south side, a huge branch of Dutch fashion retailer The Sting on the west, and the 19th-century facade of the London Pavilion, a former music hall, on the east, which is now part of the **Trocadero Centre**, a complex of shops and restaurants on Holland Street. It includes Ripley's Believe It or Not! (daily

Main Attractions
Piccadilly Circus
Old Compton Street
Soho Square
Berwick Street Market
Carnaby Street
Chinatown

Map
Page 90

Sitting under Eros, Piccadilly Circus.

Bar Italia in Soho.

10am–midnight), a collection of hundreds of weird objects, from fossilized dinosaur eggs to a replica of Tower Bridge made from matchsticks. It's also home to a Picturehouse cinema.

In 2016, the Trocadero Centre is scheduled to reopen as a budget 583-bedroom hotel across seven floors, incorporating Tokyo-style 'pod' rooms, apartments, shops and a rooftop bar.

BUSTLING SOHO

On the north side of Shaftesbury Avenue lies Soho, a bustling area of narrow streets long popular with immigrants. Flemish weavers, French Huguenots, Greeks, Italians, Belgians, Maltese, Swiss, Chinese and Russian Jews have sought refuge here at various times. Their influence is still felt in the patisseries, delicatessens, restaurants and shops.

Four hundred years ago Soho was an area of open fields, and its name is said to come from a hunting cry: 'So-ho, so-ho!'.

Bars and clip joints

Once infamous as the centre of London's sex industry, Soho occupies a middle-ground between the edgy, seedier Soho of its past and the tourist-friendly hotspot of smart bars and restaurants that populate the area today. Most of the strip joints and sex shops have been pushed towards the side streets. There are also venues for drag artists and transvestites that have been going long enough to have become almost respectable – however the forced closure of famous cabaret joint Madame Jojo's in 2014, with plans to redevelop the area, was seen as a way of 'sanitising' Soho. There are still plenty of attractive late-night bars and restaurants designed for the discerning gay crowd, drawing visitors of all persuasions.

Old Compton Street ❷

This is Soho's main artery, where a few of the celebrated continental food stores, cafés and specialist shops

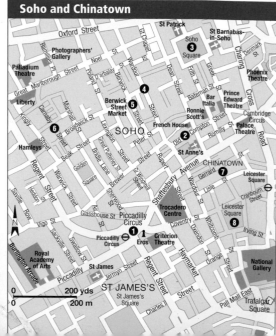

that once dominated the street, live on. Most have been replaced by modern coffee shops, bars and more outlandish establishments, such as body-piercing and tattoo parlours and erotic bookstores.

Situated at the Charing Cross Road end of Old Compton Street, the **Prince Edward Theatre**, dating back to 1930, stages long-running musicals. It was here that cabaret artiste Josephine Baker made her London debut in 1933.

Just off Old Compton Street is the French House in Dean Street, the centre of the Free French in World War II, an artists' haunt and still fiercely French. Artists such as Francis Bacon and Lucian Freud used to take advantage of the liberal licensing arrangements at the Colony Club in Dean Street. At 22 Frith Street, opposite Ronnie Scott's jazz club, is Bar Italia, a narrow café-bar with pavement seating and a retro Italian feel, which serves the best cappuccino in town and is open from 7am to 5am. It is also a great place to watch international football matches, especially Italy matches; the large screen at the back of the bar is visible from the street.

Soho Square ❸

At the top of Frith Street, leafy **Soho Square** was one of London's best addresses when it was built in the 17th century. Today various film, new media and design companies are based here, their minimalist receptions lit up by plasma screens or statement art. During the summer the garden at the heart of the square is crowded with office workers grabbing a bit of sun with their sandwich. In the centre of the square are a 17th-century statue of Charles II and a 19th-century mock-Tudor gardeners' tool shed from which steps lead down to an underground cavern, used as a workshop during World War II.

The red-brick tower of St Patrick's Catholic Church lends a bit of variety to the architectural proceedings. Established in 1893 on the site of an earlier church, a £3.5 million restoration has returned St Patrick's to its former glory.

A hint of Soho Square's former character can be seen in **St-Barnabas-in-Soho**, an 18th-century house of charitable works, caring for the destitute, on the corner of Greek Street.

The raunchier side of Soho.

Old Compton Street.

HISTORIC STREETS

Many famous people are associated with Soho, from the painters Thomas Gainsborough (1727–88) to Francis Bacon (1909–92), from Casanova (1725–98) to Oscar Wilde (1854–1900). A blue plaque reminds you that 41 Beak Street was the home of Canaletto, the Venetian painter, from 1749 to 1751. In 1926 John Logie Baird transmitted the first television images from an attic at 22 Frith Street (now Bar Italia), next door to where Mozart stayed as a boy. The house at 26 Dean Street, now Quo Vadis restaurant, is where Karl Marx wrote *Das Kapital*. Further down, at No. 49, Dylan Thomas once left the manuscript of Under Milk Wood under his chair at the French House pub.

Royal Events

The events that I have attended to mark my Diamond Jubilee have been a humbling experience.' Her Majesty Queen Elizabeth II.

For millions of visitors, London is the Royal Family. Buckingham Palace, St James's Palace, the Tower of London and Kensington Gardens all symbolise the enduring presence of a dynasty that has played a significant role in British life for more than a thousand years. The wedding of Prince William and Kate Middleton in 2011 boosted the royals' popularity, which reached its apogee in 2012 in the euphoria of the Diamond Jubilee and London Olympics.

In 2012, the Queen celebrated a landmark 60 years on the throne: only Queen Victoria has reigned for longer. The anniversary was celebrated (as her coronation had been) by street parties across the UK over an unprecedented four-day public holiday in June. Official celebrations included a Diamond Jubilee concert in front of Buckingham Palace, a rather cold and damp Thames Jubilee Pageant, a service of thanksgiving at St Paul's Cathedral and a carriage procession through London watched by a crowd

Prince William and Kate Middleton process down the aisle in Westminster Abbey.

estimated at a million people. The following year a special service was held in Westminster Abbey to celebrate the 60th anniversary of the Queen's coronation.

In May 2016, the city celebrated the Queen's 90th birthday with a spectacular 90-minute display at Windsor Castle combining a fly-past, laser show and horse parade.

Royal wedding and babies

The wedding of Prince William to Kate Middleton in 2011 attracted a global television audience of around two billion people. Thousands of onlookers descended on London to share in the party atmosphere, with many spending the night sleeping in the streets to ensure a good view of the procession and get a glimpse of the bride's much-awaited dress – an elegant ivory satin creation, designed by Sarah Burton of Alexander McQueen, decorated with lace hand-made by the Royal School of Needlework at Hampton Court.

The wedding was an intriguing mix of the ancient and modern: while the couple were making their vows, for instance, the internet practically melted as people tweeted their admiration. The couple emerged from the cathedral with new titles, the Duke and Duchess of Cambridge, and later delighted the crowds in the Mall with two balcony kisses. After a buffet reception at Buckingham Palace for around 650 guests, hosted by the Queen, William drove away his new bride in his father's borrowed Aston Martin.

As soon as William and Kate tied the knot, speculation was rife as to how long it would be before Britain would be celebrating the birth of a new heir to the throne, so the official announcement on 3 December 2012 that the Duchess was expecting her first child was met with great excitement. Prince George Alexander Louis was duly born on 22 July 2013, weighing 8lb 6oz. Described by his proud father soon after his birth as 'a little bit of a rascal', he is third in line to the throne, after Prince Charles and Prince William. Two years later, Princess Charlotte Elizabeth Diana was born, fourth-in-line.

These events have been good for Britain's economy, boosting visitor numbers to London and retail spending nationwide.

Leicester Square.

known as the only street in the world which was shady on both sides. It is still the heart of London's film and recording industries, and during weekday lunch times the surrounding bars and restaurants are full of 30-something media folk discussing the next big thing.

Wardour Street has become a restaurant hotspot, and venues such as Busaba Eathai (Thai) and Floridita (Cuban) ensure the street is busy long after office hours.

At the Shaftesbury Avenue end of Wardour Street, a tower is all that remains of Sir Christopher Wren's church of **St Anne's**, bombed in the war, though its beautifully kept gardens provide some shade and benches for a rest on a hot day.

Berwick Street Market ❺

The fruit and vegetable market in parallel **Berwick Street** is well laid out and inexpensive, and its stalls also sell cheese and flowers, plus vintage clothes and antiques. There is also a large selection of hot food stalls, a good choice for an inexpensive lunch of fresh global cuisine.

Once a residential hostel, it is now a 'life skills' centre for homeless people. Its elegant interior of fine woodcarvings, fireplaces and plasterwork is not open to the public but a monthly series of events are held here.

Wardour Street ❹

Continuing west from Soho Square past Dean Street, the next main road is **Wardour Street**, once sarcastically

FACT

Plenty of Soho's bars and pubs are still predominantly gay: a few examples are the Admiral Duncan and Comptons of Soho on Old Compton Street, Ku Bar on Lisle Street and Frith Street, and The Yard on Rupert Street with an alfresco courtyard.

Berwick Street Market.

Carnaby Street ⑥

A detour away from Soho via Broadwick Street takes you towards **Carnaby Street**. The street now hosts up-market branches of some of the hipper high-street chains, including Vans, Jack Wills, Lee Jeans and American Apparel. If you explore the pedestrianised streets to the east, off Carnaby Street, you will still find more offbeat fashions that first put the area on the map.

Chinatown ⑦

Returning to Soho and continuing down Wardour Street, walk along the south side of Shaftesbury Avenue to **Gerrard Street** and parallel **Lisle Street**, home of Chinese grocers, restaurants and stores. Kitsch Chinese street furniture, lamps and archways in Gerrard Street make this the heart of Chinatown. Established in the 1950s, after the first Chinatown in

Carnaby Street.

Chinatown building.

Limehouse was damaged by World War II bombing, it has some of the best South East Asian cuisine in town, although quality varies.

There are also Chinese herbal and medicine shops, and some very stylish cocktail bars including Opium bar (Gerrard Street). On Sundays the Chinese food market is popular with families taking a day out. Chinese New Year in late January or early February is celebrated in style, with massive papier-mâché lions dancing through the streets.

Leicester Square ⑧

Just south of Chinatown, Leicester Square is home of the big cinemas and host to the capital's film premieres. Until the 17th century, this was the garden of Leicester House, and at the four corners of the garden are busts of famous people associated with the square. At the centre is the **Shakespeare monument** (1874), surrounded by brass plates in the ground giving distances to cities all over the world. Facing the bard is a **statue of Charlie Chaplin**, born in Southwark, south London, in 1889. Around the square is a regular contingent of caricature artists, buskers and, on special occasions, a funfair carousel and amusement rides.

TRAFALGAR SQUARE AND COVENT GARDEN

With its shooting fountains and soaring Nelson's Column, Trafalgar Square is one of London's most popular open spaces. It is also a short hop from vibrant Covent Garden.

South of Leicester Square is Trafalgar Square, from where the Strand heads east, flanked on one side by Covent Garden and on the other by the riverside Victoria Embankment leading down to Waterloo Bridge.

TRAFALGAR SQUARE ❶

The closest that London has to the kind of large public square common in other European capitals was designed in 1838 by Sir Charles Barry. In 1841 it was named **Trafalgar Square** to commemorate Admiral Lord Nelson's 1805 victory against Napoleon's navy at Trafalgar, off the Atlantic coast of Spain.

At the centre of the square is **Nelson's Column**, a 169ft (51.5-metre) monument, made up of a Corinthian column topped by a statue of Horatio Nelson, battle-scarred with only one arm but without a patch on his blind eye. He is gazing towards the Mall, inspecting the fleet of model ships attached to pillars on the avenue. The four iconic lions (1847) are by Edwin Landseer.

Around the square, Canada House, South Africa House and Uganda House are memories of distant Empire days. Also celebrating the old Empire are statues of General Charles

Napier and Major General Sir Henry Havelock, on the plinths in the two southern corners of the square. The statue in the northeast corner depicts George IV.

Controversy over who should occupy the northwest corner's fourth plinth – left empty after plans in 1841 to erect an equestrian statue collapsed through lack of funds – caught Londoners' imaginations, and a committee was formed to commission works of art that could take their turn on the plinth.

Main Attractions

Trafalgar Square
National Gallery
National Portrait Gallery
St Martin-in-the-Fields
Covent Garden Market
Royal Opera House
St Paul's Church
London Transport Museum
London Coliseum
Charing Cross Bookshops

Map

Page 99

Covent Garden street performer.

SHOP

Museum shops are big business these days, and the ones at the National Gallery and National Portrait Gallery (both immediately accessible from the main entrances) do a great range of art-themed merchandise, from books to mugs, clothing, jewellery and items for children.

National Portrait Gallery.

Anthony Gormley's *One and Other* was perhaps the most popular, as members of the public were able to adopt the plinth for an hour at a time and do whatever they wished. Since then, international artists have been commissioned to create temporary pieces of artwork for the space; these have included a giant blue cockerel by Katharina Fritsch, *Gift Horse* – a full-size bronze equine skeleton – by Hans Haacke and David Shrigley's sculpture of a human hand.

The square has long been the site of public gatherings, political demonstrations and New Year celebrations. A mayoral campaign to rid it of its traditional plague of pigeons was largely successful, and in 2003 the north side of the square was pedestrianised to give people a sporting chance of reaching the fountains without being mown down by traffic.

In the southwest corner of the square, Admiralty Arch marks the start of The Mall, leading to Buckingham Palace (see page 80). Whitehall, the other exit, will lead you to the Houses of Parliament (see page 74).

The National Gallery ❷

Address: Trafalgar Square, www.nationalgallery.org.uk
Tel: 020-7747 2885
Opening Hrs: Sat–Thu 10am–6pm, Fri 10am–9pm
Entrance Fee: free except some special exhibitions
Transport: Charing Cross

Dominating the north side of Trafalgar Square is the neoclassical **National Gallery**, designed by William Wilkins in 1838 with a modern wing by Robert Venturi completed in 1991. This is the country's most important art gallery, home to around 2,000 Western European masterpieces, including works by Rembrandt, Rubens, El Greco, Vermeer and Van Gogh. For full details, see page 104.

The National Portrait Gallery ❸

Address: St Martin's Place, www.npg.org.uk

NELSON'S COLUMN

Horatio Nelson (1758–1805) is the country's greatest naval hero. A tiny figure, he was partially blinded in his right eye in Corsica, had his right arm amputated at Santa Cruz and was pacing the deck of HMS *Victory* when he was fatally shot by a French sharpshooter off Cape Trafalgar. He could be insubordinate, famously putting a telescope to his blind eye at the Battle of Copenhagen and pretending he could not read an order to disengage from battle. He is also remembered for his affair with Emma Hamilton, the wife of the British Ambassador to Naples. The three shared a *ménage à trois*.

Tel: 020-7306 0055 or 020-7312 2463
Opening Hrs: Sat–Wed 10am–6pm, Thu–Fri 10am–9pm
Entrance Fee: free except for some special exhibitions
Transport: Charing Cross

Behind the National Gallery is the **National Portrait Gallery**, housed in a Florentine Renaissance building originally designed by architect Ewan Christian and opened in 1896. Only a fraction of the collection's 10,000 artworks, plus half a million photographs of the nation's illustrious men and women, is on display at any one time. There are also temporary exhibitions. For full details, see page 106.

St Martin-in-the-Fields ❹

Address: Iratalgar Square, www.stmartin-in-the-fields.org
Tel: box office and information 020-7766 1100
Opening Hrs: Mon–Tue, Thu–Fri 8.30am–6pm, Wed 8.30am–5pm, Sat 9.30am–6pm, Sun 3.30pm–5pm; closed Mon–Fri 1–2pm
Entrance Fee: free except evening concerts
Transport: Charing Cross

Across the road is the church of **St Martin-in-the-Fields**, the oldest building in Trafalgar Square, built in 1726 by a Scottish architect, James Gibbs, when this venue was in fields outside the city. Nell Gwynne, the mistress of Charles II, is one of several famous people buried in this parish church of the royal family, which was so chic in the 18th century that pews were rented out on an annual basis. The royal box is on the left of the altar. The crypt houses the popular Café in the Crypt, a good spot for lunch or coffee, and the London Brass Rubbing Centre. This area was used as an air-raid shelter during the bombing blitz of World War II.

Regular classical music concerts are held in the church on Wednesday,

Nelson's Column.

The entrance to the National Gallery, seen from the side.

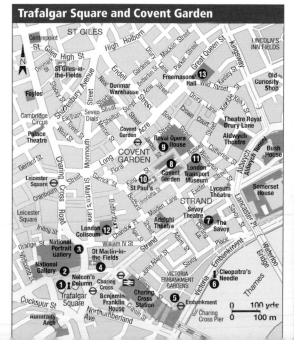

Thursday, Friday and Saturday, at either 7.30pm or 8pm. There are also free lunchtime concerts.

AROUND THE STRAND

The mundane modern architecture in the Strand, the main thoroughfare connecting the West End with the City, camouflages the fact that it was once a very fashionable street, home in the 18th and 19th centuries to the poet Samuel Taylor Coleridge and the novelist George Eliot. Although the street is past its glory days, a sense of history is not altogether lost: you can still dine in traditional style at Simpson's, opened in 1848, or take tea in the Thames Room of the graceful Savoy hotel.

At the Strand's western end, near Trafalgar Square, is **Charing Cross** railway station. In front of it is a replica of the last of 12 crosses set up by Edward I in 1291 to mark the funeral procession of his queen, Eleanor of Castile, from Nottinghamshire to Westminster Abbey. "Charing" is thought by some to come from "*chère*

One of the sphinxes flanking Cleopatra's Needle.

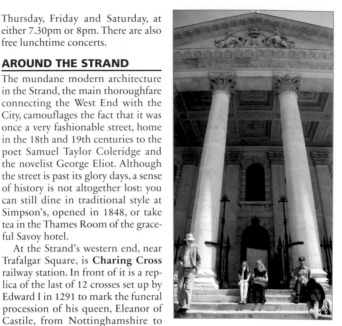

Soaking up the sunshine on the entrance steps to St Martin-in-the-Fields.

reine" (dear queen) Eleanor, although it is more likely to have come from the Old English word "*cierran*", meaning to turn.

Victoria Embankment

At this point, cut down Villiers Street, which for a while was home to Rudyard Kipling, author of *The Jungle Book* (a blue plaque marks the spot). Nearby is Craven Street, where the Founding Father of the USA, Benjamin Franklin, lived from 1757 to 1775. His Georgian mansion is now a fascinating and lively museum, the Benjamin Franklin House (36 Craven Street; tel: 020-7839 2006; www.benjaminfranklin-house.org; historical experience shows Wed–Sun noon–4.15pm; architectural guided tours Mon noon, 1pm, 2pm, 3.15pm and 4.15pm; book in advance).

Back on Villiers Street, at its southern end, is **Victoria Embankment**, built in 1870 to ease traffic congestion and carry sewage pipes needed to improve London's crude sanitation system. In the Victoria **Embankment Gardens** ❺ a restored **Water Gate** once marked the river entrance to York House, London home of the archbishops of York, birthplace of philosopher and statesman Francis Bacon (1561–1626) and home of the dukes of Buckingham.

On the river front is **Charing Cross Pier**, a starting point for boats heading east to Greenwich. This is also the site of the 60ft (18-metre) **Cleopatra's Needle** ❻, carved in Aswan, Egypt, c.1475 BC and presented to Britain in 1819 (see box). The needle is flanked by two bronze sphinxes.

The Savoy

Back on the Strand are several theatres, including the **Adelphi**, opened in 1806. Richard D'Oyly Carte (1844–1901), sponsor of Gilbert and Sullivan operas at the splendid Art Deco **Savoy Theatre**, also financed the building of the **Savoy Hotel** ❼, which opened in 1889 as one of the first in London with private bathrooms, electric lights and lifts (elevators). From the Strand, the Savoy is unimposing, but it is grand enough to have its own private forecourt and the only road in Britain where traffic drives on the right.

D'Oyly Carte is commemorated in a stained-glass window in the **Queen's Chapel of the Savoy** (www.duchyoflancaster.co.uk; Oct–July Mon–Thu 9am–4pm, Sun 10am–4pm services permitting), behind the hotel. It was founded in the 16th century when the former Savoy Palace became a hospital. Built by Peter, 9th Count of Savoy, in 1246, the palace had its heyday under John of Gaunt (1340–99), when it was 'the fayrest manor in Europe, big enough for a large part of an army'.

Browsing at the Apple Market in Covent Garden piazza.

Cleopatra's Needle, on the Victoria Embankment.

London Transport Museum.

Covent Garden ❽

Named after a convent whose fields occupied the site, **Covent Garden** was for centuries the principal market in London for vegetables, fruit and flowers. It was also the workplace of Eliza Doolittle, the flower girl in George Bernard Shaw's *Pygmalion*, who later burst into song in the film and musical *My Fair Lady*. The main piazza was originally laid out with colonnaded town houses designed by Inigo Jones c.1630, and inspired by the 16th-century Italian architect Andrea Palladio. A small market was founded here as early as 1656.

After the market moved out in 1974, the area became a blueprint for turning old commercial buildings into a mall of stores and stalls. Restaurants, cafés and shops occupy the old warehouses in the streets around the market square. There is a good line in street entertainers, who undergo auditions before they are granted a licence to perform here.

Royal Opera House ❾

Address: Bow Street, www.roh.org.uk
Tel: 020-7304 4000
Opening Hrs: box office Mon–Sat 10am–8pm
Entrance Fee: free except for performances and tours
Transport: Covent Garden

In 1733, a theatre was established in the northeast corner of Covent Garden, on the site now occupied by the **Royal Opera House**. A fire ravaged the first building in 1808, consuming Handel's organ and many of his works. The Opera House has had to contend with unimpressed audiences: price riots were common in the 19th century, and in 1809 lasted 61 nights. The Floral Hall, which acts as a reception space prior to performances and during intervals, is spectacular.

St Paul's Church ❿

Address: Bedford Street, www.actors church.org
Tel: 020-7836 5221
Opening Hrs: Mon–Fri 8.30am–5pm, Sun 9am–1pm and for services
Entrance Fee: free
Transport: Covent Garden

The portico of **St Paul's**, the actors' church, built in 1633 by Inigo Jones, and used as a backdrop in *My Fair Lady*, dominates the western end of the square. The vaults and grounds of this Tuscan-style church are said to contain the remains of more famous people than any other church except Westminster Abbey. The headstones have long been removed, but residents include master wood carver Grinling Gibbons (died 1720), the composer of **Rule Britannia**, Thomas Arne (1778) and the actress Ellen Terry (1928).

London Transport Museum ⓫

Address: Covent Garden Piazza,
www.ltmuseum.co.uk
Tel: 020-7379 6344 or 020-7565
7299
Opening Hrs: Sat–Thu 10am–6pm,
Fri 11am–6pm; last entry 45 mins
before closing
Entrance Fee: free to accompanied
children under 16
Transport: Covent Garden

The old flower market, in the south-eastern corner of the square, is now occupied by **London Transport Museum**, which brings alive the development of London's transport network, from trams and trolley-buses to the Routemaster bus. There is plenty of hands-on fun, so it's great for children. You can take the wheel of an old double-decker bus, try your hand as a Tube conductor or bump around with other passengers in the back of a train. There's also a great shop on the ground floor for stationery, books and gifts.

Around Drury Lane

Neighbouring **Drury Lane** is closely linked with the theatre. Its principal venue is the Theatre Royal, which, when it opened in 1663, was only the second legitimate playhouse in the city. The mistress of Charles II, Nell Gwynne, depicted by cartoonists as a voluptuous orange seller, trod the boards here. Being one of the largest in the West End, its stage can mount blockbuster musicals.

Opposite its white Corinthian portico is the former **Bow Street police station**, home in the 18th century of the scarlet-waistcoated Bow Street Runners, the prototype policemen.

Long Acre and St Martin's Lane

The main street Long Acre cuts through Covent Garden, from Neal Street to Leicester Square tube station. At 12–14 Long Acre is Britain's best travel bookshop, **Stanford's**. South of Long Acre is St Martin's Lane, home of the English National Opera's **London Coliseum ⓬**, where productions are sung in English, with surtitles.

Great Queen Street is the site of the **Freemasons' Hall ⓭** (tel: 020-7831 9811; www.ugle.org.uk; Mon–Fri 11am–4pm), an imposing white behemoth that houses a museum on the history of freemasonry, a library and tavern. It celebrates its tricentenary in 2017.

CHARING CROSS ROAD

Long Acre leads to **Charing Cross Road**, a hub for rare and second-hand books. **Foyles** is a maze of more than 4 million volumes but has become better organised, if duller, since the death of its eccentric former owner, Christina Foyle. It has a café, and often hosts free jazz performances. **Zwemmer's** is known for fine art and photography books. Denmark Street – also known as **Tin Pan Alley** – had dozens of music shops and studios and regarded as the home of early British rock 'n' roll, although it's a shadow of its 1960s heyday.

Music shop on Charing Cross Road.

THE NATIONAL GALLERY

Dominating Trafalgar Square is one of the world's finest art collections, bringing together masterpieces from over seven centuries – and entry is free.

J.M.W. Turner's The Fighting Téméraire, voted the nation's favourite picture in a poll in 2005.

Rembrandt's Self Portrait at the Age of 63, 1669.

The National Gallery was founded in 1824, when a private collection of 38 paintings was acquired by the British Government for the sum of £57,000 and exhibited in the house of the owner, banker John Julius Angsterstein, at 100 Pall Mall. Included in the collection were *Bacchanal* by Poussin, *St Ursula* and *The Queen of Sheba* by landscape master Claude, paintings by Van Dyck, two admirable Rembrandts, a superb Aelbert Cuyp, and William Hogarth's narrative, six pictures called *Marriage à la Mode*. As the collection grew, a new building was needed. William Wilkins' long, low construction, with its neoclassical facade and dome, opened in 1834 in the then-recently created Trafalgar Square. The building has been remodelled in various ways. The most prominent addition is the Sainsbury Wing, added in 1991.

The Essentials

Address: Trafalgar Square;
www.nationalgallery.org.uk
Tel: 020-7747 2885
Opening Hrs: Sat–Thu 10am–6pm, Fri 10am–9pm
Entrance Fee: free except some exhibitions
Transport: Charing Cross

Among the gallery's Post-Impressionist works is Georges Seurat's Bathers at Asnières.

The West Wing contains paintings from 1500–1600, including Raphael's Saint Catherine of Alexandria (c.1507), pictured, Michelangelo's The Entombment (c.1500–1) and Leonardo's The Virgin of the Rocks (1491–1508).

Botticelli's Venus and Mars (c.1485) in the Sainsbury Wing.

GALLERY LAYOUT

Constable's The Hay Wain.

The National Gallery's collection is arranged chronologically, from the 13th century to the end of the 19th century, through four wings, starting in the Sainsbury Wing containing works from the 13th–15th centuries.

Many people enter the gallery through its grand main entrance, from where a magnificent flight of stairs offers you a choice of three directions. Take the left flight to the West Wing and the Renaissance galleries. Go straight ahead, through the Central Hall, for the North Wing, where you will find several portraits by Rembrandt as well as Velázquez's *Rokeby Venus*, the Spanish painter's only surviving nude, or turn right for the East Wing. Here you will find portraits and landscapes, including work by Gainsborough, Constable, J M W Turner and Stubbs.

For special exhibitions held in the main wing, it is best to take the Getty Entrance, which also offers level access and wheelchairs.

NATIONAL PORTRAIT GALLERY

Five centuries of portraits of Britain's most famous and important figures are showcased here.

Portrait of Elizabeth I by an anonymous artist.

A British Historical Portrait gallery was founded in 1856 – the world's first portrait gallery – and was the initiative of the 5th Earl of Stanhope. With actual collection, it relied on gifts and bequests. The first was the 'Chandos' picture of William Shakespeare, attributed to John Taylor, c.1610, and arguably the only portrait of Britain's most famous playwright done from life. From the start, additions to the collection (initially comprising traditional paintings, drawings and sculpture, with photography a later addition) were determined by the status of the sitter and historical importance of the portrait, not by their quality as works of art. These criteria still pertain today. Portraits of living people were not admitted until 1968, when the policy was changed to encourage younger artists and a fresh exploration of the genre.

The Essentials

Address: St Martin's Place;
www.npg.org.uk
Tel: 020-7312 2463/7306 0055
Opening Hrs: Sat–Wed 10am–6pm, Thu–Fri 10am–9pm
Entrance Fee: free except some exhibitions
Transport: Charing Cross

Room 12 is devoted to portraits of those closely involved with the arts in the late 18th century, such as Samuel Johnson, Handel and the prolific landscape architect Capability Brown. A self-portrait of the artist Gainsborough, and a bust of poet Alexander Pope, can also be found here.

Among the 17th- and 18th-century portraits on the second floor is this one of Lady Emma Hamilton, wife of the British Ambassador to Naples and the mistress of Lord Nelson, painted by George Romney in 1785. Emma Hamilton was known for her great beauty and vitality; there are 28 portraits of her in the gallery's collection.

SPECIAL EXHIBITIONS

Changing exhibitions are held on the ground floor — check the website to see current and forthcoming listings. Recent examples in 2016 include masterpieces from Moscow's state gallery in Russia and the Arts, and Goya. Each year the annual Taylor Wessing Photographic Portrait Prize and BP Portrait Award showcase the best works of professionals and amateurs.

A visitor looks at Andy Warhol's Marilyn.

Gallery Layout
The displays are broadly chronological, starting on the second floor (reached by the vast escalator from the main hall) and ending on the ground floor. There are thematic subdivisions within each period: the Tudors, 17th-century and 18th-century portraits on the second floor; the Victorians and 20th-century portraits until 1990 (including special displays on the Balcony Gallery and landing) on the first floor. On the ground floor are the ever-popular British portraits since 1990, plus temporary shows.

The official portraits of the Victorian and Edwardian periods, filling the bulk of the first floor, are some of the last examples of stylish formality. Works are organised by theme, including the arts in Room 24, home to this Romantic portrait of poet Alfred Tennyson by Samuel Laurence.

Other themes range from science and technology in Room 27, featuring this portrait of evolutionist Charles Darwin, to politics, expansion and empire.

Getting shoes shined inside Burlington Arcade, a classy place to shop.

MAYFAIR TO OXFORD STREET

Mayfair has consistently retained its social prestige since the building of its great estates began in the 1660s. With its Georgian residences, gentlemen's clubs and exclusive shops, it is synonymous with wealth.

West of Trafalgar Square and Piccadilly Circus is Mayfair, the smartest part of town. This is where a broom cupboard costs as much as a house in the country; where shoes are handmade and where life is bespoke.

The area is divided in two by the famous thoroughfare Piccadilly. To the south lies St James's (see page 84), which grew up around the life of the royal court; to the north is Mayfair, the most expensive place to land on the English Monopoly board. The second most expensive, Park Lane, forms the western boundary of the area, while Oxford Street, the capital's most famous shopping street, is on its northern side.

PICCADILLY

Court fops and dandies were a source of moneymaking for London's traders. In the 18th century Robert Baker grew rich by selling them 'pickadils' – fashionable stiff collars – and built a mansion on what was then Portugal Street. It became known as **Piccadilly**, and it remains a fashionable street and a favourite location for airline and national tourist offices.

Royal Academy of Arts ❶
Address: Burlington House, Piccadilly,

www.royalacademy.org.uk
Tel: 020-7300 8000
Opening Hrs: Sat–Thu 10am–6pm, Fri 10am–10pm; check for 1-hour tours (free)
Entrance Fee: permanent collection free
Transport: Green Park

Behind the imposing Renaissance-style facade of **Burlington House** on the north side, fronted by a handsome courtyard, the Academy stages big, thematic exhibitions. It is most famous for its Summer Exhibition,

Fortnum & Mason.

The Royal Academy is famous for its Summer Exhibition, the world's largest open contemporary art exhibition.in the world.

the world's largest open submission exhibition; held annually since 1769 it displays thousands of works in many mediums and genres.

In the **John Madejski Fine Rooms**, tucked to the rear of the main staircase, much of the RA's permanent collection is rotated on a yearly basis. In contrast to the Academy's top-lit galleries, these smaller rooms have been restored to reveal heavy gilding and panelled doors crowned by plaster putti – the *gusto italiano* as interpreted by William Kent in the 1720s. The Academy's most famous bequests include Michelangelo's marble *Taddei Tondo* (in the high-tech Sackler wing), Constable's *The Leaping Horse* and Gainsborough's *A Romantic Landscape*.

Fine living

At No. 181 Piccadilly is the luxury **Fortnum & Mason ❷**, founded in 1707 and official grocers to the Queen, is famed not only for its exquisite food

hampers, but also for the four colonies of bees on the roof. A multi-million-pound tercentenary refurbishment saw the food hall expand into the basement, with a new gin bar and later the Diamond Jubilee Tea Salon, opened by the Queen in 2012.

A little further along Piccadilly is **The Ritz ❸**, where afternoon tea in the Palm Court is a tradition. The hotel, built in 1906, was fashionable in the 1930s and 1940s, when Winston Churchill was among the guests. In 1995 the hotel was bought for £75 million by the Barclay brothers, David and Frederick, who have restored it to its former glory. Baroness (Margaret) Thatcher lived out her final months in a luxury suite here. The Baroque-style Louis XVI dining room, in elegant pinks and golds, overlooks Green Park.

Piccadilly Arcade, known for its glass and chinaware shops, has graceful, bow-fronted Regency windows which belie the fact that it was built in 1910. Almost opposite and beside

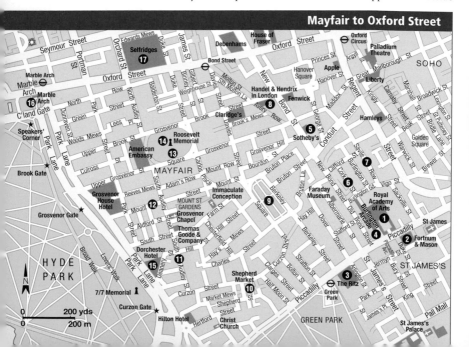

Entrance to The Ritz hotel.

the Academy, **Burlington Arcade ④**, built in 1819, is a beautiful covered shopping street lined with traditional purveyors of luxury goods. This is one of Britain's first shopping arcades; the gates are closed at night and on Sundays.

MAYFAIR

The region bounded by Piccadilly and Park Lane, Oxford and Regent streets has been a place of wealth and power since the early 18th century, when it was first laid out by the Grosvenor family, dukes of Westminster. **Mayfair** takes its name from the fair that was held annually on the site of what is now Shepherd Market. In the best British tradition, it clings to its exclusivity, although many of the magnificent Georgian homes of business barons and princes of property are now overrun with hotels, luxury offices, embassies and clubs.

The high street of Mayfair is **Bond Street**, divided into Old Bond Street at its southern end leading north to New Bond Street. Here are London's most exclusive couturiers and designer boutiques, jewellery shops, antiques emporia and art galleries.

The headquarters of **Sotheby's ⑤**, the auctioneers founded in 1744 and now American-owned, is at No. 34.

World-record prices for art works are notched up here, but not every sale is for millionaires. Admission is free, as long as you look reasonably presentable, and there is a small café.

Asprey the jeweller and Fenwick's the department store are also part of Bond Street's fabric and are worth checking out. Although some commercial galleries have moved to burgeoning east London neighbourhoods, there are still many galleries

The place to come for gentlemen's bespoke tailoring.

The Burlington Arcade was built in 1819. This Regency promenade of Lilliputian shops is patrolled by Beadles. In their top hats and livery, they ensure good behaviour, with "no undue whistling, humming or hurrying". Only a Beadle knows what constitutes undue humming.

Italian restaurant Da Corradi, Shepherd Market.

in Bond Street, adjacent Bruton Street and especially **Cork Street** ❻; prestigious premises include Waddington Custot and Browse & Darby in Cork Street, where many of Britain's top artists are represented. Plans to demolish part of the street to make way for a £90 million development may still go ahead in spite of a 'Save Cork Street' campaign.

Just beyond is **Savile Row** ❼, the home of several gentlemen's outfitters, where even off-the-peg items are highly priced. The offices of Apple, the Beatles company, were at No. 3, where in 1969 the group staged what was to be their last ever live concert from its roof.

Handel & Hendrix in London ❽

Address: 25 Brook Street, www.handel hendrix.org
Tel: 020-7495 1685
Opening Hrs: Tue–Sat 10am–6pm, Thu 10am–8pm, Sun noon–6pm
Transport: Bond Street, Oxford Circus

On **Brook Street**, which runs from the west side of New Bond Street, stands the house in which Handel

wrote his *Messiah*. His home for 35 years until his death in 1759, it has been refurbished in early 18th-century style. While the composer's life and work is well documented with information sheets, CD listening posts, and paintings, prints and old musical scores, the sparsely furnished rooms come into their own as evocative settings for intimate chamber music concerts – often with the Handel House harpsichord as their focus – and other special events.

After a major refurbishment, the venue (formerly known simply as Handel House) reopened as Handel & Hendrix in London, opening up the adjacent upstairs flat at No. 23 where the great rock guitarist Jimi Hendrix lived in the late 1960s. Detailed exhibits tell the story of his life and music while in London. There is now a new studio space, with a lift to access all floors. Look out for rehearsals, masterclasses, Saturday talks and Thursday concerts, plus family events during weekends.

Smart addresses

Brook Street is also home to **Claridge's**, one of London's premier luxury hotels, built in the 1890s, though mostly in Art Deco style. The street is also home to the Savile Club, a men-only haven of the literary establishment; past members include Thomas Hardy and the poet Yeats.

BERKELEY SQUARE ❾

Nightingales rarely sing in **Berkeley Square**, though they may have done when the song was written in 1939, and this once highly aristocratic square has been much spoilt by dull office buildings. In 1774 Lord Clive of India committed suicide at No. 45. The Earl of Shelburne, the prime minister who conceded the independence of the United States in 1783, lived in Lansdowne House, now the site of the private members' Lansdowne Club. Berkeley Square House is built

on the site of the house where Queen Elizabeth II was born in 1926.

SHEPHERD MARKET ⑩

From Berkeley Square, Curzon Street leads to Shepherd Market, Mayfair's 'village centre', by way of a side passage. This small pedestrian enclave is incongruous amid the grand town houses and exclusive hotels. Built around 1735 by the architect Edward Shepherd, it was established to supply the daily needs of local residents and obliterated the open space which had accommodated the May Fair – commemorated by a blue plaque at 7 Trebeck Street – whose riotousness offended the well-off residents.

Even today Shepherd Market maintains a quaint air in the small piazza. There are specialist boutiques, Victorian pubs and bistros, all on a village scale.

SOUTH AUDLEY AND MOUNT STREETS

Along **South Audley Street** ⑪ is the former residence of Charles X, the last Bourbon king of France, who lived here 1805–14. At No. 19, **Thomas Goode & Co**, the china, silverware and crystal shop once almost exclusively the preserve of international royalty, has occupied its own block since the 1840s.

Behind neat miniature hedges, a marble colonnade frames the window displays. Stealing the show are the pair of howdah-bearing ceramic elephants, 7ft (2 metres) tall in their regalia, which are the establishment's trademark. Produced by Minton for Thomas Goode, they took the Paris Exhibition of 1889 by storm. The shop incorporates a design archive and museum section.

The original wood panelling and chandeliers of the Audley pub set the tone for the unbridled Victoriana of **Mount Street** ⑫, whose eastern portion especially, lined with fine shops, is strikingly homogeneous. Wholly rebuilt from 1880 to 1900 in the pink terracotta Queen Anne style, its red-brick facades are enthusiastically decked out with terracotta features.

GROSVENOR SQUARE ⑬

A pleasing, friendly statue of General Eisenhower and Winston Churchill having a chat on a bench in Bond Street is a sign of the interest Americans have always had in Mayfair. In 1785 John Adams, the first United States Minister to Britain and later the nation's president, took up residence at **9 Grosvenor Square**. No fewer than 31 of the 47 households in the square then belonged to titled families. The US embassy is scheduled to move to a larger, more secure suburban location south of the Thames in 2016.

The cost of the statue of **Franklin D. Roosevelt** ⑭ in the gardens was met by grateful British citizens after World War II.

PARK LANE

Park Lane, running from Hyde Park Corner to Marble Arch, forms

FACT

In 1875 architects Messrs Ernest George and Peto were commissioned to design a frontage for Thomas Goode & Co. Many of the unusual features they incorporated still remain. One is the mechanical front door, which opens automatically under the weight of anyone standing on the platform. This rare piece of Victorian design is believed to be the only example still in use in the world.

The window of Thomas Goode & Co.

the western boundary of Mayfair. Its once magnificent homes over-looking Hyde Park (see page 197) have largely been replaced by modern hotels and apartments. These include the **Hilton Hotel** and the **Dorchester Hotel** ⑮, General Dwight D. Eisenhower's HQ in World War II, and popular with visiting film stars. To the north, the residence of the Grosvenor family (owners of a 300-acre/120-hectare estate covering Mayfair and Park Lane) was knocked down in 1928 to make way for **Grosvenor House** hotel, whose 2,000-capacity Great Room is one of Europe's largest banqueting halls.

Marble Arch and Oxford Street

At the top of Park Lane, the **Marble Arch** ⑯, designed by John Nash and based on the Arch of Constantine in Rome, was placed here, then known as Tyburn, in 1851 after being removed from the front of Buckingham Palace where it was originally erected in 1827. It now sits in the middle of a busy traffic island.

Statue of Franklin Roosevelt in Grosvenor Square.

Crowds first came to **Oxford Street** to see the condemned being taken to Tyburn (see box): this produced a ready clientele for shopkeepers, and stores first appeared along 'Ladies' Mile' between Tottenham Court Road and Marylebone Lane, just short of Bond Street Underground station.

The entrance to Claridge's.

HANGMAN'S HAUNT

A stone slab on a traffic island opposite Marble Arch at the west end of Oxford Street, London's principal shopping thoroughfare, marks the spot where public hangings took place. The first recorded one was in 1196, of populist leader William Fitz Osbern, and the last was in 1783, of highwayman John Austin. Up to 50,000 convicted felons died here. The site of London's main place of execution took its name from Tyburn Brook, which flowed into the Westbourne River at what is now the Serpentine in Hyde Park. The condemned were transported here along what is now Oxford Street (formerly Tyburn Street) from Newgate Prison or the Tower of London. The gallows stood right in the middle of the major western route into London, and so was a prominent symbol of law and order to passing travellers.

Hanging days were public holidays, attracting huge crowds, and London apprentices were given a day off to attend them. The victims dressed in their best, carried nosegays of flowers and took a last mug of ale; they were allowed to speak to the crowd before being hanged. The site of the now demolished Newgate Prison contains the Central Criminal Court.

This was where the first department stores were built. One of the finest to this day, **Selfridges** ⓱, was built further west by Gordon Selfridge, a Chicago retail millionaire. The food halls are hard to resist, and the shop window displays at Christmas are spectacular. Marks & Spencer, the drapers, opened their largest shop next door in 1930, still the site of their flagship store.

Only buses and taxis are allowed to drive down most of Oxford Street and its widened pavements are usually packed with tourists. New developments indicate that, despite the congestion, Oxford Street is still the retail heart of central London. Near Bond Street Underground station, designer boutiques in St Christopher's Place – with its pavement cafés and hanging baskets – offer an escape from the masses, as do Bond Street and South Molton Street on the south side.

At Oxford Circus, Oxford Street crosses over **Regent Street** which continues north, part of Nash's scheme to connect the Prince Regent's home at Carlton House with his newly acquired property

Shoppers on Oxford Street.

at Regent's Park. Among Regent Street's restaurants are **Veeraswamy's** (entrance on Swallow Street), London's first Indian restaurant, opened in 1926.

The Café Royal, also a haunt of Winston Churchill, and the high-living Edward VIII (when he was Prince of Wales) and George VI, has now reopened as a luxury hotel.

SHOP

Oxford Street is known for its department stores and chain stores, but Regent Street is also worth exploring. Shops include **Hamleys**, the world's biggest toy store, at Nos. 188–96 and the gigantic **Apple Store** at No. 235. Just off Regent Street on the fringes of Soho is **Liberty** (see page 52).

Fun at Hamleys.

LONDON'S PARKS

The city has more green spaces than any comparable conurbation – and they're used for everything from sunbathing to speechmaking.

Parliament Hill, Hampstead Heath.

St James's Park.

London's eight royal parks – Hyde Park, Kensington Gardens, Regent's Park, St James's Park, Green Park, Greenwich Park, Richmond Park and Bushy Park – are all owned and run by the Crown. Many were once royal hunting grounds, and they retain an elegant air.

The largest is Hyde Park (350 acres/140 hectares), a vast open space only a few paces away from bustling Oxford Street. The corner of the park near Marble Arch is known as Speakers' Corner, although the area is smaller now, where freedom of speech is given full rein on Sunday afternoons.

Hyde Park adjoins Kensington Gardens, a lovely green space on the west side of which stands Kensington Palace, home to the Duke and Duchess of Cambridge. The oldest park is St James's, beautifully landscaped with fountains and views of Buckingham Palace and Whitehall. Regent's Park, in Marylebone, houses London Zoo and has a very fine rose garden.

In addition there are several good suburban parks, some of them established in the 19th century to alleviate the unhealthy living conditions of the poor. The other great open space is Hampstead Heath in north London.

Boats on the Serpentine, Hyde Park.

Lavender beds at Kew Gardens. Main attractions include the Palm House (the Victorian glasshouse containing a tropical rainforest), a rose garden next to the Palm House, the Temperate House and the Princess of Wales conservatory.

The fountain at Regent's Park's Inner Circle.

MUSIC, WILDLIFE AND THEATRE IN THE PARKS

Enjoying live music in Regent's Park.

The sight of people sitting in striped deckchairs in a park on a warm summer's day listening to a brass band is reassuringly English. In Greenwich Park you can listen to a band or jazz orchestra playing free concerts at weekends.

Throughout the summer, all sorts of events are held in the parks; bat walks are held in Hyde Park, when you can see and hear different bat species in the park at night.

In Kensington Gardens you can follow in Peter Pan's footsteps and experience the magic that inspired J.M. Barrie's tales. A statue of Peter Pan stands on the east side of the gardens, near the lake. Or you can get a close-up view of the herons and other wildlife in Regent's Park.

Great houses provide other venues for music and theatre, with picnic concerts and opera in the grounds of Holland Park, a music festival in Hyde Park and open-air Shakespeare productions in Regent's Park's theatre in the summer. Bring cushions and blankets.

For more information, see www.royalparks.org.uk/whats-on.

Skating in Greenwich Park.

MARYLEBONE AND FITZROVIA

North of Oxford Street lies Marylebone, a characterful area of elegant squares and terraces bordered by Regent's Park. Among its attractions are Madame Tussauds, London Zoo and the Sherlock Holmes Museum.

The residential area of Marylebone (pronounced *marry-le-bun*) lies between Oxford Street and Regent's Park. It is largely Georgian in character, its streets and squares named after the Cavendish, Harley and Portland families, who progressively developed the district from the beginning of the 18th century. The need to relieve congestion in Oxford Street inspired the creation of a new road running from Paddington to Islington through the parish of St Mary-of-the-Bourne.

Today, Marylebone still retains an air of genteel village dwelling, an oasis framed by multicultural Edgware Road to the west, Oxford Street to the south and Tottenham Court Road to the east. The section known as Fitzrovia, traditionally an artists' enclave and retaining a bohemian atmosphere, nestles around the BT Tower.

NORTH OF OXFORD STREET

St Christopher's **Place**, a pedestrian enclave lined with boutiques and cafés, is accessible through a narrow passageway on Oxford Street (see page 114) and leads via cobbled James Street to Wigmore Street. The latter contains several good restaurants as well as various medical specialists spilling over from Harley Street, the preferred haunt of private physicians since the 1840s.

On the north side of the road stands **Wigmore Hall** ❶, a delightful concert venue, particularly at lunchtimes. BBC Radio 3 broadcasts live from here on Mondays. The Art Nouveau building, which has notable acoustics, was erected in 1901 by a German piano company.

Wallace Collection ❷

Address: Hertford House, Manchester Square, W1, www.wallacecollection.org

Main Attractions
Wallace Collection
Madame Tussauds
Sherlock Holmes Museum
Regent's Park
London Zoo

Maps
Page 120

Fitzrovia townhouses.

The Great Gallery in the Wallace Collection contains Old Master paintings and French and Italian furniture.

Tel: 020-7563 9500
Opening Hrs: daily 10am–5pm
Entrance Fee: free
Transport: Bond Street

This remarkable display of art ranges from 17th- and 18thcentury English and European paintings to Sèvres porcelain and huge suits of armour. In addition to pictures by Velázquez, Boucher and Fragonard, it contains Rembrandt's *Self-Portrait in a Black Cap*, Rubens' *Rainbow Landscape*, Poussin's *Dance to the Music of Time*, and Frans Hals's *The Laughing Cavalier*. There's a lovely restaurant in its light-filled atrium.

MARYLEBONE VILLAGE

Tucked amongst quiet residential terraces, **Marylebone High Street** ❸ is a hub of homeware shops, boutiques and restaurants, its urban village atmosphere providing an oasis from the surrounding bustle. It also has several specialist food shops, from charcuteries to fishmongers. On Sundays there is a good **farmers' market** (10am–2pm) at Cramer Street car park.

More pubs and small shops are dotted along narrow Marylebone Lane, which winds along the course of the subterranean River Tyburn.

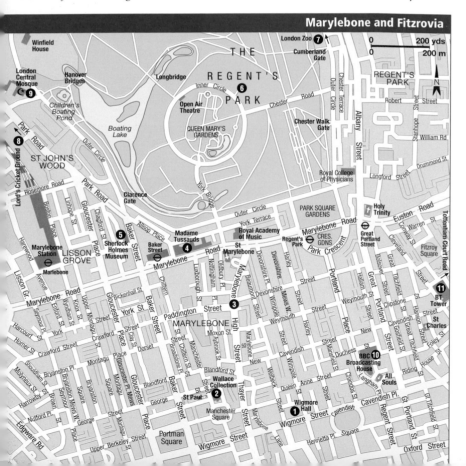

Marylebone and Fitzrovia

MARYLEBONE ROAD AND BAKER STREET

Marylebone Road is one of London's busiest east–west thoroughfares. Its intersection with north–south Baker Street is marked by two attractions, Madame Tussauds and the Sherlock Holmes Museum.

Madame Tussauds ❶

Address: Marylebone Road,
www.madametussauds.com
Tel: 0871-894 3000
Opening Hrs: Mon–Fri 9.30am–5.30pm, Sat–Sun and during peak times 9am–6pm
Transport: Baker Street

With its high-tech special effects and increasing emphasis on contemporary celebrities, Madame Tussauds waxwork museum is one of London's top attractions, especially for teenagers. For more information, see page 124.

Not far past the waiting visitors outside Madame Tussauds is the **Royal Academy of Music**, which hosts daily recitals, workshops, seminars and concerts, most of which are free (tel: 020-7873 7300). Opposite the Academy stands St Marylebone Parish Church, which was depicted by Hogarth in the wedding scene of *A Rake's Progress*. Lord Byron (1788) was baptised here, and Lord Nelson worshipped here.

Sherlock Holmes Museum ❺

Address: 221b Baker Street,
www.sherlock-holmes.co.uk
Tel: 020 7224 3688
Opening Hrs: daily 9.30am–6pm
Transport: Baker Street

On Baker Street, north of the intersection with Marylebone Road, this museum in a Grade II-listed building re-creates the Victorian home of Arthur Conan Doyle's fictional detective. Some rooms are detailed representations of his living quarters, others contain waxwork tableaux of characters and scenes described in the stories. A Victorian 'maid' is on hand to answer questions.

REGENT'S PARK

Baker Street, Marylebone High Street and Portland Place all lead to **Regent's Park ❻**, an elegant 470-acre (190-hectare) space surrounded by John Nash's Regency terraces. Shakespeare plays (and more modern productions) are performed at the Open Air Theatre throughout summer. The boating lake is a tranquil spot, the rose gardens are stunning in summer, and Regent's Canal runs through the north of the park.

London Zoo ❼

Address: Outer Circle, Regent's Park,
www.zsl.org/london-zoo
Tel: 0844-225 1826
Entrance Fee: daily Mar–Oct 10am–5.30pm, mid-July–early Sept 10am–6pm, Nov–Feb 10am–4pm; last entry one hour before closing
Transport: Camden Town

Increasingly placing an onus on conservational breeding, London Zoo is one of the world's greatest and largest zoos. Its diverse showcase includes a tropical birdwalk in the Blackburn Pavilion, the Gorilla Kingdom, and the Clore Rainforest Lookout

Regent's Park's rose garden in the heart of the Inner Circle contains some 20,000 roses. They bloom from June through to Christmas.

The Sherlock Holmes Museum.

TIP

An alternative and more romantic route to London Zoo is to take a canal boat from Camden Lock or Little Venice along Regent's Canal. The London Waterbus Company runs regular services in summer (tel: 020-7482 2550; www.londonwaterbus.com) and weekend services during winter.

displaying South American mammals, birds and reptiles.

Tiger Territory is home to Jae Jae and Melati, a pair of Sumatran tigers. You can see them hanging out in their custom-built pool, or relaxing on heated rocks in their indoor dens. Land of the Lions opened in 2016 to house several Asiatic lions and features an amphitheatre-style Lion Temple. The Penguin Beach has a pool with windows set below water level, allowing you to watch the penguins swimming underwater. On a more tactile level, the revamped children's enclosure allows visitors to handle animals such as goats and llamas.

Around the park

On the northwest side of the park is **Lord's Cricket Ground** ❽ (nearest Tube: St John's Wood), belonging to the Marylebone Cricket Club, historically known as the global centre of cricket. County (Middlesex) and England marches takes place here between May to early September. Tours are available throughout the year, including the portrait-packed Long Room through which players

All Souls' Church, Langham Place.

walk on their way to the field, the Honours Boards in the players' dressing rooms, and museum, where the original Ashes urn is on display. (tel: 020-7616 8595; www.lords.org; daily noon and 2pm, except on major match or preparation days, also 10am and 11am on weekends and Apr–Sept).

Just around the corner from Lord's is Abbey Road and the zebra crossing immortalised by the eponymous Beatles album recorded in the studios

Penguins at London Zoo.

nearby. It's hard to miss as there are usually tourists stopping to pose on the crossing.

Nearby is the **London Central Mosque** ❾ and Islamic Cultural Centre, built in 1978 and topped with a golden dome. The site for the mosque was a gift from the government to the Muslim community during World War II, in recognition of the substantial Islamic population of the British Empire. Visitors are welcome but note that clothing is modest – below the knee and covering shoulders; women can borrow headscarves from the bookshop.

Portland Place

The eastern stretch of Marylebone leads to Park Crescent and **Portland Place**, conceived by the Adam brothers as a home for the rich. John Nash included it in his grand design to connect Regent's Park with St James's but the plan was never realised. The grand Adam terraced houses in Portland Place are home to several embassies, institutes and learned societies, such as the Royal Institute of British Architects (RIBA).

Langham Place, which curves round to connect Portland Place with Regent Street, has a trio of dramatic buildings: the circular All Souls' Church built by Nash in 1822–24, the Langham hotel and the rebuilt **Broadcasting House** ❿, headquarters of the BBC, where the first public television transmission was made in 1932. In 2013 the Queen opened the new Broadcasting House, home to the BBC's television, radio, news and online services.

FITZROVIA

Dominating the skyline of this former bohemian enclave is the 620ft (189-metre) -high **BT Tower** ⓫, one of the tallest structures in London. Fitzroy Square is central to the area's literary heritage (see box); George Bernard Shaw, Virginia Woolf and Ian McEwan have all lived here.

Cosmopolitan **Charlotte Street** used to be known mainly for Greek eateries but now has a variety of chic restaurants. Running parallel is Tottenham Court Road, home to electrical goods and home furnishing stores such as Heal's, and the eastern boundary of Fitzrovia.

FITZROVIA'S LEGACY

Fitzrovia is famous for attracting a bawdy bohemian set between the 1920s and 1950s. Welsh poet Dylan Thomas and the painter Augustus John frequented the Fitzroy Tavern, while writer Julian Maclaren-Ross drank away his publishing advance at The Wheatsheaf – ultimately becoming better known for his 'King of Fitzrovia' persona, complete with silver-topped cane, than for his short stories. George Orwell was another regular and the Newman Arms on Rathbone Street features in his novels *Nineteen Eighty-Four* and *Keep the Aspidistra Flying*. Other inhabitants included Anthony Powell, Wyndham Lewis and Francis Bacon. The scene dissolved in the 1950s. Today creativity comes in other forms: many media companies are based here.

The BT Tower.

SEEING STARS AT MADAME TUSSAUDS

When computer animation creates miraculous images on screen, what is the appeal of mute life-size effigies with fibreglass bodies and wax heads?

A key ingredient in the success of Madame Tussauds is that the models are no longer roped off or protected by glass cases. You can stroll right up to them – an impertinence their bodyguards would never permit in real life. You can be photographed with your arm around the Queen or Tom Cruise. Whatever impulse draws crowds to see at the stars in real life works here in overdrive, and the reactions are similar. Is Lady Gaga really wearing a telephone hat? Is Beyoncé's skin really that perfect? A huge hit is the special *Star Wars* exhibit opened in 2015, featuring 16 of the film series' best-known characters – including Darth Vadar and Jabba – and sets, including the Death Star Throne Room.

The Essentials

Address: Marylebone Road; www.madametussauds.com
Tel: 0871-894 3000
Opening Hrs: Mon–Fri 9.30am–5.30pm, Sat–Sun and during peak times 9am–6pm
Transport: Baker Street

Madame Tussauds logo.

A waxwork of Taylor Swift was unveiled in 2015, in the museum's Pop Stars section where she joins Justin Bieber and the late Amy Winehouse, among others.

In 2015, the waxwork of Queen Elizabeth II was given a makeover and re-costumed in her diamond jubilee dress.

The waxworks of Angelina Jolie and Brad Pitt get a last-minute makeover.

Don't miss the opportunity to have a selfie taken with Kim Kardashian.

THE WOMAN BEHIND THE WAXWORKS

Marie Grosholtz.

The story began during the French Revolution in 1789 when Marie Grosholtz, trained by a doctor in modeling anatomical subjects in wax, was asked to prepare death masks of famous victims of the guillotine. She married a French engineer, François Tussaud, in 1795, but left him in 1802 to spend the next 33 years touring Britain with a growing collection of wax figures. The London waxworks began in Baker Street and moved to Marylebone Road in 1884.

Today those gory beginnings are echoed in the waxworks' Chamber of Horrors, which contains the blade that sliced off Marie Antoinette's head and re-creates various none-too-scary tableaux of torture.

You can enter a dark section of the chamber where actors portraying deranged serial killers lunge at you and yell in your face. Since you are fore-warned that this will happen and assured that they won't touch you, it's hard to be seriously terrified.

A better bet is the audio-animatronic Spirit of London ride, which carries you past well-made historical tableaux.

One of the museum's most popular sports stars, Jamaican sprinter Usain Bolt.

The glass-roofed Great Court at the British Museum.

BLOOMSBURY AND KINGS CROSS

Home to the British Museum and the traditional base of publishing in London, Bloomsbury has an intellectual reputation, while King's Cross is reinventing itself as a new cultural zone.

The eastern side of Tottenham Court Road marks the beginning of Bloomsbury, London's literary heart, and home to the British Museum and the University of London. The area was laid out in the late 17th and early 18th centuries, initially by Thomas Wriothesley, Earl of Southampton, and later by the Russell family, the Dukes of Bedford. Both are commemorated in the place names of the area.

Publishing houses occupy many of the fine Georgian properties lining the streets and squares. Bloomsbury is blue plaque territory *par excellence* (see page 132). Charles Dickens lived in Doughty Street between 1837 and 1839 (see page 130) and in the early part of the 20th century it nurtured the Bloomsbury set, a group of writers who laid the foundations for modernism in Britain. Virginia Woolf, Vanessa Bell, Duncan Grant, Dora Carrington, E.M. Forster, Roger Fry, Maynard Keynes and Queen Victoria's biographer, Lytton Strachey, all lived at addresses in the area. They probably had more influence as a body than as individuals, and were bookish men and women in a bookish world.

The ever popular Egyptian mummies.

The British Museum ❶

Address: Great Russell Street, www.britishmuseum.org
Tel: 020-7323 8299
Opening Hrs: Sat–Thu 10am–5.30pm, Fri 10am–8.30pm
Entrance Fee: free except some special exhibitions
Transport: Russell Square, Tottenham Court Road

The British Museum on Great Russell Street is the nation's greatest treasure house. It opened in 1759, in smaller premises in South Kensington, and

Main Attractions
The British Museum
Coram's Fields
King's Cross
St Pancras Station
London Canal Museum
The British Library

Map
Page 128

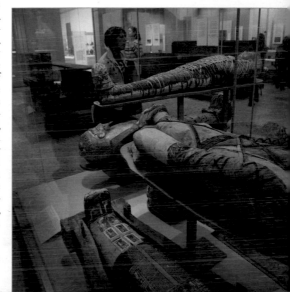

now owns more than 6.5 million items, ranging from the oldest neolithic antiquities to 20thcentury manuscripts (see page 134).

Access to the collections is via the **Great Court**, roofed with a steel-and-glass canopy in 2000 and one of the most spectacular spaces in London. The museum's famous circular Reading Room, where Karl Marx did much of his research for *Das Kapital*, is open to all as an information centre. It is also home to temporary exhibitions, its library having moved to Euston Road (see page 133).

Probably the most famous artefact in the British Museum is the Rosetta Stone, a stele from 196 BC that provided the key to deciphering Egyptian hieroglyphics.

Near the museum

From the museum three short streets (**Museum Street, Coptic Street** and **Bury Place**) lead to Bloomsbury Way. Among their antiquarian bookshops and cafés look out for the **London Review Bookshop** (14 Bury Place), which regularly hosts author readings and interviews and **Blade Rubber Stamps** (12 Bury Place), selling a

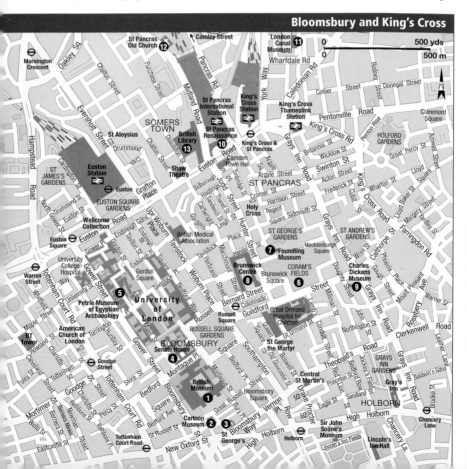

Bloomsbury and King's Cross

huge range of rubber stamps as well as everything needed to make home-made greetings cards. At the northern end of Bury Place are the adjacent **It's All Greek** and **Parthenon**, both sell-ing quality replicas of ancient arte-facts – though the British Museum's own shop is also very good for these.

In Little Russell Street, running between Museum Street and Coptic Street, the **Cartoon Museum ②** (35 Little Russell St; tel: 020-7580 8155; www.cartoonmuseum.org; Mon–Sat 10.30am–5.30pm, Sun noon–5.30pm) charts British cartooning from the 18th century to the present day; from Hogarth and Bateman to Steve Bell and Gerald Scarfe, taking in comic book characters such as Dennis the Menace and comic postcards by Donald McGill.

The British Museum's collection had an effect on the architecture of the area. Nicholas Hawksmoor's **Church of St George ③** (1731) in Bloomsbury Way was inspired by the Mausoleum of Halikarnassos, one of the Seven Wonders of the Ancient world, remnants of which can be seen in the museum (see page 135). This is best appreciated by looking at its unusual stepped tower, with lions and unicorns at its base and a statue of George I wearing a toga on top. The church often holds free choral performances on Sunday afternoons (www.stgeorgesbloomsbury.org.uk).

THE UNIVERSITY OF LONDON

Just north of the British Museum is the University of London, identified by the grey turret of **Senate House ④**, built in 1936, on the western side of Russell Square.

Close by, at 46 Gordon Square, is the house to which Virginia Woolf and her siblings moved after their father's death in 1904, thus becoming a magnet for other 'Bloomsberries'.

The **Petrie Museum of Egyptian Archaeology ⑤** (University College London, Malet Place; Tue–Sat 1–5pm; free) is a two-room museum crammed with an estimated 80,000 treasures, of interest especially to students, academics and anyone fas-cinated with Egypt.

CORAM'S FIELDS ⑥

East of the British Museum, across **Russell Square**, the area is dissected by Southampton Row. On the east

Cartoon Museum.

TIP

Opposite Euston Station is the excellent **Wellcome Collection** (183 Euston Road; tel: 020-7611 2222; www.wellcomecollection.org; Tue–Wed, Fri–Sat 10am–6pm, Thu 10am–10pm, Sun 11am–6pm; free), a museum and art space devoted to medicine and its relationships with art and society. It mixes items from Henry Wellcome's (1853–1936) eclectic collection of medical objects, interactive exhibits, paintings and much more. Other draws include a café and a intriguing bookshop.

side of the square, just beyond the children's hospital in Great Ormond Street, are Coram's Fields, where children rule the roost (adults may only enter the park if accompanied by children). As well as playgrounds, sports facilities, and a nursery, it has rabbits, chickens and sheep.

Thomas Coram was a sea captain who started a hospital and school for foundling (abandoned) children and persuaded artists of the day, including William Hogarth, to donate works of art to raise funds. The collection, which includes paintings by the great 19th-century portraitists Thomas Gainsborough and Joshua Reynolds, is displayed in **The Foundling Museum** ❼, adjacent to the site of the old Foundling Hospital on the north side of Coram's Fields (40 Brunswick Square; tel: 020-7841 3600; http://foundlingmuseum.org.uk; Tue–Sat 10am–5pm, Sun 11am–5pm; children free).

The ground floor traces the history of the hospital and of the philanthropic movement set against the background of 19th-century social conditions. Upstairs, in a fine rococo drawing room, are items belonging or related to George Frideric Handel, one of the hospital's benefactors.

Nicholas Hawksmoor's tower on the Church of St George.

Shopping and eating

The **Brunswick Centre** ❽, a 1960s shopping-cum-housing development on the west side of Coram's Fields, has been given a makeover. It includes several good eating options as well as a large art-house cinema. Alternatively, south of Coram's Fields is **Lamb's Conduit Street**, a characterful street with interesting shops and The Lamb pub.

CHARLES DICKENS MUSEUM ❾

Address: 48 Doughty St, www.dickensmuseum.com
Tel: 020-7405 2127
Opening Hrs: daily 10am–5pm, last admission 4pm
Transport: Russell Square

A five-minute walk southeast of Coram's Fields is the house-museum where Dickens lived with his family from 1837 to 1839, and wrote *Oliver Twist* and *Nicholas Nickleby*. In a reverential atmosphere, visitors can

Charles Dickens Museum.

inspect a huge collection of furniture, memorabilia, paintings, books and documents. The displays on the upper floors illustrate his one great passion besides literature – the plays that he produced, directed and acted in at various times.

South of Dickens Museum, **John Street**, lined with handsome Georgian properties, some with a full complement of 18th-century ironwork, leads to Theobald's Road and Holborn (see page 139). North of Coram's Fields, and best reached along Hunter Street, lies the newly booming area of King's Cross and St Pancras.

King's Cross and St Pancras

The area around St Pancras and King's Cross stations, for many years run down and sleazy, has undergone massive regeneration in the 21st century. Triggered by the construction of the Eurostar rail terminal, which opened in 2007, the area is fast becoming a new cultural zone, called King's Cross Central, attracting creative industries and contemporary art galleries, as well as bars, restaurants and luxury apartments.

Housing the new terminal, **St Pancras Station ⑩**, an immense red-brick edifice by Sir George Gilbert Scott, the master of Victorian Gothic, has been superbly restored, with a 5-star hotel and a spa.

Regent Quarter

The area behind the two stations, for long an industrial backwater crossed by roads and railway lines, is also being regenerated, especially the so-called Regent Quarter, near the Regent's Canal. Occupying an old icehouse on the wharf of Battlebridge Basin is the **London Canal Museum ⑪** (12–13 New Wharf Road, accessed from Wharfdale Road; tel: 020-7713 0836; www.canalmuseum.org.uk; Tue– Sun 10am–4.30pm). As well as portraying canal life, the museum tells

Playing in Coram's Fields.

the hard story of London's 19th-century ice trade, when ice was imported from Norway. One of two ice pits is open to view.

Camley Street

Behind St Pancras Station, Camley Street leads north towards Camden.

The King's Cross Central development.

Blue Plaques

Numerous famous writers, artists and intellectuals have made Bloomsbury their home. Commemorating their presence are scores of blue plaques.

One of many pointers to London's varied past are the blue plaques on many sites to commemorate famous people, events and buildings. There are plenty in Bloomsbury, but they are also strewn across London. Almost 900 have appeared on the former homes of the famous and the long dead. The first plaque was erected by the Royal Society of Arts in memory of the poet Lord Byron in 1867. In those days the round plaques were often brown rather than blue, and were pithily known as 'indications of houses of historical interest in London'.

A blue plaque marking one of John Lennon's former London residences

Today the service is administered by English Heritage and relies on donations.

Bona fide plaques are ceramic with white lettering on a circular blue base. To ensure legibility, the design allows for only 19 words of inscription, including dates; they are bald statements of fact, giving little biographical information – simply the name, dates, profession and usually the period he or she lived in the building.

Who gets a plaque?

The awarding of a plaque is almost haphazard: there is no overall register of famous people who have lived in London. Many plaques are put up because descendants or adherents of the deceased put forward the suggestion to English Heritage. Thus plaques function as a barometer of public taste, as notions change about what constitutes fame. The range has been dominated by 19th-century politicians and artists, but in 1997 the first plaque to commemorate a rock star – Jimi Hendrix – went up in Brook Street (see page 112). In 2013 Harry Beck, the man who designed London Underground's iconic tube map, received a blue plaque on the house where he was born in Leyton.

A plaque-spotting tour is packed with variety. Captain William Bligh (of Bounty fame) lived at 100 Lambeth Road, SE1; Charlie Chaplin lived at 287 Kennington Road, SE1; Sir Winston Churchill lived at 34 Eccleston Square, SW1; Benjamin Franklin lived at 36 Craven Street, WC2; Charles Dickens lived at 48 Doughty Street, WC1; Henry James lived at 34 De Vere Gardens, W8; Karl Marx lived at 28 Dean Street, W1; George Bernard Shaw lived at 29 Fitzroy Square, W1; and Mark Twain lived at 23 Tedworth Square, SW3.

Most candidates for traditional plaques are submitted to lengthy scrutiny. They must have been dead for at least 20 years; they must be regarded as eminent by luminaries in their profession; they should have made an important contribution to human welfare; the well-informed passer-by should recognise their name; and they should, by the kind of infuriatingly nebulous 'general agreement' that has characterised British decision-making, deserve recognition.

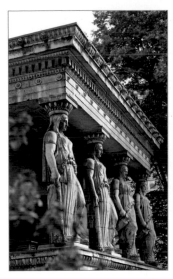

Opposite Euston Station, on Euston Road, look out for St Pancras New Church. Its eight caryatids (four on each side) were inspired by the Erechtheum on the Acropolis in Athens.

On the left is **St Pancras Old Church** ⑫, one of the oldest Christian sites in London. Its cemetery contains the graves of several notable figures, including the celebrated architect and art collector Sir John Soane (see page 141).

On the same street is **Camley Street Natural Park** (free), opposite the cemetery and flanking the canal, with a trail, wildlife pond and child-friendly activities at weekends.

The British Library ⑬

Address: 96 Euston Road, www.bl.uk
Tel: 0843 208 1144
Opening Hrs: Mon and Fri 9.30am–6pm, Tue–Thu 9.30am–8pm, Sat 9.30am–6pm, Sun 11am–5pm; some reading rooms and cafés close earlier; tours available
Entrance Fee: free, charge for some special exhibitions
Transport: King's Cross, Euston

Back on Euston Road, next door to St Pancras, is the British Library, which moved here from the British Museum in 1998. It houses over 14 million books and periodicals, including a Gutenberg Bible, the Magna Carta and original texts by Shakespeare, Dickens and Leonardo da Vinci. In addition to guided tours of the highlights, the library holds temporary exhibitions. The spacious courtyard (with café) is a peaceful refuge from busy Euston Road.

Inside the British Library.

THE BRITISH LIBRARY

Researchers can use the reading rooms by applying in person or through the website (www.bl.uk) for a reader's pass. Two forms of identification, including proof of home address and proof of signature, must be produced. Free 45-minute induction sessions help users find their way around the vast resources.

Members of any local library in the UK can also access the collection, if the book required cannot be obtained from any other library. This is done through the local library service.

THE BRITISH MUSEUM

Opened in 1759, this world-class institution on Great Russell Street contains some 6.5 million objects.

Devote just 60 seconds to each object owned by the British Museum and you'd be there, without a break, for more than 12 years. Even though only 50,000 objects are on display at any given time, this is not a place to 'do' in a couple of hours. It is a treasure house that caters for scholars as well as tourists and, as the scholars do, it is best to concentrate initially on what interests you most. A tour of the highlights is a good start (see page 135).

The best time to visit is soon after opening. This is also an ideal time to appreciate the Great Court – a dramatic glassed-over space in the heart of the complex, added for the millennium – and the round Reading Room, where Marx and Lenin once studied, which now functions as an information and research centre.

A huge new wing, the light-filled World Conservation and Exhibition Centre, opened in 2014 and houses large-scale temporary exhibitions.

The Essentials

Address: Great Russell Street, WC2; www.thebritishmuseum.org
Tel: 020-7323 8299
Opening Hrs: Sat–Thu 10am–5.30pm, Fri 10am–8.30pm
Entrance Fee: free except some exhibitions
Transport: Russell Square, Tottenham Court Road

THE MAIN COLLECTIONS

Greece and Rome

The museum's vast holdings from the Classical world are divided between Rooms 11–23 and Rooms 69–73 on the first floor.

Room 18, the **Parthenon Gallery**, is lined with an exquisitely detailed frieze from the colonnade of the Parthenon, removed from the

The Parthenon or Elgin Marbles have been the source of controversery ever since they were taken from the Parthenon by Lord Elgin between 1801 and 1805.

The reconstructed facade of the Nereid Monument, which dates back to the early 4th century.

The British Museum has the largest collection of Egyptian antiquities outside the Egyptian Museum in Cairo. Colossal busts and statues of ancient kings and pharaohs dominate the space.

The Portland Vase, a superbly crafted cameo glass vessel from the early 1st century.

The museum exterior.

TOP 10 HIGHLIGHTS

The Egyptian mummies
This is the richest collection of Egyptian funerary art outside Egypt.
The Sculptures of the Parthenon
Commonly known as the Elgin Marbles, these 5th century BC sculptures have a wondrous muscular detail.
The Rosetta Stone
This granite tablet from the 2nd century BC provided the elusive key to deciphering ancient Egypt's hieroglyphic script.
The Nereid Monument
The imposing facade of this 4th-century monument from Xanthos in Turkey was reconstructed after an earthquake.
The Mausoleum of Halikarnassos
This giant tomb, finished around 350 BC in southwest Turkey, was one of the Seven Wonders of the Ancient World.

The gilded wooden inner coffin of Henut-mehyt, a Theban priestess, dating from c.1250 BC.

The Sutton Hoo Ship Burial
The richest treasure ever dug from British soil, an early 7th-century longboat likely to have been the burial chamber of an East Anglian king.
The Lewis Chessmen
82 elaborately carved 12th-century chess pieces, found in the Outer Hebrides, off the Scottish coast.
Lindow Man
A well-preserved 2,000-year-old body found in a peat bog in England and dubbed Pete Marsh.
The Benin Bronzes
Brass plaques found in Benin City, Nigeria, in 1897. They depict court life and ritual in extraordinary detail.
The Cassiobury Park Turret Clock
This intricate 1610 weight-driven clock is part of a remarkable collection of timepieces.

The 12th-century Lewis Chessmen, found in the Outer Hebrides.

Acropolis by Lord Elgin, British Ambassador in Constantinople, at the turn of the 19th century.

Room 17 has the **Nereid Monument**, a magnificent Lycian tomb (c.390–380 BC) from Xanthos, and nearby Room 21 has fragments and sculptures from the **Mausoleum of Halikarnassos** (modern day Bodrum; mid-4th century BC), the tomb of Maussollos and considered to have been one of the Seven Wonders of the Ancient World. A large-scale model of the mausoleum shows how it would have looked in its splendid entirety.

Early Europe

As well as highly crafted Celtic artefacts and Roman treasures, look out for Lindow Man, a 1st-century man discovered in a peat bog in Cheshire.

Medieval and Modern Europe

Apart from the Sutton Hoo treasure, objects include richly decorated ecclesiastical artefacts such as an intricately decorated 12th-century gilt cross from Germany.

Africa

The Sainsbury African Galleries in the basement combine ancient and modern, showing how cultural traditions are still alive today. This is one of the most colourful and vibrant collections in the museum.

Of special interest are the Benin Bronzes, from the Kingdom of Benin (now in Nigeria), a powerful state in West Africa between the 13th and 19th centuries.

A 16th-century European mechanical galleon.

The Americas

The museum has superb collections from Central and North America in Rooms 26–27 on the ground floor (far-right corner off the Great Court). There are a number of impressive Olmec statues and other works from around 1000 BC, plus magnificent carved Mayan slabs from the 8th century AD. Relics from the Aztec civilisation include turquoise

mosaic work that may have been given to Hernán Cortés by Moctezuma II and a very rare pre-Conquest manuscript painted on deer skin.

Asia

The museum's collections of Chinese, Japanese and Korean artefacts are astonishingly large, with a series of vast galleries given over to them (33–33b on the ground floor, 67 and 92–95 on the upper floors).

Human-headed winged bull, one of a pair of marble bulls that guarded either side of a gateway at Khorsabad, Assyria (710 BC), in modern day Iraq.

Nebamum hunting birds in the marshes (1450 BC).

The ceremonial helmet from the Sutton Hoo treasure.

Lindow Man, the 1st-century bog man.

TREASURES OF ANCIENT EGYPT

The Egyptian Galleries are a must-see.

The Egyptian Galleries filled with funerary arte-facts (Rooms 61–66, on the upper floor), are the rooms to see first, simply because they can get overcrowded as the day goes on – 98 percent of visitors want to see the Egyptian mummies in rooms 62–63. They're worth seeing, too: thanks to the enthusiastic plundering by 19th-century explorers, this is the richest collection of Egyptian funerary art outside Egypt.

The size and ornamentation of the coffins and sarcophagi are immediately striking. The richly gilded inner coffin of the priestess Henutmehyt (see page 135), for example, dating from 1250 BC, is a work of considerable art. Scans displayed beside the coffin of Cleopatra (not the Cleopatra) show how well the body inside is preserved, and the process of embalming is explained in detail.

Apart from the noble humans who were destined to spend their afterlife in London's Bloomsbury, there are various mummified cats, dogs, fish and crocodiles, plus amulets and assorted jewellery.

Look out for the paintings from the Tomb of Neba-mun, a Theban official, dating from the 18th Dynasty (c.1350 BC), in Room 61.

TOURS WORTH TALKING ABOUT

Free 'eye-opener' tours (30–40 minutes) each focus on a specific area of the collection. A variety of multimedia sets can be hired, including one for children. Handling sessions take place daily in various galleries, and there are free lunchtime talks Tue–Fri at 1.15pm and 20-minute evening tours, Fri 5–7pm.

Assistant to a Judge of Hell, a 16th-century stone figure from Ming-Dynasty China. The figure is holding a bundle of scrolls recording the sins of the deceased.

The dragon at Temple Bar.

HOLBORN AND THE INNS OF COURT

Once the haunt of Samuel Johnson, Dickens and Thackeray, this area on the cusp of the City has long been the centre of the legal profession. For centuries it was also the irrepressible hub of Britain's newspaper industry.

Holborn encompasses what can be termed legal London, with landmarks such as the Royal Courts of Justice, the Old Bailey and the historic Inns of Court clustered around Fleet Street, the former centre of the national newspaper industry. The area is wedged in between London's financial and political centres, and is markedly different from both: away from the busy thoroughfares, quiet courtyards, leafy parks and some of the city's oldest buildings lend a sense of a bygone London.

KINGSWAY AND THE EASTERN STRAND

Somerset House ❶

Address: The Strand, www.somerset house.org.uk; www.courtauld.ac.uk
Tel: 020-7845 4600
Opening Hrs: Courtauld Institute of Art daily 10am–6pm
Entrance Fee: reduced entry Mon
Transport: Temple
Somerset House became the city's first office block in 1775 when the original 16th-century palace was rebuilt. For many years it housed the official registry of births, marriages and deaths; the Inland Revenue offices remain, but the northern and southern wings now accommodate a

series of galleries and museums. The complex is divided into two main sections by its large courtyard, which contains a fanciful statue of George III wearing a toga. From mid-November to early January the courtyard is turned into a huge **skating rink**, the classical facade providing a magical setting. In summer there are outdoor film screenings and concerts.

Entering from the Strand, you'll come to the **The Courtauld Gallery**, home to a fine collection of 20th-century European art, notably some

Main Attractions
Somerset House
The Inns of Court
Lincoln's Inn Fields
Sir John Soane's Museum
Dr Johnson's House
St Bride's Church

Map
Page 140

Middle Temple Lane.

The Royal Courts of Justice.

Lincoln's Inn Fields.

major Impressionist and post-Impressionist paintings: works include Van Gogh's *Self-Portrait with Bandaged Ear* and *Manet's A Bar at the Folies-Bergère*. Temporary exhibitions are held in the Embankment galleries.

The Seamen's Hall gives access to the splendid River Terrace, which in summer has a café with great views.

Across the Strand from Somerset House is **Bush House ❷**, the former headquarters of the BBC's World Service, which is due to be transformed into offices in a £52 million refurbishment deal. The World Service has moved to the BBC's expanded Broadcasting House near Oxford Circus. To the north, Kingsway marks the western boundary of Holborn and legal London. It was named after George V, and its tunnel, opened in 1906 for trams to dive beneath the buildings of Aldwych before emerging at Waterloo Bridge, was a miracle of urban engineering in its day.

Two baroque churches sit on traffic islands in the Strand: by Bush House is **St Mary le Strand**, built by James Gibbs from 1715; a short distance further east by a statue of Gladstone is **St Clement Danes ❸**, completed by Wren in 1682. The name is a reference to the first structure on the site, built by the Vikings in the 9th century. The church has an association with the Royal Air Force, who rebuilt it after bomb damage in World War II.

At the end of the Strand on the left are the **Royal Courts of Justice ❹**, dealing with libels, divorces and all civil cases. The courts moved here from Westminster Hall in 1884. The neo-Gothic confection of towers and spires has around 1,000 rooms, and newspaper and television journalists often hang around its entrance awaiting verdicts. Visitors can sit in the public galleries of the 58 courts when trials are in session. Check for 2-hour public tours of the building; advance booking necessary (tel: 07789-751248).

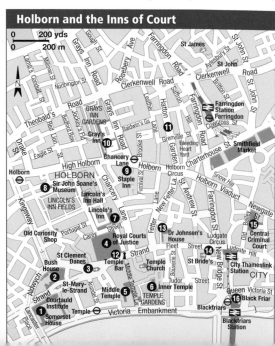

Holborn and the Inns of Court

THE INNS OF COURT

All around this area are the **Inns of Court**, home of London's legal profession. The 'Inns' were once, much as they sound, places of rest and comfort for trainee lawyers. From the 19th century onward, law was taught at King's College, next to Somerset House in the Strand, and at University College in Gower Street. Before then, the only way to obtain legal training was to serve an apprenticeship in one of the Inns.

Four still remain, and still function as accommodation and offices for the legal profession: **Middle Temple** ❺ and **Inner Temple** ❻ between Fleet Street and the Embankment, and Gray's Inn (see page 142) and Lincoln's Inn further north. With their cobbled lanes and brass plaques bearing Dickensian names, they are atmospheric places to stroll around. Note that the entrances to Middle Temple Lane and Inner Temple Lane are easily missed – the gates are usually closed and access is via a small side passageway.

These Inns take their name from the crusading Knights Templar, who bought land here in the 12th century and built the **Temple Church** (charge), inspired by the Church of the Holy Sepulchre in Jerusalem. There are a number of the knights' tombs inside, and a tiny punishment cell by the altar. The church contained one of the clues featured in Dan Brown's *The Da Vinci Code*. Sloping down to the Embankment, the grassy swards of the Temple Gardens are a pleasant place to take a break from sightseeing.

North of the Royal Courts of Justice, between Kingsway and Chancery Lane, is **Lincoln's Inn** ❼, alma mater of Oliver Cromwell, and the two great 19th-century prime ministers, William Gladstone and Benjamin Disraeli.

Lincoln's Inn Fields were created for the students' recreation, but the best sport was watching the early city planners try to outmanoeuvre each other: Inigo Jones sat on a 17th-century Royal Commission to decide the area's fate.

Sir John Soane's Museum ❽

Address: 13 Lincoln's Inn Fields, www.soane.org

TIP

There are free guided tours of the buildings of Somerset House every Thursday at 1.15pm and 2.45pm, and Saturday at 12.15pm, 1.15pm, 2.15pm and 3.15pm. Tickets are available on the day from 10.30am from the Information Desk.

Courtauld Institute gallery.

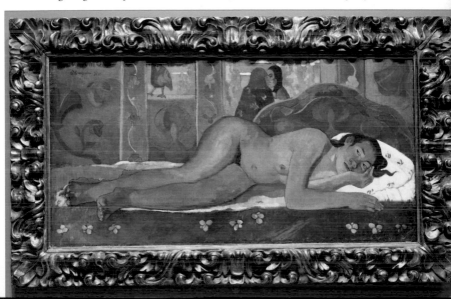

Barrister's wig in a Middle Temple Lane shop window.

Temple Church.

Tel: 020-7405 2107
Opening Hrs: Tue–Sat 10am–5pm; also 6–9pm (candlelit opening) first Tue of each month
Entrance Fee: free except Tue evenings
Transport: Holborn

This marvellous museum is a self-endowed monument to John Soane (1753–1837), one of London's most important architects and collectors, who left his house and collection much as they had been during his lifetime. He built his private home on three sites along the edge of Lincoln's Inn Fields (No. 13) and it is a delight to visit, like being in a miniature British Museum.

Among the highlights are an Egyptian sarcophagus, Hogarth's *Rake's Progress* and some fine Canalettos, but much of the pleasure of visiting is derived from the building itself and how there are treasures tucked into every corner.

Dickens's world

The ghost of the great Victorian writer Charles Dickens (1812–70) haunts the streets of Holborn. Just south of Lincoln's Inn Fields is the **Old Curiosity Shop**, a tiny 16th-century structure – now a shoe shop – likely to have been the inspiration for Little Nell's antiques shop.

On the other side of Lincoln's Inn, Dickens's first marital home was on the site of the neo-Gothic Prudential Assurance building in Holborn, opposite a half-timbered row of shops at the bottom of Gray's Inn Road. This is **Staple Inn ❾**, one of the former Inns of Chancery that dealt with commercial law. Dating from 1586 and a survivor of the Great Fire of London, it shows how much of the city must have looked before 1666.

Dickens underwent his legal apprenticeship at **Gray's Inn ❿** (Mon–Fri 10am–4pm), one of Holborn's four Inns of Court. Dating from the 14th century, its grounds lie just to the west of Gray's Inn Road. The magnificent garden (Mon–Fri noon–2.30pm) was laid out by Francis Bacon, the Elizabethan philosopher and statesman. With an irony that must have tickled

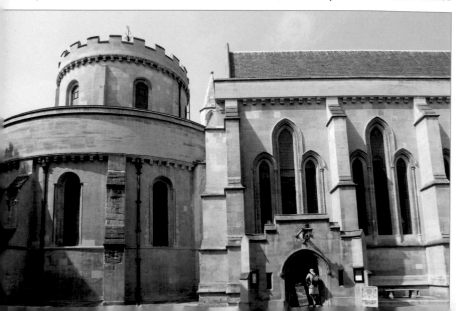

Dickens's sense of the law's ridiculousness, Gray's Inn Hall saw the first production of Shakespeare's *Comedy of Errors*.

Further east is **Bleeding Heart Yard**, scene of much of the domestic action in *Little Dorrit*. Only a step or two away is **Hatton Garden** ⓫, the centre of London's diamond trade, and Leather Lane, where market stalls sell fresh food and household goods.

FLEET STREET

Just beyond the Temple Inn and the Royal Courts of Justice is **Temple Bar** ⓬, where a mean-looking heraldic dragon marks the boundary between Westminster and the City of London, beyond which, theoretically, the monarch cannot pass without the Lord Mayor's permission.

Stretching eastwards is **Fleet Street**, the former home of Britain's national newspapers from 1702, when the first daily newspaper, the *Daily Courant*, was published here. In the 1980s, new technology enabled the press barons to move to cheaper sites in Docklands and elsewhere.

There is still evidence of the street's illustrious past. Dr Samuel Johnson – who famously quipped, 'A man who is tired of London is tired of life' – lived in the back courts at 17 Gough Square from 1748 to 1759. Here, with the help of six assistants, he compiled the first comprehensive English dictionary. **Dr Johnson's House** ⓭ is an evocative museum of this great man of letters (tel: 020-7353 3745; May–Sept Mon–Sat 11am–5.30pm, Oct–Apr 11am–5pm; cash only). The creaky old building dates from 1700; Johnson paid rent to the tune of £30 per year, equivalent to around £3,000 today. (The alleyway leading to Gough Square is immediately east of No. 167 Fleet Street.)

The crime writer Edgar Wallace (1875–1932) is immortalised on a plaque on the northwest corner of **Ludgate Circus**, at the far end of Fleet Street. As an 11-year-old he sold newspapers at this junction.

Wedged in behind the Reuters Building designed by Sir Edwin Lutyens in 1935 is 'the journalists'

On top of the Old Bailey's dome, a golden figure of justice stands with a sword in her right hand and, in her left, scales to weigh the evidence.

Lincoln's Inn.

The Old Curiosity Shop.

Johnson portrayed in a window of his former home.

and printers' church', **St Bride's** ⑭ (tel: 020-7427 0133; www.stbrides. com). It was near here that the aptly named Wynkyn de Worde, an associate of William Caxton, set up the street's first press. There is a small museum of Fleet Street in the crypt, where a magpie collection of Roman mosaics from a villa on this site, Saxon church walls, and human remains are stored – much was revealed when the building was bombed in World War II. The ossuary is visible if you join a guided tour (Tue 3pm; charge; check website for dates). Samuel Pepys was baptised at St Bride's (he was born in 1633 in Salisbury Court, off Fleet Street) and he records in his diary how he had to bribe the sexton to find room for his brother's corpse here. The church's elegant spire is Sir Christopher Wren's tallest and is said to have inspired the first tiered wedding cake. Lunchtime concerts are held here on Tuesday and Friday at 1.15pm except for Lent, August and December.

DR JOHNSON'S DICTIONARY

Samuel Johnson (1709–84) was one of the great figures of the Enlightenment, rising from a humble background to become a member of London's intellectual elite. Having arrived in the city in 1737 after his attempt at a teaching career failed, he started writing for The Gentleman's Magazine, as well as penning various plays and poems. In 1746 he was commissioned by a group of publishers to produce a dictionary for a fee of £1,575 – a large sum at the time, but the work ended up taking 10 years instead of the three originally estimated, and Johnson had to pay for his staff and materials out of it. In 1762, however, his financial stability was assured with the award of a £300 annual pension by the king in recognition of his efforts (and thanks to his influential friends, actor and educator Thomas Sheridan and the Earl of Bute).

While some words in the dictionary have changed in meaning over the years (for example, 'nice' was defined as 'superfluously accurate'), many of his pithy definitions still fit the bill. One of the more oblique entries is for 'lexicographer', which Johnson ruefully defined as 'a harmless drudge'.

SAMUEL JOHNSON, LL.D
BORN AT LICHFIELD, Sept. 18ᵗʰ 1709

Ye Olde Cheshire Cheese pub is just off Fleet Street.

LUDGATE HILL

The River Fleet, which once marked the division between Westminster and The City, used to be a 'disembouging stream' according to the 18th-century poet Alexander Pope. Acting as a sluice for Smithfield Market, and notorious since the 14th century for its foetid stench, it was bricked over in the 18th century, although the subterranean waters still have the propensity to make their presence felt by periodically flooding basements in the area.

The Fleet Prison for debtors was on the Fleet's right bank, Newgate Prison on the left. Public executions took place here until 1868, when a law brought an end to the rowdy spectacles they had become.

On the site of the former prison, just beyond Ludgate Circus, is the **Central Criminal Court** ⓯, universally known by the name of the street in which it is located: Old

Bailey. Some of the country's most unpleasant criminals have been brought to account here. In the forbidding No. 1 Court, until the abolition of the death penalty in 1965, convicted murderers were sentenced to be hanged, the judges placing black caps on their heads as they passed sentence. You can still watch cases from the visitors' gallery (Mon–Fri 10am–1pm and 2–5pm approx, closed Aug).

BLACKFRIARS

The underground river enters the Thames at Blackfriars Bridge, named after a friary that was here from 1278 to 1538. A fine monument to this Dominican order is the 1905 **Black Friar** ⓰, on the corner of Queen Victoria Street: a most spectacular Arts and Crafts pub.

Heading west along Victoria Embankment from Blackfriars takes you back to Somerset House, past the permanently moored ships HMS *President* and HQS *Wellington*, opposite the gardens of the Inns of Court.

Diamond merchant in Hatton Garden. This part of London has retained a core of shops selling a particular item: opticians and other optical-related goods (such as camera lenses) as well as watch repair shops along Fleet Street, and diamonds in Hatton Garden.

The Black Friar pub.

ST PAUL'S AND THE CITY

The City, covering just one square mile, is Britain's main financial centre. This was the original London, once contained by Roman walls, and it retains its own government and police force.

The City, London's financial quarter, is a world apart from the rest of the capital. It runs its own affairs, has its own police force and a distinct set of hierarchies. Even the Queen treads carefully here: on her coronation drive in 1953, she was obliged – if only by tradition – to stop at Temple Bar and declare that she came in peace. The name 'Square Mile' is given to this financial district that was at one time regarded as 'the clearing-house of the world', but it signifies far more than a limited geographical area. For most of its 2,000-year history, the City was London.

Today, more than 300,000 workers stream into the City every weekday. Known for their work-hard-play-hard attitude, they are driven by competition and substantial annual bonuses. On weekends, less than 9,000 City residents are left to savour the stillness that settles across the Square Mile, an area where a strong sense of tradition has helped a potentially faceless financial world retain a certain degree of character.

The City has been devastated twice. In 1666 the Great Fire devoured four-fifths of the area, and during the winter of 1940–1 Germany's Luftwaffe left one-third of it in ruins.

St Paul's Cathedral ❶

Address: www.stpauls.co.uk
Tel: 020-7246 8357
Opening Hrs: Mon–Sat 8.30am–4.30pm, last admission 4pm; free 90-minute tours at 10am, 11am, 1pm, 2pm (reserve at desk on arrival)
Transport: St Paul's

At the top of Ludgate Hill, the western approach to the City, stands St Paul's, the first cathedral built after the English Reformation and Sir Christopher Wren's greatest work. A tablet above his plain marble tomb

Main Attractions
St Paul's Cathedral
St Bartholomew the Great
Smithfield Meat Market
Charterhouse Square
Museum of London
Bank of England
Leadenhall
Monument
Tower of London

Map
Page 148

30 St Mary Axe, aka The Gherkin.

TIP

Like any closed world,
the City doesn't open up
easily to outsiders.
Peering out of a tourist
bus at acres of glass and
concrete is far too super-
ficial an examination;
time and legwork in the
network of alleys and
backstreets which thread
through the office blocks
will reveal much more.

reads: *'Lector, si monumentum requiris, circumspice'* ('Reader, if you wish to see his memorial, look around you'). For full coverage of St Paul's, see page 162.

Paternoster Square

St Paul's needs room to breathe, but the area around it – in particular the ancient market site known as **Paternoster Square** – has been intensively developed. In spite of recent remodelling, it forms a disappointing setting for Wren's masterpiece.

In 2004 the **London Stock Exchange** abandoned its long-held

base near the Bank of England in Threadneedle Street for new premises in Paternoster Square that were better suited to electronic trading.

With origins going back to merchants trying to raise money for a Far Eastern trip in 1553, the Stock Exchange has changed enormously since the Big Bang reforms of 1986, when it agreed to radically change its practices. Fixed commission systems were abolished, and jobber and broker functions were merged and transferred to a computerised quotation system. The trading floor, once crowded with frantic pin-striped

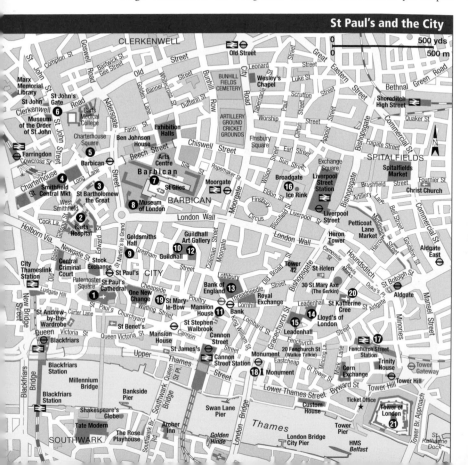

St Paul's and the City

figures engaged in open outcry, fell silent. As a result, the Stock Market is a fairer but duller place. It is no longer open to the general public.

Historic churches

In the warren of roads that lead from St Paul's to the river, there are several Wren churches. **St Andrew-by-the-Wardrobe** in St Andrew's Hill was so named because it stood near a royal storage area. **St Nicholas Cole Abbey** is followed by **St Benet's**, which serves as the Metropolitan Welsh Church.

On the other side of Queen Victoria Street is the **College of Arms** (www.college-of-arms.gov.uk; entrance hall open when receptionist is present Mon–Fri 10am–4pm; free; Record Room tours by arrangement, tel. 020-7248 2762), which has a handsome, refurbished 17th-century interior by William Emmett and a library of heraldry and genealogy, which, for a fee, deals with genealogy enquiries.

Other Wren churches in the vicinity include **St James Garlickhythe** on busy Upper Thames Street, which was disastrously struck by a crane that

Sign on the College of Arms.

demolished its rose window in 1991, and **St Michael Paternoster Royal**, the burial place of Dick Whittington (1423), a Lord Mayor of London, who, with his cat, has entered British mythology as a pantomime figure. This rags-to-riches story sets out to prove that even country bumpkins could be elected Lord Mayor of the City, though the real Whittington came from a wealthy county family and amassed a fortune as a merchant.

St Paul's Cathedral.

WEST SMITHFIELD

Northwest of St Paul's is the great block of St Bartholomew's Hospital.

Barts Hospital ❷

Address: Museum, North Wing, West Smithfield
Tel: 020-3465 5798
Opening Hrs: Tue–Fri 10am–4pm, tours by arrangement Fri 2pm
Entrance Fee: free; charge for tour
Transport: Barbican, St Paul's

Founded in 1123, St Bartholomew's Hospital is the oldest in London. Like many early hospitals, it was founded as a monastery offering 'hospitality' to pilgrims and the needy. The care provided was initially a combination of shelter, comfort, food and prayer, and only in later centuries evolved into medical treatment. Patients were tended by monks and nuns (hence the term 'sister' still in use today).

The hospital includes an interesting little **museum** on changes in medicine over the centuries. A door at the rear of the museum opens to reveal two William Hogarth murals dressing the staircase of the entrance hall of the North Wing. Some of the figures are believed to have been modelled on patients. For a closer look, book one of the guided Friday tours.

Opposite the hospital, on the wall at the corner of **Giltspur Street** and **Cock Lane**, is a golden figure of a urinating boy, symbolising the extinguishing of the 1666 Great Fire at this point. Just beyond, in **West Smithfield**, are memorials to the Scottish hero William Wallace, victim of a spot of judicial butchery here in 1305, and to the 270 'Marian martyrs,' Protestants burned at the stake for religious heresy by Queen Mary in the 1550s.

St Bartholomew the Great ❸

Address: West Smithfield, www.great stbarts.com
Tel: 020-7600 0440
Opening Hrs: Mon–Fri 8.30am–5pm, mid-Nov–mid-Feb until 4pm; Sat 10.30am–4pm, Sun 8.30am–8pm
Transport: Barbican

One of the oldest and finest churches in the City stands in a corner of the square, perhaps a trifle shocked by what has passed before, for this was

Barts Hospital.

also the site of the Bartholomew Fair, immortalised in Ben Jonson's play of the same name. Film-makers, too, have been drawn to this corner of London: scenes in *Four Weddings and a Funeral* and *Shakespeare in Love* were filmed inside the church. The monk Rahere, who founded St Bartholomew's Hospital, is buried here.

SMITHFIELD TO CLERKENWELL

The unlikely confection of iron and plaster adjacent to St Bartholomew's is **Smithfield Central Markets ❹**, at its busiest early in the morning. Here the porters and workers known as 'bummarees' thunder about with barrow loads of carcasses and the knife grinders shower sparks out of the backs of their vans. Through all the commotion, it's still possible to hear 'backchat', Smithfield's equivalent of Billingsgate profanity, designed to fool unwanted listeners.

The last of the great markets still on its original site, Smithfield is now one of the most modern meat markets in the world, thanks to a £70 million overhaul. The renovation was accomplished without sacrificing the Victorian shell of the Central Markets. Although Smithfield has resisted becoming a shopping piazza like Covent Garden, the area has gone up-market, with a number of good-quality restaurants in St John Street.

Just north of Smithfield is Georgian **Charterhouse Square ❺**. With its gas lamps and cobbles, it is a favourite location for period film-makers. The Carthusian order **London Charterhouse** still has around 40 residents, some of whom conduct guided tours between April and September (tel: 020-7253 9503; www.thecharterhouse. org; book in advance).

St John's Gate ❻

Address: St John's Lane, www.museum stjohn.org.uk
Tel: 020-7324 4005

Opening Hrs: Mon–Sat 10am–5pm, 60-minute tours Tue, Fri and Sat at 11am, 2.30pm
Entrance Fee: free
Transport: Farringdon

To the left of London Charterhouse, approached through the medieval St John's Gate off Clerkenwell Road, is **St John's** Priory, founded by the crusading Order of the Knights of St John. Little remains of the buildings dissolved by Henry VIII, but there is a small **museum** in the Gate House, and guided tours of the Grand Hall and remains of the Priory Chapel, which, like the Temple Church off Fleet Street, was round.

Smithfield butcher.

Clerkenwell

Further north, beyond Old Street is **Clerkenwell**, historically a district of immigrants (notably Italian) and revolutionary traditions, as well as the traditional centre of the city's watchmaking industry. In the 19th century, Chartists and campaigners for Home Rule collected around Clerkenwell Green.

Guiseppe Mazzini, the Italian revolutionary, lived at No. 10 Laystall

Inside St Bartholomew the Great.

Tombstones in Bunhill Fields, where many famous people are buried, including John Bunyan, author of The Pilgrim's Progress.

Barts Hospital museum.

and John Bunyan. Across the road is **Wesley's House and Chapel** (tel: 020-7253 2262; www.wesleyschapel.org. uk; Mon–Sat 10am–4pm, Sun worship 12.30–1.45pm), built by the founder of Methodism, John Wesley, in 1778. There is a museum in the crypt and Wesley's house, next to the chapel, is also open to the public. In the men's public toilets are Victorian fixtures manufactured by Thomas Crapper.

THE BARBICAN

Based around three 42-storey towers, the **Barbican Centre ⑦** (www. barbican.org.uk; check for architecture tours and hidden Barbican tours) is the main residential block in the City and contains Europe's largest arts centre. It was devised as council housing by the Corporation of London in the 1950s to attract residents and boost a falling City population. It took more than 20 years to build and is renowned for its inaccessibility and maze-like design. Later the flats were sold at exorbitant prices. The complex contains two art galleries, a cinema, two theatres and the London Symphony Orchestra, and is

Street and Lenin edited a newspaper in what is now the Marx Memorial Library at 37a Clerkenwell Green (tel: 020-7253 1485; www.marx-memorial-library.org; open to the public Mon–Thu noon–4pm; guided tours Tue and Thu 1pm).

To the east, just south of Old Street Underground station on City Road, is **Bunhill Fields** (Apr–Sept Mon–Fri 8am–7pm, Sat–Sun 9.30am–7pm; Oct–Mar Mon–Fri 8am–4pm; Sat–Sun 9.30am–4pm), the burial ground for many notable nonconformists including Daniel Defoe, William Blake

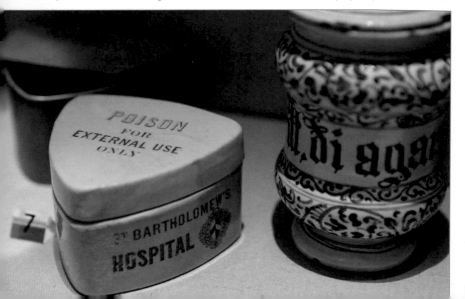

now listed as being of architectural and historical importance.

Beside the Barbican Centre, on the site of a Roman fort, is the Museum of London.

Museum of London ❽

Address: London Wall, www.museumof london.org.uk
Tel: 020-7001 9844
Opening Hrs: daily 10am–6pm, last admission 5.30pm
Entrance Fee: free
Transport: Barbican

With more than a million objects in its stores, this is the world's largest urban history museum and an essential stop for understanding how the City developed.

Aside from important prehistoric and Roman collections, it has a vast archaeological archive, a costume and decorative arts collection, a photographic archive of 280,000 images and more than 5,000 hours of oral life-story recordings.

London's history is presented chronologically from prehistory to the early Stuarts. The same thematic threads run through each period:

The Barbican apartments.

architecture, trade and industry, transport, health, religion, fashions, leisure pursuits. There are many detailed information panels; you may find that, an hour into your visit, you're still with the Romans.

Get your bearings and find key attractions.

CITY OF LONDON

Here are some highlights:

London Before London
This surveys life in the Thames Valley from 450,000 BC to AD 50. The centrepiece of the exhibition is the 'River Wall' displaying 300 artefacts found in the Thames.

Roman London
This gallery has a hoard of gold coins (1st–2nd century AD), a Roman leather bikini, and the gilded arms of what must have been a life-size statue of a god or emperor.

Medieval London
Telling the story of London from the end of Roman rule to the accession of Elizabeth I, this gallery displays items such as a gold and garnet brooch found in a Covent Garden grave, and some extremely pointy medieval shoes.

War, Plague and Fire
This tells the story of London in the turbulent 17th century, when Civil War, plague and then the Great Fire of 1666 ravaged the city. Objects include a death mask of Oliver Cromwell, primitive fire-fighting equipment and fire-damaged floor tiles from Pudding Lane (where the fire began in a baker's shop).

Galleries of Modern London
These galleries bring the story of London up to the present day, and display the stunning Lord Mayor's Coach. There is also a reconstructed 18th-century pleasure garden and pavilion, a cell from a debtors' prison, an Art Deco lift from Selfridges, and exhibits such as the elaborate Fanshawe dress made from Spitalfields' woven silk.

THE GUILDS
Craftsmen with the same trade tended to congregate in small areas, and clubbed together to form medieval guilds. Like trade unions, the guilds operated to ward off foreign competition and established an apprenticeship system. They set standards for their goods and working practices, and ran mutual-aid schemes which helped members in difficulty. The more prosperous guilds built halls to meet and dine in and wore lavish uniforms or 'liveries', in due course becoming livery companies.

Museum of London exhibit.

Down the centuries the livery companies joined the establishment, promoting charities and founding some of England's better educational institutes, including Haberdashers' College and Goldsmiths' College.

The Livery Halls

Today some of the most impressive portals in the City belong to livery halls. Behind their elaborate carvings members dine as lavishly as ever.

Most spectacular is **Goldsmiths Hall** ❾ in Foster Lane (tel: 020-7606 7010; www.thegoldsmiths.co.uk/hall), between the Museum of London and St Paul's, where the integrity of coins made by the Royal Mint are checked in an annual ceremony. The use of the word 'hallmark' as a seal of value originated here and the company is still responsible for assaying gold. Unfortunately, visitors are not usually allowed inside the livery halls, except on open days held a few times a year (see website for dates and bookings).

While the 108 livery companies today have little connection with their original crafts, they still exert influence in their home territory. The City is governed by the City Corporation, chaired by the **Lord Mayor** (whereas the rest of the capital comes under the wing of the Mayor of London, who presides over the Greater London Authority). The office of Lord Mayor dates from 1189. The new Mayor is elected each year on Michaelmas Day (29 September) when the reigning Lord Mayor and his aldermen parade through the streets carrying posies of flowers to ward off the stench which filled the City in medieval times.

Guildhall ❿

Address: Gresham Street, www.guild hall.cityoflondon.gov.uk
Tel: 020-7332 1313
Opening Hrs: Mon–Sat 10am–4.30pm; Sun noon–4pm
Entrance Fee: free
Transport: St Paul's

In November the Mayor is sworn in here, taking up his symbols of office in a ceremony known as the Silent Change, so called because no words are spoken. The Guildhall is the best

The Lord Mayor's Coach in the Museum of London.

Postman's Park delivers a soothing antidote to the over-scale Barbican. Small, secluded and a short walk from the Museum of London walkway exit, this is a good place to take a break. Rows of hand-lettered Doulton plaques placed in an open gallery by socialist artist George Watts (1817–1904) commemorate tragic acts of bravery by ordinary people. The General Post Office, from which the park derives its name, closed long ago.

Mansion House.

place to glimpse the guilds' past. Dating from the 15th century, and several times restored, the Great Hall is decorated with the liveries' banners and shields, and contains statues of Gog and Magog, the legendary founders of London. A small museum (tel: 020-7332 1868; Mon–Sat 9.30am–4.45pm; free) in a room adjacent to the Library displays the timepieces owned by the Clockmakers' Company. This splendid collection is the oldest and largest of its kind. There are 15 marine timekeepers, including one by John Harrison.

The Lord Mayor's Show is held a day after his swearing in. This colourful parade starts at the Guildhall and passes through the City, culminating at **Mansion House ⓫**, opposite the Bank of England. This is the Lord Mayor's official residence, designed by George Dance the Elder in 1758, but its magnificent rooms are not open to the public. However, there are guided tours every Tuesday at 2pm (charge) – meet at the A-board

near the porch entrance to Mansion House, in Walbrook.

Guildhall Art Gallery ⓬

Address: Guildhall Yard, www.cityoflondon.gov.uk
Tel: 020-7332 3700
Opening Hrs: Mon–Sat 10am–5pm, Sun noon–4pm
Transport: Mansion House or St Paul's

Established in 1886, the Guildhall's gallery was destroyed in the Blitz but reopened in 1999. John Singleton Copley's immense *The Defeat of the Floating Batteries at Gibraltar*, around which the new gallery was designed, commands attention, but allow time to linger over the smaller-scale works depicting London life. You can take a free tour of the collection's highlights on Fridays (hourly between 12.15 and 3.15pm).

Shortly before work began on the present building, the remains of a **Roman amphitheatre** were discovered under the yard. The arena, including well-preserved timber drains bearing original carpentry tool marks, may now be viewed in a lower-level gallery.

AT SIXES AND SEVENS

For years there was fierce rivalry between the craftsmen's guilds. In 1515 the Lord Mayor interceded and named a top 12 who could process in that order at the Lord Mayor's Show: Mercers (dealers in fine cloth), Grocers, Drapers, Fishmongers, Goldsmiths, Skinners, Merchant Taylors, Haberdashers, Salters, Ironmongers, Vintners and Clothworkers. Competition between the Skinners and Merchant Taylors, which were founded in the same year and both claimed the number six slot, was particularly fierce. The Lord Mayor decreed they should alternate positions six and seven every year, which is said to have originated the expression 'at sixes and sevens', meaning 'in disarray'.

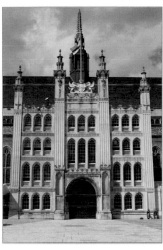

The Guildhall.

Bank and Beyond

The triangular intersection known as **Bank** can intimidate. Imposing civic architecture abounds, with Sir Edwin Lutyens' **HSBC** building on the north west side, Mansion House on the western corner, the **Royal Exchange** building to the east and Sir John Soane's implacable facade of the **Bank of England** to the north.

All the City's great institutions grew from the fulfilment of the most basic needs and only later acquired their grandiose headquarters. Banking first came to the City in the 12th century when Italian refugees set up lending benches (*banca* in Italian) in **Lombard Street**, running eastwards from the Bank of England.

The Bank of England ⓲

Address: Museum entrance in Bartholomew Lane, www.bankof england.co.uk
Tel: 020-7601 5545;
Opening Hrs: Mon–Fri 10am–5pm
Entrance Fee: free
Transport: Bank

The **Bank of England** dominates the Bank square as it does the British financial scene. Popularly known as the Old Lady of Threadneedle Street, a nickname probably originating from a late 18th-century cartoon

> **FACT**
>
> Behind Mansion House is St Stephen Walbrook, the Lord Mayor's church, rebuilt after the Great Fire and considered by many to be Christopher Wren's best. Its dome is believed to be a dry run for St Paul's and its controversial 'cheeseboard' altar is by Henry Moore.

An ornate memorial to Admiral Horatio Nelson (1758–1805), the Guildhall.

SHOP

The Royal Exchange, where animated young traders in traditional garish blazers once shouted and waved instructions, is now occupied by a clutch of luxury retailers including Cartier, Bulgari, Tiffany, Hermès, De Beer and Chanel. To round off a spree here, head for one of the Exchange's posh restaurants or bars.

Exterior of the Lloyd's of London building.

depicting an old lady (the bank) trying to prevent the then prime minister, Pitt the Younger, from securing her gold. The name stuck because it aptly describes the conservative, maternalistic role the bank played in stabilising the country's economy – a role strengthened in 1997 when the new Labour government freed it from direct government control.

The Bank of England was set up in 1694 to finance a war against the Dutch. In return for a £1.2 million loan, it was granted a charter and became a bank of issue (with the right to print notes and take deposits). Today it prints 5 million notes daily, destroys another 5 million and stores the nation's gold reserves. Its present home was largely rebuilt between 1925 and 1939.

It covers 3 acres (1.2 hectares) and contains the **Bank of England Museum**. The presentations narrate how the bank helped to finance Britain's war effort against France in 1688, how it became one of the first institutions in the City to employ women and how it controlled

The 30 St Mary Axe building, aka the Gherkin.

government borrowing during World War II. There is a display of gold, including Roman and modern bars.

Lloyd's of London

The financial boom of the 1980s brought immediate demands for new office buildings which would be purpose-built for modern communications and, by 1991, 1.7 sq miles (4.4 sq km) of office space had been built in the City. One of the first, and the most dramatic, was the 1986 **Lloyd's of London** ⓮ building in Lime Street, designed by Sir Richard Rogers (now Lord Rogers).

For so long the biggest insurance group in the world, Lloyd's started in the 17th-century coffee house of Edward Lloyd, where underwriters, shippers and bankers gathered and began to strike deals. Its practices remained largely unchanged for 300 years, but in the late 1980s sundry international disasters led to some huge payouts and millions of pounds

were lost. Many of the 'names' – investors who shouldered the insurance risks, often through syndicates – lost life savings and owed more than they could ever possibly pay; tragically a few committed suicide.

The building is no longer open to visitors, but the exterior is a highlight of the City. Hidden from sight on a magnificent marble floor is a rostrum housing the **Lutine Bell**, which was rung once for bad news and twice for good. It was rung following the 9/11 terrorist attacks in 2001.

Beside this modern building is the more accessible **Leadenhall ⑮**, once the wholesale market for poultry and game, and now a handsome commercial centre. The magnificent airy Victorian cream-and-maroon structure has a collection of up-market chain shops, bookshops, sandwich bars and stylish restaurants, attracting City workers at breakfast and lunch time.

Grand stations

London's other steel-and-glass Victorian constructions – the railway stations – were also given facelifts

during the 1980s building boom. **Liverpool Street** was overhauled along with neighbouring **Broadgate ⑯**, one of the most ambitious developments in the City, with 16 office-block buildings around three squares including, at Broadgate Square, an ice rink with sushi, coffee and sandwich stalls dotted around the perimeter. There are now plans afoot to redevelop the site.

Fenchurch Street ⑰ with its arched roof and graceful windows was the City's first railway station. Originally situated in the Minories, it moved in 1854 to its present location and has the 1930s Manhattan-style office building, **1 America Square**, over its railway lines.

To stand out in such an architectural playground, new buildings have to be innovative. A much-loved new feature of the London skyline is the **30 St Mary Axe building**, a 40-storey tapering glass tower designed by Lord Foster and better known as **the Gherkin**. Richard Rogers' latest addition to the novelty silhouettes in the City is the 'Cheesegrater', a 740ft

Leadenhall Market sits on the site of the Roman Forum.

Leadenhall Market.

(225-metre) -tall skeletal glass-and-steel wedge that soars skywards. And at 20 Fenchurch Street is the latest skyscraper to be built, also with an affectionate nickname, the Walkie-Talkie, because of its distinctive top-heavy shape.

Less obvious is **One New Change** on Cheapside, the City's newest shopping centre designed by Jean Nouvel. Its 6th floor roof terrace offers stunning views of the City and St Paul's.

Monument ⑱

Address: Monument Yard, www.the monument.info
Tel: 020-7626 2717
Opening Hrs: viewing gallery Apr–Sept daily 9.30am–6pm, Oct–Mar 9.30am–5.30pm
Transport: Monument

Erected according to Wren's designs to commemorate the 1666 fire, this Roman Doric column stands 202ft (61 metres) high. The height happens to be the same as the distance between the monument's base and the king's baker's house in Pudding Lane where the fire began.

Climb the 311 steps of Monument, commemorating the Great Fire of London, for superb views.

The Great Fire lasted four days and spread through 460 streets, destroying 87 churches and more than 13,000 houses. Inside the column,

Liverpool Street station.

311 steps wind up to a small platform, from which the view is spectacular. Appropriately enough, the gallery affords a chance to appreciate the remarkable vision Wren imposed on the City through his spires. (There are so many Wren spires that you risk severe Wren-fatigue if you attempt to see them all.)

St Mary-le-Bow  is the home of the famous Bow bells, which define a true cockney – you have to be born within earshot. There have been many sets of bells over the centuries; the current ones were cast after World War II. The church interior after restoration is rather plain, but the Norman crypt, now a restaurant called The Café Below, is worth a visit. Wren was able to leave his significant mark on London because so much of it had been destroyed in the Great Fire, but some churches survived the conflagration, including **St Katherine Cree** , a mix of Classical and Gothic, in Leadenhall Street. Henry Purcell played its fine 17th-century organ, and the painter Hans Holbein, a plague victim, was buried here in 1543.

Tower of London

Address: Tower Hill, www.hrp.org.uk
Tel: 020-3166 6000
Opening Hrs: Mar–Oct Tue–Sat 9am–5.30pm, Sun–Mon 10am–5.30pm; Nov–Feb Tue–Sat 9am–4.30pm, Sun–Mon 10am–4.30pm; last admission 30 minutes before closing
Transport: Tower Hill

East of the Monument, across the river from the oval-shaped City Hall, from which the Greater London Authority's power is exercised, is the City's oldest structure. At first sight the **Tower of London** can look like a cardboard model rather than a former seat of power, but closer inspection reveals an awesome solidity which encompasses much of Britain's history. The Tower has contained at various times a treasury, public record office, observatory, royal mint and zoo, and was so frequently remodelled for these purposes that its interiors look less ancient than one expects.

For full coverage of the Tower of London, see page 164.

The Tower of London.

ST PAUL'S CATHEDRAL

Sir Christopher Wren built more than 50 churches in London after the Great Fire of 1666, but this is the one that remains his masterpiece.

Sir Christopher Wren.

Historians believe that the first church on the St Paul's site was built in the 7th century, although it only really came into its own as Old St Paul's in the 14th century; by the 16th century it was the tallest cathedral in England. Much of the building was destroyed in the Great Fire of 1666. Construction on the new St Paul's Cathedral began in 1675, when its architect, Sir Christopher Wren, was 43 years old.

The architect was an old man of 76 when his son Christopher finally laid the highest stone of the lantern on the central cupola in 1710. In total, the cathedral cost £747,954 to build, and most of the money was raised through taxing coal imports. As part of the cathedral's 300th anniversary in 2008, a major £40 million restoration project involved a thorough clean of the exterior, scrubbing away centuries of soot and grime.

The Essentials

Tel: 020-7246 8350; www.stpauls.co.uk
Opening Hrs: Mon–Sat 8.30am–4.30pm, last admission 15 minutes before closing; tours 10am, 11am, 1pm and 2pm
Transport: St Paul's

Just below the 24 windows in the dome is the Whispering Gallery, nearly 100ft (30 metres) of perfect acoustic. A whisper can be heard across the gallery, 107ft (33 metres) away.

Admiral Lord Nelson (1758–1805) is entombed in the crypt.

A chapel behind the High Altar, damaged during the Blitz, was restored as the American Chapel, with a book of remembrance paying tribute to the 28,000 American citizens based in the UK who died in World War II.

The iconic dome of the cathedral forms a distinctive shape on the London skyline.

The superb craftsmanship was supervised during the 35-year construction by the master builder, Thomas Strong, and by Wren himself.

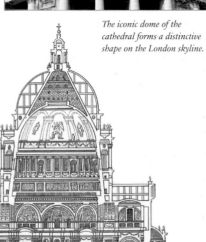

The cathedral's appearance is deceptive. The famous dome viewed from afar would look huge if seen from inside the building. The dome you see from within is in fact a much smaller dome, on top of which is built a brick cone. The cone's purpose is to support the massive weight of the external Portland stone dome, which weighs more than 64,000 tonnes.

THE TOWER OF LONDON

Queens were beheaded here, princes murdered and traitors tortured. Once a place to be avoided, it is now one of London's top visitor attractions.

The Imperial State Crown.

Encircled by a moat (now dry), with 22 towers, the Tower, begun by William the Conqueror around 1078, is Britain's top military monument and a reminder of how power was once exercised in the nation.

Two of Henry VIII's wives, Anne Boleyn and Catherine Howard, were beheaded here, in 1536 and 1542. So were Sir Thomas More, Henry's principled Lord Chancellor (1535), and Sir Walter Raleigh, the last of the great Elizabethan adventurers (1618). The uncrowned Edward V, aged 12, and his 10-year-old brother Richard were murdered here in 1483, allegedly on the orders of Richard III. William Penn, the future founder of Pennsylvania, was imprisoned here in 1669, and the diarist Samuel Pepys in 1679. As recently as 1941, Rudolph Hess, Germany's deputy führer, was locked in the Tower.

The Essentials

Address: Tower Hill; www.hrp.org.uk
Tel: 020-3166 6000
Opening Hrs: Mar–Oct Tue–Sat 9am–5.30pm, Sun–Mon 10am–5.30pm; Nov–Feb Tue–Sat 9am–4.30pm, Sun–Mon 10am–4.30pm, last admission 30 minutes before closing
Transport: Tower Hill

Tower of London armoury.

Given that the Tower's 18 acres (7.3 hectares) contain enough buildings and collections to occupy three hours, you may prefer to skip the one-hour Beefeater-led tour and strike out on your own. A multimedia guide can be hired.

In summer, it's best to arrive early to beat the queues, giving priority to the Crown Jewels and the Bloody Tower. Note that the spiral staircases in some of the towers require a degree of agility. Within the Tower walls, picnics are permitted on

At the centre of the fortress is the imposing White Tower with its four weathervane-topped turrets, each of a different style. The name followed Henry III's order to whitewash the exterior.

Traitors' Gate.

THE SIGHTS WORTH SEEING

Historic view of the Tower.

The Medieval Palace

Just before Traitor's Gate is the entrance to the residential part of the Tower, used by monarchs when they lived here. St Thomas's Tower, built in 1275–79 but much altered, displays archaeological evidence of its many uses. Parts of the Wakefield Tower (1220–40), such as the King's Bed Chamber, are furnished in 13th-century style and a torture exhibition has been added. A spiral staircase leads to a walkway on top of the south wall, which provides a good view of the riverside defences. The wall runs to the Lanthorn Tower (1883) containing 13th-century artefacts.

The White Tower

The oldest part of the fortress, the White Tower, was probably designed in 1078 by a Norman monk, Gandulf, a prolific builder of castles and churches. It has walls 15ft (5 metres) thick. Its original form remains, but nearly every part has been refurbished or rebuilt: the door surrounds and most windows were replaced in the 17th and 18th centuries, and much of the Normandy stone was replaced with more durable Portland stone from Dorset. The first floor gives access to the austere Chapel of St John the Evangelist, a fine example of early Norman architecture. Much of the remaining space is devoted to displays of armour, swords and muskets, taken from the Royal Armouries. Legend has it that London will fall if the ravens who nest here ever leave the Tower – so their wings are clipped to ensure they stay.

A Tower raven.

any of the seats. There are also snack kiosks and a restaurant in the New Armouries. In winter you can go ice-skating just outside the Tower's walls, with lovely views of the river.

Visitors can apply to take part in Ceremony of the Keys, a 700-year-old event that happens at the end of each night (see website for advance booking).

MORE MODERN THAN MEDIEVAL

Given that so much of the country's turbulent history was played out within these walls, the Tower conspicuously lacks the romantic aura that many visitors expect. The reason is that, until comparatively recently, its buildings were functional – as well as serving as a fort, arsenal, palace and prison, it also contained at various times a treasury, public record office, observatory, royal mint and zoo. As a result, it was frequently remodelled and renovated, especially in the 19th century, so that many floors and staircases, for example, look more modern than medieval. But then, how could the boards that Henry VIII trod hope to survive the footfalls of 2.5 million tourists a year?

Any sense of awe is also undermined by the brightly uniformed 'Beefeaters'. Although all have served in the armed forces for at least 22 years, some have enthusiastically embraced showbiz, apparently auditioning for the role of pantomime villain by alternating jocular banter with visitors and melodramatically delivered descriptions of torture and beheadings. In contrast, pike and musket drills by the English Civil War Society are conducted with the masterful lethargy of confirmed pacifists.

Sir Walter Raleigh's room in the Bloody Tower (1603–16).

Attired in Tudor uniforms, Yeoman warders first took up their posts under Edward VI and have been guarding the Tower for more than 500 years. Their nickname "Beefeaters" may derive from the French word buffetier, meaning servant, although an "eater" was also used in English to describe a servant. In 2007 the first female Beefeater, Moira Cameron, was appointed; like her fellow male Beefeaters she has a military background. Among the perks of the job of a Beefeater is the use of a subsidised apartment within the Tower of London.

The upper chamber of Wakefield Tower was used as a throne room by Henry III and later converted into an anteroom of the King's private chambers by his son, Edward I. Wakefield Tower also housed the state archives from 1360 to 1856 and, for a time, served as the Jewel House.

In character as Isaac Newton, former Master of the Royal Mint at the Tower of London.

THE HIGHLIGHTS

The Wall Walk
The walk along this defensive outer wall takes in the eastern towers. Access is through the Salt Tower, which was often used as a prison. Next are the Broad Arrow Tower, also once a lock-up, the Constable Tower, which contains a model depicting the Tower in the 14th century, and the Martin Tower, which houses an exhibition on the Crown Jewels.

The Fusilier Museum
In the centre of the Tower is the modest but elegantly housed museum. Opened in 1962, it follows the regiment's campaigns from its first battle for William of Orange against the French in Walcourt up to its more recent peacekeeping involvement in the Balkans and Northern Ireland. The regiment was almost destroyed in the American War of Independence.

The Crown Jewels
These are displayed in the neo-Gothic Waterloo Barracks, built in 1845. The queues here can be long, with airport-style barriers. At the centre of the display are a dozen crowns and a glittering array of swords, sceptres and orbs used on royal occasions. A moving walkway ensures that visitors cannot linger over the principal exhibits, but many other glass cases contain gold dishes, chalices and altar dishes that can be viewed at leisure. The collection includes the notorious Koh-i-Noor diamond.

The Fusilier Museum charts the story of the British infantry regiment, founded here in 1685.

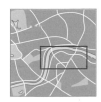

SOUTHWARK AND THE SOUTH BANK

The historic area south of the Thames has been transformed into a vibrant entertainment centre. Its multiple attractions, ranging from the London Eye and Tate Modern to Tower Bridge, are linked by an attractive riverside walk.

S outhwark is one of the oldest parts of the capital. The first bridge across the Thames was built by the Romans near London Bridge, and the community around it developed separately from the City, as it lay beyond the City's jurisdiction. In Shakespeare's day it was the place for putting on unlicensed plays and for setting up brothels, and it retained its reputation as an area of vice well into the 19th century. The regeneration around Tate Modern, Borough Market and Butler's Wharf – coupled with Renzo Piano's giant tower, The Shard – has transformed the area.

AROUND LAMBETH BRIDGE

Opposite the Houses of Parliament, beside Lambeth Bridge, is the red-brick **Lambeth Palace ❶**, which has been the London residence of the Archbishops of Canterbury since the 12th century. The fine Tudor brick-work of the entrance tower dates from 1485, but much of the rest is Victorian. The rare occasions on which the palace is open to the public include the annual Open House weekend (see page 57).

Adjacent, by Lambeth Bridge on Lambeth Palace Road, the

garden and deconsecrated church of **St Mary** contains the **Garden Museum** (tel: 020-7401 8865; www. gardenmuseum.org.uk; check web-site for opening times), which is due to reopen in early 2017 after a 15-month refurbishment. The museum is based on the work of two 17th-century royal gardeners, the elder and younger John Tradescant, father and son, who introduced exotic fruits such as pineapples to Britain. The old-fashioned roses and herbaceous

Main Attractions
Imperial War Museum
London Sea Life Aquarium
London Eye
Southbank Centre
Tate Modern
Shakespeare's Globe
Southwark Cathedral
Borough Market
Tower Bridge
Design Museum

Map
Page 170

Second-hand book market outside the BFI.

Lambeth Palace.

perennials are delightful, and the church's rich history is evident in its memorials, including one remembering HMS Bounty's Captain William Bligh, who lived locally in his later years.

Imperial War Museum ❷

Address: Lambeth Road, www.3iwm.3org.3uk
Tel: 020-7416 5000
Opening Hrs: daily 10am–6pm
Entrance Fee: free except some special exhibitions
Transport: Elephant & Castle, Lambeth North

A 15-minute walk south from Lambeth Bridge, along Lambeth Road, leads to the **Imperial War Museum** (IWM London). The museum reopened in 2014 after extensive remodelling, creating new gallery spaces and improved facilities to do justice to this incredible collection. It also marked the centenary of the outbreak of World War I in 2014.

The museum, of what Churchill termed 'the Age of Violence', was founded in 1917; at the opening ceremony it was stated that the museum 'was not a monument of military glory, but a record of toil and sacrifice'. In 1936 the museum was moved to the present building, which stands on the site of a 19th-century psychiatric hospital known as Bedlam, an inspired choice for a museum chronicling the horrors of modern warfare.

After World War II the museum began to gather material from this and later conflicts, and three smaller sites, including the warship HMS Belfast (see page 180), were acquired.

As part of the refit, the atrium space at the heart of the museum was reworked to display iconic objects, including aircrafts, tanks and artillery, plus new shops and a park-side café. Other exhibits include one of Britain's leading collections of 20th-century art.

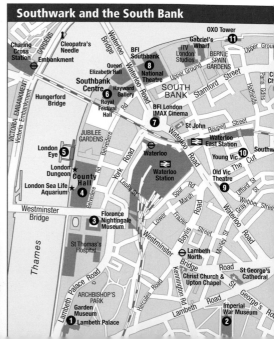

St Thomas's Hospital

Back by the river, close to West-minster Bridge, **St Thomas's Hospital** includes a reminder of warfare's nobler side: the **Florence Nightingale Museum ③** (2 Lambeth Palace Road; tel: 020 7620 0374; www.florence-nightingale.co.uk; daily 10am–5pm). Don't be deterred by the uninspiring walk down Lambeth Palace Road; this small museum is worth the detour. It has a rich collection of memorabilia, and there are audio hotspots around the museum on the life and achievements of Florence Nightingale and Mary Seacole, whose work in the Crimean War of 1853–6 helped transform nursing.

COUNTY HALL ①

Just downstream from Westminster Bridge and facing the Houses of Parliament is the majestic **County Hall**, designed in 1908 by architect Ralph Knott and for years the seat of the Greater London Council, which

ran London until the government of Margaret Thatcher abolished it in 1986. It now incorporates the London Aquarium, the London Dungeon, the five-star Marriott hotel, a budget hotel (a Premier Inn), a Namco games arcade and several restaurants.

The first attraction as you walk eastwards along the river is **Namco Funscape** (www.namcofunscape-london-events.co.uk; 10am–midnight), home to bumper cars, video games and a bowling alley. Better for children is the **London Sea Life Aquarium** (tel: 0871-663 1678; www.visitsealife.com/london; Mon–Thu 10am–6pm, last admission 5pm, Fri–Sun 10am–7pm, last admission 6pm). Thousands of specimens represent some 500 species of fish, and atmospheric sounds, smells and lighting are all employed to great effect. Highlights include the sharks and the touch pool.

County Hall is also the new home of the **London Dungeon** (tel:

KIDS

At the London Sea Life Aquarium, it's worth catching the feeding times. Sharks are usually fed at 2.30pm on Tuesday, Thursday and Saturday, but do check times beforehand.

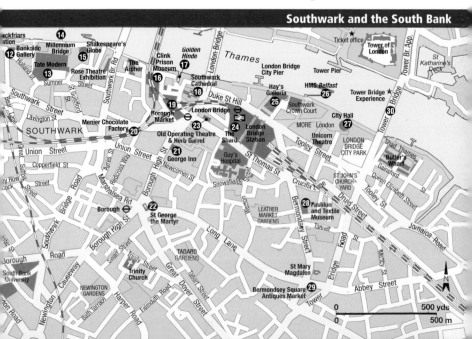

Southwark and the South Bank

The tour of the **London Dungeon** begins with an obligatory photo opportunity – head in the stocks, a blackened chopper at your neck. It's lots of fun for kids who are keen on the macabre, but it is pretty scary and the entire visit is spent in darkened corridors (often made more atmospheric by bloodcurdling shrieks), so it's not recommended for children under eight. Even under-12s must be accompanied by an adult. Queues tend to be long, so book in advance.

The London Eye.

0871-423 2240; www.thedungeons.com; Fri–Wed 10am–5pm, Thu 11am–5pm, weekends until 6pm; longer opening hours in school holidays). Lasting about 1.5 hours, the actor-led tour features ghoulish exhibits of the Black Death, the Great Fire of 1666, Jack the Ripper's exploits, Sweeney Todd the barber's gruesome deeds, and a boat ride to hell. Guaranteed to make you jump at some point.

London Eye ❺

Address: County Hall,
www.londoneye.com
Tel: 0871-781 3000
Opening Hrs: daily Sept–Mar
10am–8.30pm, Apr–June 10am–
9pm, July–Aug 10am–9.30pm.
Closed 1 week in Jan
Transport: Waterloo

Towering over County Hall is the **London Eye**, one of the world's largest observation wheels, designed by architects David Marks and Julia Barfield for the turn of the millennium.

The wheel, with 32 enclosed capsules, takes 30 minutes to make a full rotation – a speed slow enough to allow passengers to step in and out of the capsules while the wheel keeps moving. On a clear day, you can see for 25 miles (40km). Book ahead (by phone or online) if you hope to ride the Eye at busy periods, although check the weather forecast first.

The grassy area around the London Eye has been redeveloped into a pleasant park, called the Jubilee Gardens.

SOUTHBANK CENTRE ❻

The Southbank Centre (tel: 020-7960 4200; www.southbankcentre.co.uk) is Britain's most vibrant arts centre. Its cafés, bars, book and gift shops are open throughout the day, and there's usually a free event in one of the foyers.

Concert halls

The 2,900-seat **Royal Festival Hall** (RFH), the oldest and largest of the three concert halls on the South Bank, was constructed on the site of the Lion Brewery, destroyed by bombing during World War II. The building was opened in 1951 as part of the Festival of Britain, intended to improve the country's morale after

Skateboarders on the South Bank.

years of post-war austerity. Reopened in 2007 after extensive renovation, the hall now has improved acoustics, better facilities in the foyer and a renovated restaurant, Skylon.

There are two other concert halls within the complex, the 917-seater Queen Elizabeth Hall, opened in 1967 for music theatre and opera, and the 372-seater Purcell Room, intended for solo recitals and chamber music. Both of these are closed for renovations, and due to reopen in late 2017.

Hayward Gallery

Set on the upper level of the Southbank Centre complex is the **Hayward Gallery** (tel: 020-7960 4200; www.haywardgallery.org.uk; closed for until late 2017). This is an outstanding example of 1960s brutalist architecture, with a cutting-edge programme focusing on the world's most adventurous and innovative artists.

The Hayward's mirrored **Waterloo Sunset Pavilion**, designed by Dan Graham as part of the regeneration of the Southbank, remains open in between main exhibitions. The gallery roof is often used as exhibition space.

BFI Southbank

Next door is BFI Southbank (the former National Film Theatre; www.bfi.org.uk), Britain's leading art house cinema since 1952. With four cinemas, it holds over 2,400 screenings and events each year, from restored silent movies (with live piano accompaniment) to world cinema productions.

In the Mediathèque, visitors can browse the British Film Institute's archive free. The Riverfront Bar in front of the building, with trestle tables sheltering under Waterloo Bridge, is run by Benugo Bar & Kitchen.

The BFI also runs the **BFI London IMAX Cinema** ❼, which rises from the roundabout at the south end of Waterloo Bridge. Large format film is projected onto a screen 66ft high by 85ft wide (20 by 26 metres), the biggest in the UK. It also specialises in screening films in 3-D.

The National Theatre ❽

On the other side of Waterloo Road, still by the river, is the concrete

Fountain outside Queen Elizabeth Hall.

TIP

The area around the Southbank Centre is great for free entertainment, from lunchtime concerts to photographic exhibitions in the National Theatre's foyer. Further along the river, there are often free concerts and talks at Tate Modern.

National Theatre (www.national theatre.org.uk). The theatre company first opened its doors in 1963 as the Old Vic under Laurence Olivier, but in 1976 the company moved to its new premises on the river, which incorporates three theatres: the large 1,200-seater Olivier; the 900-seater Lyttelton, a two-tier proscenium theatre; and the Dorfman (formerly the Cottesloe), a more intimate space, accessed at the side of the building.

For a peek behind the scenes, book a backstage tour (tel: 020-7452 3000; mailto:tours@nationaltheatre.org. uk); 75-minute tours run daily; check for times.

At this point, a detour down Waterloo Road, past the IMAX cinema (see page 173), leads to The Cut and the elegant **Old Vic Theatre** ❾ (www.oldvictheatre.com), erected in 1811. A music hall in its early days, it is now a repertory theatre, where Hollywood star Kevin Spacey was artistic director from 2003 to 2015, bringing huge prestige (and funding) to the venue. Legendary actors such as Laurence Olivier and Judi

The Oxo Tower.

Dench have trodden the boards here. Backstage tours are available (tel: 020-7928 2651 for dates).

Located a little further along The Cut is the **Young Vic** ❿, a theatre especially known for nurturing the talent of young theatre directors.

The BFI London IMAX Cinema.

GABRIEL'S WHARF TO BANKSIDE

Back on the riverfront, to the east of the National Theatre, is Gabriel's Wharf, a cluster of artisanal shops and restaurants. East again is the Art Deco Oxo Tower ⑪ Architect Albert Moore had grand ideas for this project: as well as erecting what was to become London's second highest commercial building, he wanted to use electric lights to spell out the name of the gravy powder. When planning permission was refused due to an advertising ban, Moore came up with the idea of using three letters – O, X and O – as 10ft (3-metre) -high windows looking out north, south, east and west. Inside the tower are several smart restaurants.

Beyond Blackfriars Bridge, the riverside walk leads past the **Bankside Gallery** ⑫ (tel: 020-7928 7521; www. banksidegallery.com; daily 11am–6pm), home of the Royal Watercolour Society and the Royal Society of Painter-Printmakers, which holds exhibitions.

Tate Modern ⑬

Address: Bankside, www.tate.org.uk
Tel: 020-7887 8888
Opening Hrs: Sun–Thu 10am–6pm, Fri–Sat 10am–10pm
Entrance Fee: free except for special exhibitions
Transport: Southwark or London Bridge

Easily identifiable by its tall brick chimney, Tate Modern occupies the former Bankside Power Station and houses the Tate's international modern art collection and part of its contemporary collection. An extension to the south of the Tate building was completed in 2016, creating new galleries and more public space, including a roof terrace.

In addition to the art, a highlight of the Tate Modern is the view across the Thames to St Paul's Cathedral from the upper floors. (For full coverage, see page 182.)

Tate Modern.

TIP

A novel way to travel between Tate Modern and Tate Britain (see page 77) is to take the Tate Boat. It runs every 40 minutes during gallery hours and also stops at the London Eye.

Millennium Bridge ⑭

Giving easy access to Tate Modern from St Paul's Cathedral, the Millennium Bridge was the first new river crossing in central London since Tower Bridge opened in 1894.

Designing the footbridge was tricky: it had to be slender enough not to spoil the view of St Paul's

THE NATIONAL THEATRE

The idea of a National Theatre was suggested in 1848, but it wasn't until 1912, when Lilian Baylis became manager of the Old Vic Theatre, that the basis for a National Theatre was established. Baylis turned the old Victorian music hall into 'the home of Shakespeare and opera in English', but finding a site for a permanent theatre proved difficult. During World War II, the government introduced funding for the arts as part of the war effort, the London County Council made land available on the South Bank, and in 1949 the National Theatre Bill was passed through Parliament. In 1962 Laurence Olivier was named artistic director, and his first play opened the following year.

The Old Vic remained the company's home while the new theatre was being built, by architect Denys Lasdun. In 1976, after more than a century of controversy, the National Theatre was opened by the Queen, by which time Peter Hall was the director. He was succeeded by Richard Eyre in 1988 and Trevor Nunn in 1997. The director from 2003 to 2015, Nicholas Hytner, had some success in broadening the theatre's appeal by offering some cheaper seats. There are tickets available from £15.

Street performer.

The Millennium Bridge, looking towards St Paul's Cathedral.

from Bankside, yet it also had to make an impact as a significant millennial sculpture. The solution, a sort of stainless-steel scalpel, was provided by architect Norman Foster, sculptor Anthony Caro and engineers Ove Arup and Partners. However, opening-day crowds caused the bridge to sway excessively, and it had to be closed for two years for adjustments. For its first year or so it was dubbed the 'wibbly-wobbly bridge'.

Shakespeare's Globe ⑮

Address: New Globe Walk, www.shakespearesglobe.com
Tel: box office 020-7401 9919
Opening Hrs: tours regularly
Entrance Fee: charge for tours
Transport: London Bridge or Southwark

Bankside and Southwark are the most historic areas of the South Bank. They grew up in competition with the City opposite, but by the 16th century had become vice dens. Bankside was famous for brothels, bear- and bull-baiting, prize fights

and the first playhouses, including the Globe.

The replica of the 1599 building opened in 1996 and is worth a visit even if you're not seeing a play. It has been painstakingly re-created using the original methods of construction and has an open roof (the season runs from May to mid-October). It can accommodate around 1,500 people – 600 standing (called 'groundlings' and liable to get wet if it rains) and the rest seated. The wooden benches feel rather hard by Act III, but you can bring or rent cushions.

A new indoor theatre opened in 2014, named after the Globe's founder Sam Wanamaker. This is an intimate venue with performances by beeswax candles in ornate chandeliers, in keeping with theatre performances in Shakespeare's time. The performances are selected to fit in with the theatre's ambience and often feature music from period instruments. There are also concerts in the winter months, and regular tours year round.

Note that there are no tours of Shakespeare's Globe theatre during performances. If you are visiting when a matinée is on, you will be given a tour of the Rose, Bankside's first playhouse, instead.

The Rose Playhouse

Shakespeare also acted at the Rose Playhouse, whose foundations were discovered close to the Globe in 1989. Turn down New Globe Walk (by the Globe's box office) and then left into Park Street. This was Bankside's first theatre, built in 1587. Events are staged here and tours take place when guided tours of the Globe are not possible (tel: 020-7261 9565; charge).

BANK END

Back on the riverside walk, past Southwark Bridge on the stretch known as Bank End, is the Anchor Bankside inn. The present building (1770–5) is the sole survivor of the 22 busy inns that once lined Bankside. Dr Samuel Johnson, of dictionary fame, drank here.

Clink Street

Like most country bishops, the bishops of the powerful see of Winchester had a London base. A single gable wall remains of Winchester Palace, their former London residence. They had their own laws, regulated the many local brothels and were the first authority in England to lock up miscreants. The prison they founded, in what is now Clink Street, remained a lock-up until the 18th century. The **Clink Prison Museum** ⑯ (tel: 020-7403 0900; www.clink.co.uk; July–Sept daily 10am–9pm, Oct–June Mon–Fri 10am–6pm, Sat–Sun 10am–7.30pm) recalls the area's seedy past.

Shakespeare's Globe.

The Golden Hinde.

Clink Street leads on to Pickfords Wharf, built in 1864 for storing hops, flour and seeds, and now converted into an apartment block. At the end of the street, in **St Mary Overie Dock**, is a replica of Sir Francis Drake's splendid galleon, the **Golden Hinde** ⑰ (tel: 020-7403 0123; www.goldenhinde.com; daily 10am–5.30pm).

Launched in 1973, the ship is the only replica to have completed a circumnavigation of the globe, and has now clocked up more nautical miles than the original, in which Drake set sail on his voyage of discovery in 1577.

Southwark Cathedral ⑱

Address: London Bridge, http://cathedral.southwark.anglican.org
Tel: 020-7367 6700
Opening Hrs: daily 8am–6pm
Entrance Fee: free
Transport: London Bridge

Southwest of London Bridge and hemmed in by the railway, Southwark Cathedral is a rich fund of local history. A memorial to Shakespeare in the south aisle, paid for by public subscription in 1912, shows the bard reclining in front of a frieze of 16th-century Bankside. Above it is a modern (1954) stained-glass window

Southwark Cathedral.

Historical characters at the Clink Prison Museum.

depicting characters from his plays. Shakespeare was a parishioner for several years. John Harvard, who gave his name to the American university, was baptised here, and is commemorated in the Harvard Chapel.

The cathedral holds free organ recitals every Monday (1pm) and classical concerts on Tuesday (3.15–4pm).

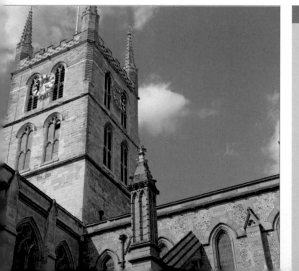

LONDON BRIDGE

The present London Bridge, dating from 1967–72, is the latest of many on this site. Until Westminster Bridge opened in 1750, the crossing here was the only bridge across the Thames in London. A wooden bridge had existed here since the Romans, but the first stone bridge, later lined with houses, was erected in 1176 and completed 33 years later. In 1823–31 a new bridge of five stone arches was built, but in 1972, having been sold to American businessman Robert P. McCulloch for US$2.46 million, it was dismantled and re-erected in Arizona. Some claimed that McCulloch bought London Bridge in error, thinking that it was the much grander Tower Bridge. He denied this.

BOROUGH

The area around London Bridge has undergone a major regeneration programme. Much of its Dickensian character lingers, adding greatly to its appeal. In addition to Borough Market, there are several quirky museums and many restaurants, cafés and specialist shops.

Borough Market ⑲

Address: Southwark Street, www.boroughmarket.org.uk
Tel: 020-7407 1002
Opening Hrs: lunch Mon–Tue 10am–5pm, full market Wed–Thu 10am–5pm, Fri 10am–6pm, Sat 8am–5pm
Transport: London Bridge

The highlight of the area is Borough Market, a wholesale food market dating from the 13th century. This is a popular retail market offering gourmet and organic products – it is busiest on Friday and Saturdays. Apart from basics such as fruit and vegetables, you will find stalls specialising in seafood, game, oils and vinegars, cakes, preserves, fresh pasta, juices, wines and beers. It's a great spot for lunch.

Southwark Street

A brief diversion down Southwark Street is the splendid Victorian Hop Exchange (now offices), with The Wheatsheaf in its cellar. A cross between bar and pub, it serves hearty pub grub, shows Sky Sports, has black-and-white photographs decorating its walls and is often lively.

Further along Southwark Street, the **Menier Chocolate Factory** ⑳ (51–3 Southwark Street; box office: 020-7378 1713; www.menierchocolatefactory.com) sits on the corner of O'Meara Street. Housed within this 1870s chocolate factory is a 150-seat theatre, plus bar and restaurant.

Borough High Street

Situated on Borough High Street, the main road south from London Bridge, is the 17th-century **George Inn** ㉑ (No. 77), the only remaining galleried coaching inn in London and mentioned in Dickens' *Little Dorrit*. Further down the street is the renovated **Church of St George the Martyr** ㉒ (www.stgeorge-themartyr.co.uk), also known as 'Little Dorrit's

EAT

There are lots of opportunities to sample the produce free at Borough Market. Many stalls also do takeaway food, from venison burgers to scallops that are pan-fried while you wait. For a posh sit-down meal, try Roast, on the first floor; breakfast (Mon–Fri until 11am, later on Saturday) is a great way to enjoy the upmarket dining experience at a fraction of the cost of lunch or dinner.

The George Inn.

1676

THE GEORGE

DRINK

Further east along the south bank from Tower Bridge is Rotherhithe, which has several good traditional pubs, including the Mayflower, where the Pilgrim Fathers moored their ship before sailing to Plymouth and America in 1620. It is close to the Brunel Museum Thames Tunnel (Railway Avenue; www.brunel-museum.org.uk; tel: 020-7231 3840; daily 10am–5pm) on the site of the Thames Tunnel: built by Isambard Kingdom Brunel it was the world's first under-river tunnel.

Church', because Dickens' heroine was baptised and married there. She is represented in stained glass in the east window. There are free classical recitals (usually piano) on Thursdays at 1pm.

London Bridge area

Back towards London Bridge, at 9a St Thomas Street, is the **Old Operating Theatre Museum & Herb Garret** (tel: 020-7188 2679; www.thegarret.org.uk; daily 10.30am–5pm), the only surviving 19th-century operating theatre in Britain. It offers insights into the fearsome medical techniques of the day. The Herb Garret displays herbs and equipment used in the preparation of medicines.

Next to London Bridge station is **The Shard** ㉔. The tallest building in Western Europe, at 1,106ft (310 metres) high, it is a mix of residential and office space, and includes a restaurant and 5-star hotel. You can take a lift to the 72nd floor for unobstructed views of the city and beyond (www.theviewfromtheshard.com; check website for opening times; advance booking recommended).

Down Tooley Street is **Hay's Galleria** ㉕, a setting for shops, craft stalls

and restaurants. In the centre is the 60ft (18-metre) kinetic sculpture, David Kemp's *The Navigators*.

HMS *Belfast* ㉖

Downstream from Hay's Galleria is HMS *Belfast*, the last of the warships to have seen action in World War II (tel: 020-7940 6300; www.iwm.org.uk/visits; daily Mar–Oct 10am–6pm, Nov–Feb 10am–5pm; last admission one hour before closing). You can explore the whole ship, from the bridge to the engine rooms; there's an interactive Operations Room, and a taste of battle in the Gun Turret Experience. The Upper Deck Bar, on the roof of the visitor entrance, has fabulous views of HMS *Belfast*, Tower Bridge and other impressive landmarks.

To its east, the oval-shaped building is **City Hall** ㉗, seat of the Greater London Authority, the body that governs London. In front is The Scoop, a sunken amphitheatre staging free theatre, music and films in summer.

Bermondsey Street

A 10-minute detour southeast leads to hip Bermondsey Street, lined with stylish restaurants, bars, boutiques and galleries. At No. 83, you can't miss the pink-and-orange **Fashion and Textile Museum** ㉘ (tel: 020-7407 8664; www.ftmlondon.org; Tue–Sat 11am–6pm, Thu 11am–8pm, Sun 11am–5pm, last admission 45 minutes before closing), the creation of British designer Zandra Rhodes. It celebrates fashion via exhibitions and its own academy.

At the other end of the street, on Friday morning only, is **Bermondsey Square Antiques Market** ㉙. Although it doesn't have the same attractive surroundings as Portobello Road market, it does have a wide selection of antiques, with everything from Victorian silver jewellery to religious icons. Arrive early if you are after a bargain as the market opens at 6am – there are some good cafés around the market for breakfast.

City Hall.

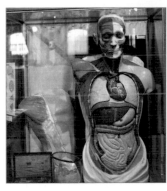

The Old Operating Theatre Museum.

Tower Bridge ③⓪

Dating from 1894 the Victorian Gothic Tower Bridge is one of London's most iconic structures. Despite its mock-medieval cladding, it contains 11,000 tons of steel, and sophisticated engineering raises its middle portion to allow tall ships through. When the capital was a flourishing port, it opened several times a day. In 1954 a bus driver was awarded a medal for putting his foot on the accelerator when, to his horror, he saw the bridge yawn open before him. The bus leapt over a 3ft (1-metre) gap. These days the bridge opens around 500 times a year, with its bascules taking 90 seconds to lift.

The structure contains **Tower Bridge Experience** (tel: 020-7403 3761; www.towerbridge.org.uk; Apr–Sept 10am–6pm, Oct–Mar 9.30am–5.30pm), an exhibition detailing the history of the bridge and explaining how the mechanism works. The view from Tower Bridge's high walkways is magnificent – and even better since 2015, when the Glass Walkway gave visitors a unique view of London, 42 metres (138ft) above the River Thames. For vertigo sufferers – don't look down!

Around Butlers Wharf

The old warehouses east of Tower Bridge contain a gourmand's delight. The gourmet in question is Habitat founder Sir Terence Conran, who opened several restaurants, such as Le Pont de la Tour in the biscuit-coloured **Butlers Wharf**.

Tower Bridge.

TATE MODERN

Once it generated electricity; now it is a powerhouse of modern and contemporary art.

Exploring the exhibits.

Tate Modern has caught the public's imagination in a quite unprecedented way, both for its displays and its building, a magnificent presence on the South Bank. The redundant Bankside Power Station, a massive horizontal block with a huge central tower, has been transformed into a gallery showcasing the Tate's collection of modern and contemporary art. Machinery from within the power station was removed to create an entrance the height of the building; three gallery floors, shops and cafés, a restaurant and an auditorium were piled into a compact bank on one side. From the windows are fabulous views of St Paul's Cathedral across the river. On the other side is the vast Turbine Hall, a stunning exhibition space. A new 11-storey gallery to the south of the Tate Modern opened in 2016, with 60 percent more gallery space and a roof terrace; a bridge across the Turbine Hall provides the link between the two galleries.

The Essentials

Address: Bankside; www.tate.org.uk
Tel: 020-7887 8888
Opening Hrs: Sun–Thu 10am–6pm, Fri–Sat 10am–10pm
Entrance Fee: free except for special exhibitions
Transport: Southwark or London Bridge

Whaam! by Roy Lichtenstein (1923–97), part of the permanent collection. Lichtenstein's interest in Americana dated from the early 1950s, but his involvement in pop art received a crucial boost from one of his young sons, who showed him a Mickey Mouse comic book and said: "I bet you can't paint as good as that."

Kandinsky's Swinging (1925). Kandinsky began his artistic career as a figurative landscape painter in Russia, but moved towards abstraction through the influence of German Expressionism. He used colour for emotional effect. Also in Tate Modern's permanent collection is Kandinsky's Cossacks (1910–11).

Chinese artist Ai Weiwei's Sunflower Seeds, one of the many installations that have graced the Turbine Hall. This installation was made up of around 100 million individually crafted ceramic 'seeds' that covered 1000 sq m (10,764 sq ft).

THE COLLECTION

An exhibit from the permanent collection.

In order to make the permanent collection more accessible and popular with the general public, the works are ordered by theme. Note that the displays change from time to time, so the examples picked out here may not all be on show when you visit.

The permanent collection is hung in four suites, over three floors. On level 2 is Poetry and Dream, where the focus is on Surrealist artists and their associates. A large central room (Room 2) includes works by Joan Miró, Picasso, Giacometti, Max Ernst, Salvador Dalí, Francis Bacon, Joseph Beuys and Giorgio de Chirico. Transformed Visions is on level 3, exploring abstract art and its influences. This is where you'll find Mark Rothko's Seagram Murals, paintings which were originally commissioned for the Four Seasons Restaurant in Manhattan but which Rothko eventually decided to give to the Tate.

On level 4 are Energy and Process and Structure and Clarity, with the former showcasing artists, such as the Italian Arte Povera movement of the 1960s and 70s, who are interested in transformation and natural forces. Structure and Clarity explores the development of abstract art since the early 20th century, including Cubism, Futurism and Vorticism, with work by Georges Braque, Paul Cézanne, Fernand Léger, Roy Lichtenstein, Auguste Rodin, Henri Matisse and Bridget Riley.

Tate Modern posters.

THE IMPERIAL WAR MUSEUM

It vividly chronicles a century of conflict around the world.

The building that now houses the Imperial War Museum opened in 1815 as Bethlem Royal Hospital for the insane, popularly known as Bedlam. After the hospital moved out of London in the 1930s, the central block of the building was turned over to the Great War collection of the Imperial War Museum, previously housed in South Kensington. The former psychiatric hospital was an inspired choice for a museum chronicling the horrors of modern warfare.

After World War II the museum began to gather material from this and later conflicts, and three smaller sites, including the warship HMS *Belfast* (see page 180), were acquired.

In recent years, the museum has expanded its remit from the purely military to include a rolling programme of exhibitions covering many aspects of modern history, from World War I to today. Some are only loosely connected with conflict – from code breaking and refugees to fashion and sport.

The Essentials

Address: Lambeth Road; www.iwm.org.uk
Tel: 020-7416 5000
Opening Hrs: daily 10am–6pm
Entrance Fee: free except for special exhibitions
Transport: Elephant & Castle or Lambeth North

The First World War Galleries.

Temporary exhibitions, such as Fashion on the Ration, take a wider look at issues that affect people during times of conflict.

Throughout the museum there are interactive displays and activities designed to engage children.

The museum's dramatic atrium houses a Spitfire used in the Battle of Britain, a V1 'doodlebug' flying bomb and a Harrier fighter jet that saw service in Afghanistan.

Displays in the First World War Galleries explore the lives of those who experienced it both at home and on the battlefield.

MUSEUM LAYOUT

The World War I exhibition on the ground floor

Following a major £40-million refurbishment, the Imperial War Museum reopened in 2014. As you enter the main hall, your direction will depend on where your interest lies, with both permanent galleries and temporary exhibitions.

The dramatic atrium houses permanent exhibits in the Witnesses to War collection, with nine objects including a Harrier jet and Spitfire plane suspended from above.

The First World War Galleries depict the war through those on the front line or at home. Here artefacts, art, photography, and film and sound recordings weave an atmosphere as close as possible to the mood of the time, while interactive screens give access to further information.

The Holocaust Exhibition is a powerful display that traces the Nazi persecution of Europe's Jews from 1933 to 1945, and explains how Hitler's rise to power affected the suffering of so many around the world.

Some parts of the museum are harrowing and not recommended for young children. The Holocaust Exhibition, built around the testimonies of survivors and with poignant exhibits, is not recommended for children under 14.

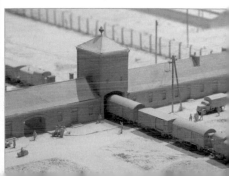

KNIGHTSBRIDGE, KENSINGTON AND NOTTING HILL

Knightsbridge and Kensington have long been the home of the British upper classes, and the areas' cultural attractions reflect their dilettantish interests. Neighbouring Notting Hill Gate is more diverse, younger and edgier.

These three areas of London encompass many of its best features: Knightsbridge has grand architecture, designer shops and two of London's top department stores; Kensington is home to three world-class museums and Queen Victoria's monuments to her husband Prince Albert; Notting Hill Gate, the stamping ground of the young, hip and famous, has Portobello Road, one of London's funkiest street markets.

In the heart of all this is a huge area of parkland, where you can skate, jog, hire a boat or just stroll around and forget you're in the city. Throughout the area are pretty cobbled mews and squares lined with elegant town houses that make venturing off the main streets rewarding.

This chapter begins at Hyde Park Corner, proceeds via Knightsbridge to Kensington and Notting Hill Gate, and then dips into Kensington Gardens and Hyde Park.

HYDE PARK CORNER

At the junction of Piccadilly, Park Lane and Knightsbridge, **Hyde Park Corner** is a major hub of traffic now, but it used to stand on the outskirts of London.

Apsley House ❶

Address: 149 Piccadilly, Hyde Park Corner, www.english-heritage.org.uk
Tel: 020-7499 5676
Opening Hrs: Apr–Oct Wed–Sun 11am–5pm, Nov–late Mar Sat–Sun 10am–4pm
Transport: Hyde Park Corner

The mansion on the northern side of Hyde Park Corner is known colloquially as No. 1, London, as it was the first house you came to after passing through the tollgates at the top of Knightsbridge. Built in

Main Attractions

Harrods
Victoria and Albert Museum
Natural History Museum
Science Museum
Royal Albert Hall
Albert Memorial
Kensington Square
Notting Hill
Portobello Road Market
Kensington Palace

Map

Page 188

Outdoor drinks on Beauchamp Place.

1770 by Robert Adam, and owned by Arthur Wellesley, the first Duke of Wellington, in 1816, just after he had defeated Napoleon at Waterloo, it is still lived in by the Wellesley family. Inside are collections of furniture, silver and porcelain, and paintings by Velázquez, Rubens, Van Dyck and Goya. Among its sculptures is a huge nude of Napoleon by Canova.

Wellington Arch ❷ (tel: 020-7930 2726; Apr–Oct Wed–Sun 10am–5pm, Nov–early Dec 10am–4pm; may close for functions so ring ahead), in the middle of Hyde Park Corner, was designed in 1828 as part of a grand approach to London. The huge bronze statue of a charioteer and four horses (the *Quadriga*) depicts the angel of peace descending on the chariot of war.

KNIGHTSBRIDGE

Running west of Hyde Park Corner is Knightsbridge, where you'll find two of London's most famous stores: Harrods and Harvey Nichols.

Harvey Nichols ❸, well known for its innovative window displays, opened on the corner of Knightsbridge and Sloane Street in the 1880s; with eight floors of fashion, beauty and home collections, it caters to a discerning – and affluent – clientele. The Fifth Floor is a very smart place to eat, and has a roof terrace.

Harrods ❹

Address: 87–135 Brompton Road, www.harrods.com
Tel: 020-7730 1234
Opening Hrs: Mon–Sat 10am–9pm, Sun 11.30am–6pm
Transport: Knightsbridge

Nearby in Brompton Road, **Harrods** is hard to miss, especially at night when it is brightly illuminated. The food hall is ornately decorated and sells a wide range of gourmet items; it's worth looking, even if you only come out with a tin

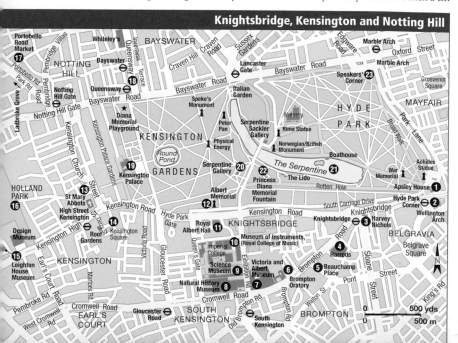

Knightsbridge, Kensington and Notting Hill

Harrods at night.

of speciality tea. The store's famous January sales see the British lose their dignity in the scramble to save hundreds of pounds.

The store was started by Henry Charles Harrod when his grocery business opened in 1849, although the present building was opened in 1905. The Egyptian Al-Fayed brothers bought the store and other House of Fraser outlets for £615 million in 1983, and the flamboyant Mohamed Al-Fayed (whose son Dodi died with Princess Diana in the 1997 Paris car crash) owned the store until 2010, when he sold it to Qatar Holdings.

Beauchamp Place ❺ (pronounced *Beecham*), a stylish street west of Harrods lined with designer stores and expensive restaurants, is the stamping ground of the well-heeled, including sundry royals.

Beyond Harrods, at the point where Brompton Road branches left, is the Roman Catholic **Brompton Oratory** ❻ (www.brompton oratory.com; daily 7am–6pm), a flamboyant Italian baroque building designed by a 29-year-old architect, Herbert Gribble. Opened in 1884, its huge dome, extravagant decor and gilded mosaics are seldom seen in British churches. There are regular music recitals.

You can take a lift inside Wellington Arch up to the galleried balconies, from where there are good views, including into the gardens of Buckingham Palace.

Exhibition Road is pedestrianised.

A cabmen's shelter in front of the V&A Museum, one of 13 still dotted around London. Now Grade II-listed, they provide shelter and refreshment for cab drivers.

SOUTH KENSINGTON

South Kensington exudes affluence; Christie's has an auction house here, in Old Brompton Road, and there are plenty of designer shops and upmarket restaurants.

It's also very cosmopolitan: the Lycée Français is at 35 Cromwell Road, teaching the children of the many French people who live in the area, and the German Goethe Institute is in Princes Gate.

Three Victorian museums

At the heart of South Kensington are three world-class museums: The Victoria and Albert Museum, the Natural History Museum and the Science Museum, which owe their existence to the spirit and enterprise of the Victorian age. In 1851, the Great Exhibition, held in Hyde Park, was an astonishing success. For the first time elements of the far-flung Victorian Empire were brought under the curious gaze of the public. The idea for the exhibition had come from Henry Cole (1808–82), chairman of the Society of Arts, and it had been taken up enthusiastically by Prince Albert.

More than 6 million visitors came to the park to see the Crystal Palace, and after it moved to Sydenham, south London, the following year, the profits were used to purchase 87 acres (35 hectares) of land in adjoining South Kensington to build a more permanent home for the arts and sciences.

Greatest of them all is undoubtedly the **Victoria and Albert Museum** ❼, popularly known as the V&A, which Henry Cole began assembling the year after the Great Exhibition, though Queen Victoria did not lay the foundation stone of the current building until 1899, 38 years after Albert died. It was the first museum to be gas-lit, allowing working people to visit in the evening after finishing their jobs. For a detailed guide to its collections, see page 200.

On the other side of Exhibition Road is the neo-Gothic pile of the **Natural History Museum** ❽, built between 1873 and 1880. With its collection of 75 million plants, animals, fossils, rocks and minerals and, of course, its dinosaurs, it is justly celebrated and a big hit with children. For details, see page 202.

Facade of the Natural History Museum.

Wellcome Wing focuses on contemporary science and technology. See page 198 for more details.

On the corner of Queen's Gate Terrace, opposite the Natural History Museum, is **Baden-Powell House**, with a statue of the Boy Scouts' founder standing on watch outside. It is now a budget hostel, but there is a small exhibition area dedicated to Lord Baden-Powell (1857–1941).

Music and geography

Further up Exhibition Road, on Prince Consort Road, is the **Royal College of Music**, containing the **Museum of Music 🔟** (tel: 020-7591 4842; www.rcm.ac.uk; Tue–Fri 11.30am–4.30pm in term time and summer holidays only; free)   due to reopen after renovation in 2019 – and regular free afternoon recitals.

The **Science Museum 9**, round the corner in Exhibition Road, traces the history of inventions from the first steam train – Stephenson's Rocket – to the battered command module from the Apollo 10 space mission, and is a particular favourite of children. The

On the corner of Exhibition Road and Kensington Gore is the **Royal Geographical Society** (tel: 020-7591 3000; www.rgs.org; Mon–Fri 10am–5pm). Exhibitions in the Pavilion, and the Foyle Reading Room are open to the public. There are also ticketed lecture events.

Dinosaur in the Natural History Museum.

Royal Albert Hall ⓫

Address: Kensington Gore, www.royalalberthall.com
Tel: 020-7838 3105 (tours); 020-7589 8212 (tickets)
Transport: South Kensington

The **Royal Albert Hall**, an ornate building with a capacity of 5,500, was opened in 1871 in honour of Prince Albert. The frieze around the outside illustrates 'The Triumph of Arts and Sciences'. Events here range from boxing bouts to rock concerts, but the hall is best known for the Proms, a series of BBC-sponsored classical concerts running for eight weeks in the summer. Named after the promenading audience, they provide a rich diet of affordable music. Throughout the year there's a rich programme of classical concerts.

The Royal Albert Hall.

Queen Victoria's most expressive tribute to her **husband is the Albert Memorial ⓬** in Kensington Gardens, opposite the Albert Hall. Designed by Sir George Gilbert Scott, it depicts the prince as a god or philosopher, clutching in his right hand the catalogue of the Great Exhibition which he masterminded. Marking the corners of the monument are symbols for the spread of the British Empire: a camel for Africa, a bull bison for America, an elephant for Asia and a cow for Europe (Australia, then the Empire's dumping ground for convicts, failed to merit a mention). It looks stunning when lit up at night.

In a 1960s building next door to the Albert Hall is the **Royal College of Art**, where annual graduation exhibitions allow the public to buy the works of future greats. David Hockney and Henry Moore studied here.

KENSINGTON HIGH STREET

Kensington Gore runs into Kensington High Street, a useful shopping area – more compact and stylish than Oxford Street but with most of the big-name stores and fewer people. **Kensington Church Street,**

Statue of Lord Holland in Holland Park.

and a fine example of Victorian Gothic Revival. Walk through the cloisters to reach St Mary Abbots Gardens, a quiet spot away from the crowds. To the right, Kensington Church Walk is lined with exclusive boutiques. At the top, Holland Street, running off Kensington Church Street, has designer shops and a pretty pub, the Elephant and Castle.

Back on Kensington High Street, walk down Derry Street to the entrance to the **Roof Gardens** (tel: 020-7937 7994; www.roofgardensclub. com; check for opening hours), a members' club and restaurant (Babylon), six storeys above street level. With 1.5 acres (0.6 hectares) of ornamental gardens and views over west London, this is one of the most original places to eat in the city. The gardens are themed with Spanish and English woodland areas and have resident flamingos.

Further down Derry Street is **Kensington Square ⓮**, one of the oldest in London, and an elegant mix of architectural styles dating from the late 17th century. The Pre-Raphaelite painter Edward Burne-Jones lived at No. 41, and the philosopher

branching off to the right towards Notting Hill Gate, is the place for antiques. On the corner behind the flower stall stands **St Mary Abbots Church ⓭**, designed by Victorian architect Sir George Gilbert Scott,

The Albert Memorial has been restored to its former gilded – some say gaudy – glory.

John Stuart Mill, another eminent Victorian, at No. 18.

West down Kensington High Street is the former Commonwealth Institute, which from late 2016 was home to the **Design Museum**. At the end of the street is **Leighton House Museum** (12 Holland Park Road; tel: 020-7602 3316; www.rbkc.gov. uk; Wed–Mon 10am–5.30pm; free guided tour Wed 3pm). The red-brick exterior conceals an extraordinary interior. The home of the Victorian artist Lord Leighton (1830–96), president of the Royal Academy, it is a mix of lavish Orientalism and conventional Victorian comforts. It contains his highly romanticised works, as well as many by fellow Pre-Raphaelites, but the centrepiece of the house is the grand Arab Hall, displaying Leighton's collection of Islamic tiles.

Portobello Market stallholder.

Edward Burne-Jones's house in Kensington Square.

South of here is cosmopolitan **Earl's Court**, named after the earls of Oxford who owned the land in the 12th century. It is famous for its massive exhibition centre, built in 1937, which hosted the volleyball events in the 2012 Olympics.

To the west is **Olympia**, another exhibition centre. To the north is **Holland Park** , the grounds of the Jacobean Holland House, mostly destroyed in World War II. Peacocks preen among the formal gardens, and the ruins provide an appealing set for open-air concerts. For refreshments, try the restaurant in the Orangery, or the more informal café nearby.

NOTTING HILL

The northeastern exit of Holland Park leads to Holland Park Avenue, at the top of which is Notting Hill Gate, a hip area of London.

Portobello Road Market

Address: Portobello Road, www.portobelloroad.co.uk
Opening Hrs: Mon–Wed, Fri–Sat 8am–6pm, Thu 8am–1pm; antiques

market Sat 8am–6pm

Transport: Ladbroke Grove, Notting Hill Gate

Although it's open every day, Notting Hill's Portobello Road is busiest on Saturdays when it's lined with antiques stalls. The antiques are concentrated in the more genteel southern end of the street, while further north, under the Westway flyover, a flea market mixes junk, cutting-edge fashion and arts and crafts (Fri–Sun). Between these two, the traditional fruit, veg and flower stalls blend with traders selling global foodstuffs.

As a backdrop to the stalls, the refurbished Electric Cinema is London's oldest surviving cinema (1905); it also houses a retro-style American diner.

Off Portobello Road, on Blenheim Crescent, is the former **Travel Bookshop** (now a Book Warehouse), the setting for the 1999 romantic comedy *Notting Hill*, in which Hugh Grant improbably wooed Julia Roberts. What the film didn't convey is that Notting Hill is a melting pot in which many races and just about every social class rub shoulders.

Ladbroke Grove

Notting Hill's main north–south artery, **Ladbroke Grove**, is the parade route for the **Notting Hill Carnival**, a three-day Caribbean festival which takes over the area on the last weekend of August. West of Notting Hill (Shepherd's Bush or White City tube stations) is **Westfield**, a huge urban shopping centre where high street names rub shoulders with Armani, Louis Vuitton and Ted Baker. There is a larger branch by the Olympic Stadium in Stratford.

Queensway and Kensington Gardens

Westbourne Grove heads eastwards to **Queensway** ⑱, home to Whiteleys Shopping Centre, which has cafés, restaurants and a cinema. At the top of Queensway, past the ice rink, is Kensington Gardens.

London's great green lung is **Hyde Park** and **Kensington Gardens**, which cover 1 sq mile (2.5 sq km) – the same area as the City of London. Although they are a single open space, they are two distinct parks, divided by West Carriage Drive.

Dating from 1912, Peter Pan's statue in Kensington Gardens was erected secretly one night so it might seem as if it had appeared by magic.

Vintage shops line Portobello Road.

In the northwestern corner of Kensington Gardens is the popular Diana Memorial Playground, perhaps a more fitting tribute to the princess than the Princess Diana Memorial Fountain.

Hyde Park.

Kensington Palace ⑲

Address: Kensington Gardens, www.hrp.org.uk
Tel: 020-3166 6000
Opening Hrs: Nov–Feb daily 10am–5pm. Mar–Oct 10am–6pm; last admission one hour before closing
Transport: Notting Hill Gate, Queensway

On the west side of Kensington Gardens, overlooking the Round Pond, is **Kensington Palace**, the former home of Diana, Princess of Wales.

The palace was given its present appearance by Sir Christopher Wren and Nicholas Hawksmoor, and was the centre of the Court after William III bought the mansion in 1689. Several monarchs were born here, the last of them Victoria in 1819, who 18 years later was called from her bed to be told she had become Queen.

The state apartments have undergone major redevelopment. There is now a display focussing on Princess Diana's clothes and style, while another exhibition explores Queen Victoria's story; visitors can see the room in which she was born, and the spot where she met Prince Albert.

Around the palace grounds are an attractive sunken garden and an Orangery, designed by Nicholas Hawksmoor in 1704 and modified by Sir John Vanbrugh. It has wood carvings by Grinling Gibbons and is now a café.

A path east of the gilded main gates of Kensington Palace leads to **Kensington Gardens**. The lake on the eastern side (called The Long Water here, and the Serpentine in Hyde Park) has, at its northern edge, the delightful **Italian Garden**, commissioned by Prince Albert. There are fountains and a statue of Edward Jenner, who developed the vaccination against smallpox. The loggia in Italian Renaissance style was originally the fountains' pumphouse.

Along the path by the water is a statue, by George Frampton, of J.M. Barrie's **Peter Pan** – the full title of this classic children's story is *Peter Pan in Kensington Gardens*.

Addressing the crowds at Speakers' Corner.

The Serpentine Gallery ⑳ (tel: 020-7402 6075; www.serpentinegallery. org; daily 10am–6pm; free) by the road bridge is a dynamic exhibition space for contemporary art. Each summer, the Serpentine Gallery in the museum's grounds is specially designed by a new architect each year, and hosts events. In 2013 the dynamic Serpentine Sackler Gallery opened nearby, designed by prize-winning architect Zaha Hadid. Formerly this was the Magazine, a Grade II listed building. The modern extension, used as a café/restaurant and social space, presents the best in emerging talent across all art forms.

HYDE PARK

Across the road is Hyde Park which, as the *Domesday Book* of 1086 records, was inhabited by wild bulls and boars. First owned by the monks of Westminster Abbey, it was turned into a royal hunting ground by Henry VIII and then opened to the public in the 17th century. The **Serpentine ㉑**

was created in the 1730s as a royal boating lake, and boats can still be hired from the north bank. **Rotten Row**, William III's Route du Roi, running along the southern edge, is where the Household Cavalry, based in the barracks on Knightsbridge, exercise their horses.

The **Princess Diana Memorial Fountain ㉒**, a ring of flowing water surrounding a landscaped area, was designed by Seattle-based landscape architect Kathryn Gustafson.

At the northeast corner, near Marble Arch, is **Speakers' Corner ㉓**, where anyone can pull up a soap box and sound off, especially on Sunday afternoons. This tradition goes back to when the Tyburn gallows stood here (1388–1783; see page 114) and condemned felons were allowed to make a final unexpurgated speech to the crowds before being hanged. Close by, in Park Lane, is the monument Animals in War, a reminder of the role played by millions of animals in warfare.

Italian Garden, Kensington Palace.

THE SCIENCE MUSEUM

This museum is an astounding tribute to the ingenuity of human beings over the centuries.

With more than 10,000 exhibits, plus additional attractions such as an IMAX theatre and a huge new interactive gallery based on maths and science, opened in 2016, this museum could take days to explore. It's best to assign priorities before you start.

An important point to note is the distinction between the main wing, dating to 1928 and containing the classic steam engines and planes, and The Wellcome Wing, opened in 2000, concentrating on information technology. You can walk between the two wings at five of the museum's seven levels, but the ambience of the wings is quite different and it is more satisfying to explore one wing at a time.

The Essentials

Address: Exhibition Road, SW7;
www.sciencemuseum.org.uk
Tel: 020-7942 4000
Opening Hrs: daily 10am–6pm, last admission 45 minutes before closing
Entrance Fee: free except special exhibitions, IMAX cinema and simulators
Transport: South Kensington

The Making the Modern World gallery brings together many of the museum's most exciting exhibits. "Modern" is defined as post-1750 and the stars include the world's oldest surviving steam locomotive, the coal-hauling Puffing Billy (circa 1815), a Ford Model T (1916), a Lockheed Electra airliner hanging in silvery splendour from the ceiling (1935), a copy of Crick and Watson's DNA double helix model (1953) and the Apollo 10 command module (left, 1969).

The first gallery you enter is the Energy Hall, dominated by a 1903 mill engine.

Vintage car.

OTHER HIGHLIGHTS

Wellcome Wing.

The Wellcome Wing looks to the future rather than the past. On the ground floor, Antenna is a series of changing exhibits based around current science news, while an IMAX film theatre conjures up dinosaurs or outer space. The theme of the first floor is 'Who am I?', asking such questions as 'How does your brain make you so special?' and 'Do we all come from Africa?'. In Future, on the third floor, is a series of large digital board games on which contestants are invited to vote on health, communications and lifestyle topics – for example, 'Should men be allowed to give birth?'.

The Flight Gallery (third floor) is a favourite with all ages; exhibits range from a seaplane to a Spitfire, from hot-air balloons to helicopters. The 1919 Vickers Vimy in which Alcock and Brown made the first non-stop transatlantic flight is here, as is Amy Johnson's *Gipsy Moth Jason*. There's also a replica of the Wright Flyer in which Wilbur and Orville Wright pioneered powered flight in 1903.

The Launchpad (third floor) for older kids is packed with experiments they can try out; 'explainers' help them understand what's going on. There are over 50 interactive exhibits from the world of physics, such as a thermal imaging camera.

The Secret Life of the Home (basement) displays domestic appliances and gadgets, with buttons to press and levers to pull, two of which show the internal workings of a flushing lavatory and a CD player.

The ever-popular Exploring Space gallery has been revamped to include a range of new exhibits, including the huge Spacelab 2 x-ray telescope – the actual instrument that was flown on the Space Shuttle – and full-size models of the Huygens Titan probe and Beagle 2 Mars Lander. The replica of the Apollo 11 lunar excursion module has been reconfigured to a new level of accuracy.

The Rocket, George Stephenson's 1829 passenger locomotive, is on display in the Making of the Modern World gallery.

VICTORIA AND ALBERT MUSEUM

The world's largest collection of decorative and applied arts covers everything from massive sculptures to knitting.

With 5 million objects and almost 8 miles (13km) of galleries, the Victoria and Albert Museum (founded in 1852) is colossal. Its exhibits range from exquisite Persian miniatures to a whole room designed by Frank Lloyd Wright. One minute one can be admiring Raphael's cartoons for the tapestries in the Sistine Chapel, and the next examining E.H. Shepard's illustrations for *Winnie-the-Pooh*. In 2013 its exhibition *David Bowie is* was the first international retrospective of the great musician, and drew record numbers.

The Islamic Galleries have been recently redesigned with the superb Ardabil carpet, the oldest carpet in the world, as a centrepiece. The Ceramics galleries include porcelain animals crafted for Augustus the Strong, while highlights from the Gilbert collection (gold and silver objects, and enamel portrait miniatures), are in rooms 70–73.

The Essentials

Address: Cromwell Road, SW7; www.vam.ac.uk
Tel: 020-7942 2000
Opening Hrs: daily 10am–5.45pm, Fri some galleries until 10pm
Entrance Fee: free except some exhibitions
Transport: South Kensington

The Iranian Ardabil carpet (1539–40) in the Jameel Gallery of Islamic arts.

The British Galleries document British taste, exploring "what was hot and what was new from the time of Henry VIII and the Tudors to William Morris". The exhibits include the Great Bed of Ware, a 16th-century four poster.

A British Empire builder is savaged in Tippoo's Tiger (Mysore, 1793), in the South Asia Gallery.

The Paul and Jill Ruddock Gallery features Renaissance-era artworks.

An immense glass sculpture by the American glass artist Dale Chihuly hangs in the foyer of the Cromwell Road entrance.

OTHER HIGHLIGHTS

Museum exterior detail.

The Sculpture Courts. British and neoclassical works from the late 18th and early 19th centuries.
Plaster Casts. Fine copies, from Trajan's Column to Michelangelo's David.
Raphael Cartoons (1515–6). Templates for a series of tapestries in the Sistine Chapel.
Medieval and Renaissance. Renaissance pieces include Andrea Briosco's 16th-century Shouting Horseman.
The Fashion Galleries. Fashions through the ages from the 18th century to the present day.
The Ceramic Staircase. Completed in 1869, it symbolises the relationship between art and science.
The Hereford Screen. An intricate choir screen (1862) studded with semi-precious stones.
Henry Cole Wing. Prints, drawings, paintings and photographs ranging from John Constable's paintings to Beatrix Potter's watercolours. Don't miss the Frank Lloyd Wright Gallery.
Refreshment Rooms. Three fabulously ornate café interiors from the 19th century, interlinked and opening onto the courtyard garden.
The Museum Shop. Quite simply irresistible.

Platform shoes in stamped leather by Vivienne Westwood (1993). As well as a fascinating permanent collection, the Fashion Galleries also display temporary exhibitions.

THE NATURAL HISTORY MUSEUM

This colossal collection has 75 million plants, animals, fossils, rocks and minerals – and it's growing by 50,000 new specimens a year.

In spite of the museum's vast size, the layout is easy to master due to colour-coded zones: the Red Zone (entrance on Exhibition Road), which explores the forces that shape our planet; the Green Zone, which looks at Earth's ecology; the Blue Zone, which investigates earth's biodiversity; and the Orange Zone covering the wildlife garden and the Darwin Centre.

One of the museum's delights is the way it presents high-tech exhibits alongside lovely Victorian-style galleries filled with meticulously labelled cabinets. Many of the latter are found in quiet byways of the museum, but one vintage member of the collection is the wood and plaster model of a blue whale, which has been the centrepiece of the Mammals section since being built in 1938.

The Essentials

Address: Cromwell Road, SW7; www.nhm.ac.uk
Tel: 020-7942 5000
Opening Hrs: daily 10am–5.50pm, last admission 5.15pm
Entrance Fee: free except for some special exhibitions
Transport: South Kensington

Dinosaur skeleton.

The Central Hall of the museum. The extravagant Gothic Romanesque building, by architect Alfred Waterhouse, was the first in Britain to be faced entirely in terracotta. Its soaring arches and rich ornamental detail bring to mind a cathedral, an effect intended by Sir Richard Owen, the superintendent of the collection. Owen wanted the building to be a temple of nature.

The skeleton and dramatic full-size model of a blue whale is a big attraction. Many families also make a bee-line for the Dinosaurs section (Life Galleries), the highlight of which is a full-scale animatronic T-Rex that roars and twists convincingly, impressing most children.

OTHER HIGHLIGHTS

The Human Biology section.

Investigate (basement). Here children can touch, weigh, measure and examine under a microscope a range of specimens. A team of explainers is on hand to help.

Human Biology. This section is packed with interactive exhibits: you can test your memory and senses or be tricked by optical illusions.

Mammals. As well as displaying an astonishing array of taxidermy, these galleries contain sobering statistics on the rapid rate at which species are becoming extinct.

Creepy Crawlies. Wander through a house and learn about the many uninvited housemates in an average home. Sit in a life-size model of a termite mound or watch a colony of leaf-cutter ants.

Earth's Treasury. This conveys the planet's beauty, displaying rocks, gems and minerals glittering in the gallery's semi-darkness.

The Jerwood Gallery. This houses a superb collection of watercolours, oils, prints and drawings, some of which are the original illustrations to books by 19th-century explorers.

The Darwin Centre. This cocoon-shaped centre for scientific study and repository for 20 million specimens gives visitors the opportunity to see scientists in action.

The Wildlife Garden *(enter via the Darwin Centre).* This lush spot is a refreshing way to end a visit (Apr–Oct 10am–5pm; winter visits by appointment only).

A cross-section of a giant redwood.

An escalator transports visitors into a vast globe, the entrance to the Earth Galleries, where Restless Surface covers earthquakes and volcanoes. The tremors of an earthquake are simulated in a mock-up of a Japanese mini-market.

Well-heeled cyclist crossing King's Road.

CHELSEA

Backing on to a secluded stretch of the Thames, Chelsea has a village feel, but also a strong bohemian side. Running through it is the King's Road, the centre of Swinging London in the 1960s and, later, of punk.

Sandwiched between Kensington and the Thames, Chelsea's tranquil enclaves still hint at the riverside hamlet it was until the late 18th century. Despite a modest character, by the 16th century Chelsea had become known as a 'Village of Palaces', with strong royal links – King Henry VIII among them – and was destined to be the site of Wren's Royal Hospital in 1682.

A reputation for art took root with the Chelsea Porcelain Works and the illustrations generated by the Chelsea Physic Garden's botanical publications. By the 19th century, a bohemian set had moved in wholesale, including the painters Rossetti, Whistler and Sargent and writers such as George Eliot (and later, T.S. Eliot).

BELGRAVIA TO SLOANE SQUARE

When the squares and terraces of **Belgravia** were built around 1824, these streets west of Hyde Park Corner were intended to rival Mayfair. From Knightsbridge, the best entrance to Belgravia is via **Wilton Place**. The stucco terraces were developed by architect Thomas Cubitt, who gave his name to the modern construction company known for

its motorway bridges. Like much of Mayfair, **Belgrave Square** is largely occupied by embassies and various societies and associations. The square usually has a heavy police presence.

Eaton Square, to the south, is more residential. However, many of its supposed residents live in other parts of the world and the houses are dark and obviously under-used. Chopin gave his first London recital here at No. 88.

In 1895 the playwright Oscar Wilde was arrested in the Cadogan

Main Attractions
Sloane Square
King's Road
Duke of York Square
Royal Hospital
National Army Museum
Chelsea Physic Garden
Cheyne Walk
Chelsea Old Church

Map
Page 206

Chelsea Physic Garden.

The Royal Court Theatre.

Hotel in Sloane Street, tried and sent to prison for his homosexual conduct. Sloane Street leads from Knightsbridge to **Sloane Square** ❶, where **Chelsea** proper begins. On the east side of the square is the **Royal Court Theatre**, where John Osborne's mould-breaking anti-establishment play *Look Back in Anger* was first staged in 1956. The company still has a robust reputation for shaping the classics of the future.

Sloane Square was named after the physician Sir Hans Sloane (1660–1753), whose personal collection formed the basis of what is now the

British Museum. He laid out much of this area and his name crops up often on street plans. He also unwittingly gave his name to a typical young upper-class urbanite living in Chelsea in the 1980s: the Sloane Ranger, a lady in flat shoes, pearls, gathered skirt and a quilted jacket.

ALONG THE KING'S ROAD

Until 1829 the **King's Road** ❷, leading west from Sloane Square, was a private royal road leading from Hampton Court to the court of King James. It rose to fame during the 1960s, and was later linked

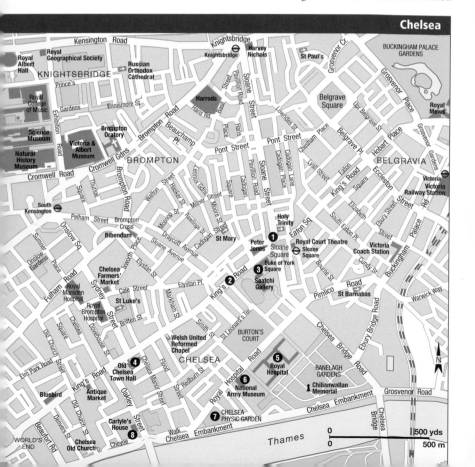

Dressed for summer on King's Road.

to punk fashions, after Vivienne Westwood and Malcolm McLaren opened their designer shop, Sex, at No. 430 in 1972. Westwood still sells her designs from these premises, renamed World's End, which is what this part of Chelsea is called. Sloane Square's GTC (General Trading Company), and Peter Jones department store are also long-established shops.

Duke of York Square ❸

Lately, the biggest innovation on the King's Road's retail front has been the redevelopment of the Duke of York's Headquarters, formerly a military campus. The main building with its Tuscan portico (1801), designed as a school for the orphans of soldiers, houses the **Saatchi Gallery** (www.saatchi-gallery.co.uk), which contains the work of contemporary British artists assembled by former advertising mogul Charles Saatchi. The gallery holds themed temporary exhibitions, selected works by the gallery's huge range of international artists.

Old Chelsea Town Hall ❹

Prettily painted 18th- and 19th-century terraces leading off the King's Road have a tradition of housing artists and intellectuals. On the left-hand side of the road opposite Sydney Street stands the Old Chelsea Town Hall. The old borough of Royal Kensington, given its royal appellation by Queen Victoria in 1901, was merged much against its wishes with Chelsea in 1965, and took over the administration of both. The Old Chelsea Town Hall continues to provide a cultural and social focus for residents. The Register Office next door is well-known for society and celebrity weddings.

SYDNEY STREET

In 1836, Charles Dickens was married more conventionally – in **St Luke's**, a stunning Gothic church halfway up Sydney Street, running north of the King's Road. Eagle-eyed Disney fans may recognise it from the 1996 film version of *101 Dalmatians*. If the weather is fine its gardens are a lovely spot to unwind.

Old Chelsea Town Hall.

Sydney Street is also home to the popular Chelsea Gardener nursery and the **Chelsea Farmers' Market**, a small shopping enclave with a boho feel thanks to its organic supermarket and one-storey units where the emphasis is on natural remedies and ingredients.

At the top of Sydney Street is **Brompton Cross**, a network of streets containing upmarket shops and restaurants, including Bibendum Restaurant, in the Art Deco-style former headquarters of the Michelin Tyre Company on Fulham Road.

ROYAL HOSPITAL ROAD

Among the leggy would-be models gliding along the King's Road are uniformed old gents with the initials RH on their caps. These are Chelsea Pensioners, retired war veterans who live in the **Royal Hospital**, built by Christopher Wren in 1692 on Royal Hospital Road. From the King's Road, a practically uninterrupted vista is afforded down the length of **Royal Avenue**, the hospital perfectly framed in the distance. The gravelled boulevard, now lined with

Royal Hospital.

19th-century houses, was laid out by Wren with the purpose of providing a direct route from the hospital to Kensington Palace. The scheme failed to materialise when Charles

Pastel-coloured mews houses.

II, the sponsor, died, and this first and only section now stands as testimony to Wren's grand vision. Royal Avenue was the fictional home of James Bond.

Royal Hospital ❺

Address: Royal Hospital Road, www.chelsea-pensioners.org.uk
Tel: 020-7881 5200
Opening Hrs: museum Mon–Fri 10am–4pm, tours Mon–Fri 10am and 1.30pm (booking required), grounds year round Mon–Sat 10am–sunset, Sun from 2pm.
Entrance Fee: free
Transport: Sloane Square

The idea behind this magnificent building housing the Chelsea Pensioners was inspired by the Hôtel des Invalides in Paris. The main buildings, two residential wings linked by the Great Hall and Chapel, were designed in English Baroque style.

The wood-panelled Great Hall, the dining room, features a vast mural with Charles II on horseback, painted by Verrio. It was in this hall in 1852 that Wellington lay in state. Decorated with regimental colours,

the adjoining Wren Chapel features *Christ Rising from the Tomb*, a fresco by Sebastiano Ricci. A huge painting of the Battle of Waterloo by George Jones hangs in the entrance to a small museum. It overlooks a 1:300 scale model that, with an audio presentation, illustrates the hospital and its massive grounds in the 18th century.

National Army Museum ❻

Address: Royal Hospital Road, www.nam.ac.uk
Tel: 020-7730 0717
Opening Hrs: daily 10am–5.30pm
Entrance Fee: free
Transport: Sloane Square

The museum reopened in 2016 following a £23-million refurbishment. Founded in 1960 by Royal Charter, the National Army Museum was established for the purpose of collecting, preserving and exhibiting objects and records relating to the Land Forces of the British Crown. It also explores the complex, shifting relationship Britain has with its Army. The museum has amassed a huge international collection, touching on some of the rawest elements

Chelsea Farmers' Market.

Artwork at the Royal Hospital.

FACT

Chelsea Physic Garden can lay claim to having the oldest rock garden in England, if not Europe. Dating back to 1773, it is made of salvaged building stone from the Tower of London and basaltic lava from Iceland.

of human experience: love, loss, death, sacrifice, endeavour, bravery and loyalty. The collections also tell the stories of some of the hundreds of thousands of Empire and Commonwealth troops who served for the British Army over the last 400 years.

Chelsea Physic Garden ❼

Address: 66 Royal Hospital Road, www.chelseaphysicgarden.co.uk
Tel: 020-7352 5646
Opening Hrs: late Mar–Oct Tue–Fri, Sun 11am–6pm; Nov–late Mar gardens only Mon–Fri 10am–dusk
Transport: Sloane Square

Behind a high wall is the Chelsea Physic Garden, founded in 1673 for the study of medicinal plants. The 3.5-acre (1.5-hectare) garden is divided into four contrasting sections: a Garden of World Medicine, a Pharmaceutical Garden,

Chelsea Physic Garden.

and systematic order beds in the two southern quadrants. The Pharmaceutical Garden displays plants according to their medical uses while the Garden of World Medicine details the use of specific plants in different parts of the world.

You will also find a pond rockery, perfumery and aromatherapy borders, glasshouses, and herb and vegetable gardens. A woodland area has birds' nesting boxes, and there are themed trails for adults and children.

CHELSEA EMBANKMENT

At the foot of Royal Hospital Road, a fine row of Queen Anne houses make up **Cheyne Walk** (see box). Cheyne Walk sits back from the flagstoned, windblown sweep of **Chelsea Embankment**, roaring with traffic in the shadows of old plane trees but beautiful nonetheless. Flanked by greenery it is also known as Chelsea Gardens and opened to great fanfare in 1874. It retains its sculptural lampposts with their fat, milky globes, and its cast-iron benches with end supports shaped like sphinxes. The views stretch out across the Thames to the Battersea Park Peace Pagoda

THE ULTIMATE DES RES

Cheyne Walk has long been one of London's most exclusive streets. A host of famous people have lived in its fine, mainly 18th-century, properties, from writers George Eliot and Hilaire Belloc to the artist J.M.W. Turner and the engineer Isambard Kingdom Brunel. It is still a choice address today, with Paul Getty, Mick Jagger and Keith Richards having all been resident at one time.

The pre-Raphaelite artist Dante Gabriel Rossetti lived with the poet Swinburne in No. 16, and they kept peacocks in their back garden. The birds so disturbed the neighbours that nowadays every lease on the row prohibits tenants from keeping them.

Carlyle's House.

on the opposite bank, built by Japanese monks and nuns in 1985; east to the iconic chimneys of the Battersea Power Station – restoration of the Grade II listing building is due to be completed in 2017 (which includes dismantling and rebuilding the chimneys); and west to the pink-and-cream confection of the **Albert Bridge** (1873).

Carlyle's House ❽

Transport: 24 Cheyne Row, www.nationaltrust.org.uk
Tel: 020-7352 7087
Opening Hrs: mid-Mar–Oct Wed–Sun 11am–5pm
Transport: Sloane Square
A statue of the Scottish essayist Thomas Carlyle (1795–1881) watches the traffic grind by further down the Embankment. The dour essayist lived here between 1834 and 1881. The house is preserved exactly as it was – to the point of not having electricity – and it is easy to imagine Mr and Mrs Carlyle sitting in their kitchen, although it may not have been a cosy scene. It was fortunate the Carlyles married each other, it was said, otherwise there would have been four miserable people in the world instead of two. Yet leading intellectuals, including Charles Dickens, John Ruskin

and Alfred, Lord Tennyson, used to visit Carlyle here.

Sir Hans Sloane's tomb is outside **Chelsea Old Church** (All Saints) on Cheyne Walk. The church has several fine Tudor monuments and was painstakingly rebuilt after being destroyed by a landmine in 1941.

The site was formerly occupied by a 12th-century Norman church. Henry VIII, who had a large house on the river where Cheyne Walk now is, supposedly married Jane Seymour in secrecy here, several days before the official ceremony. Thomas More (1478–1535), author of *Utopia*, which sketched out an ideal commonwealth, had a farm here. His stormy relationship with Henry VIII, which resulted in his execution, was the subject of Robert Bolt's 1960 play *A Man For All Seasons*.

FACT

The telltale enormous windows looking out onto Tite Street (off Royal Hospital Road) betray the origins of these houses: in the 1870s, this street was crammed with artists' studios, including The Studios, at No. 33. These were once used by the American painter John Singer Sargent (1856–1925) who died at No. 31, while Oscar Wilde once occupied No. 34.

There are blue plaques aplenty on Cheyne Walk.

William Blake's former home in Hampstead.

VILLAGE LONDON

London grew by swallowing up surrounding villages. But many are still there in spirit, each with its own distinctive character. Here we explore them by the four points of the compass.

At its widest point, from South Croydon to Potter's Bar, the metropolis is nearly 60 miles (100km) from top to bottom, and London remains one of the world's most populous and multicultural cities. Perhaps because it is so big, many of those who live within its confines hardly think of it as a unified city at all, but as a collection of largely independent villages or communities. While Londoners may commute many miles to work, they are likely to do their shopping in their local high streets and build their social lives on their home patch.

Cows grazing on Petersham Meadows, Richmond.

The River Thames cuts through London, forming an effective physical and psychological block to free movement. While south Londoners stream across London Bridge to work in the City every day, they are more likely to go shopping in Croydon or Bromley than in the West End, and north Londoners will head further north to such shopping citadels as Brent Cross. Many people born within the metropolis rarely move far from their home – unless moving to the suburbs for cheaper properties – and rarely relocate to the other side of the river.

The 24-hour Shepherd Gate Clock at the Royal Observatory.

Where to go

While most visitors are busy with the tourist haunts of the West End and the City, those who go further afield are rewarded with a glimpse of what the locals call 'real London'. Head west to Kew for Kew Gardens, and river walks at Chiswick and Richmond. Venture north to Islington and Camden for good shopping, nightlife, restaurants and Regent's Canal, or to Highgate and Hampstead for historic pubs and Hampstead Heath. Travel east of the centre to see high-rise Docklands, historic Spitalfields and the main 2012 Olympics site. In the southern suburbs are Greenwich, famous for its observatory and naval museum, neighbouring Blackheath and Brixton.

All can be reached by public transport, using either the Tube, Docklands Light Railway, buses or, in the case of the southern suburbs, overground railway from London Bridge, Victoria or Charing Cross stations.

Village London

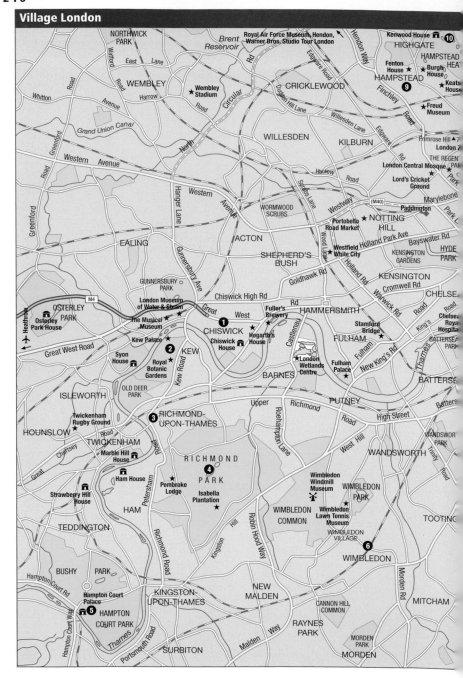

Royal Air Force Museum, Hendon,
Warner Bros. Studio Tour London

NORTHWICK PARK

Brent Reservoir

Kenwood House ⑩

HIGHGATE

HAMPSTEAD HEATH

East Lane

Watford

Fenton House ★

★ Burgh House

HAMPSTEAD ⑨

★ Keats House

WEMBLEY

★ Wembley Stadium

CRICKLEWOOD

Harrow

Circular

Road

Finchley

★ Freud Museum

Grand Union Canal

North

WILLESDEN

KILBURN

Primrose Hill ▲

London Z

Whitton

Greenford

Western   Avenue

Willesden Lane

Duggan Hill Lane

Edgware Road

Hendon Way

London Central Mosque

THE REGEN PAR

Lord's Cricket Ground

Greenford

Road

Hanger Lane

Western

Avenue

WORMWOOD SCRUBS

Harrow

Road

Scrubs Lane

Westway

(M40)

Marylebone

Park L.

Paddington

EALING

ACTON

SHEPHERD'S BUSH

Portobello Road Market

NOTTING HILL

Wood Lane

Holland Park Ave

Bayswater Rd

GUNNERSBURY PARK

Gunnersbury Ave

Goldhawk Rd

Westfield White City

Holland Park Ave

KENSINGTON GARDENS

HYDE PARK

Chiswick High Rd

Rd

Holland Rd

KENSINGTON

Cromwell Rd

London Museum of Water & Steam

Great

West

Fuller's Brewery

HAMMERSMITH

Warwick Rd

CHELSEA

M4

① CHISWICK

Stamford Bridge ★

FULHAM

King's

Road

Chelsea Royal Hospital

OSTERLEY PARK

The Musical Museum

Osterley Park House ★

Chiswick House

★ Hogarth's House

Castlenau

Road

BATTERSE PARK

Kew Palace ★

② KEW

London Wetlands Centre ★

New King's Rd

King's

BATTERSE

Great West Road

Syon House ★

Royal Botanic Gardens

Kew Road

BARNES

Fulham Palace ★

Thames

Heathrow

ISLEWORTH

OLD DEER PARK

Upper

Richmond

PUTNEY

High Street

Batters

Twickenham Rugby Ground ★

③ RICHMOND-UPON-THAMES

Roehampton Lane

Road

West Hill

WANDSWORTH

WANDSWOR PARK

HOUNSLOW

TWICKENHAM

Road

RICHMOND

Chertsey

Marble Hill House ★

④ PARK

Wimbledon Windmill Museum ✕

WIMBLEDON PARK

Great

Ham House ★

Pembroke Lodge ★

Robin Hood Way

Kingston

Wimbledon Lawn Tennis Museum

WIMBLEDON COMMON

Trinity

TOOTING

Strawberry Hill House ★

Petersham

Isabella Plantation ★

Richmond Road

Road

WIMBLEDON VILLAGE

⑥

TEDDINGTON

HAM

Richmond Road

WIMBLEDON

Morden Rd

BUSHY PARK

Hampton Court Rd

Hampton Court Palace ★

KINGSTON-UPON-THAMES

NEW MALDEN

Way

Malden

MITCHAM

⑤ HAMPTON COURT PARK

Portsmouth Road

CANNON HILL COMMON

RAYNES PARK

MORDEN PARK

Hampton Court Way

Thames

SURBITON

RAYNES PARK

MORDEN

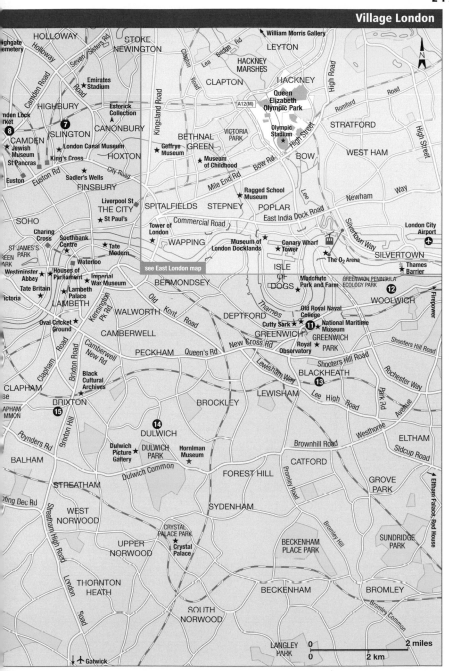

William Morris Gallery

HOLLOWAY

STOKE NEWINGTON

ighgate emetery

Holloway

Seven Sisters Rd

LEYTON

Clapton Road

Lea Bridge Rd

HACKNEY MARSHES

Camden Road

Emirates Stadium

CLAPTON

HACKNEY

High Road

Romford Road

Road

Highbury Road

Kingsland Road

A12(M)

Queen Elizabeth Olympic Park

STRATFORD

High Street

HIGHBURY

Estorick Collection

STRATFORD

nden Lock rket

7

CANONBURY

BETHNAL GREEN

VICTORIA PARK

Olympic Stadium

High Street

WEST HAM

High Street

8

ISLINGTON

CAMDEN

Jewish Museum

St Pancras

London Canal Museum

Geffrye Museum

HOXTON

BOW

Euston

King's Cross

City Road

Museum of Childhood

Bow Rd

BOW

Newham

Way

Euston Rd

Sadler's Wells

Mile End Rd

FINSBURY

Ragged School Museum

Lee

Liverpool St

THE CITY

St Paul's

SPITALFIELDS

STEPNEY

POPLAR

East India Dock Road

London City Airport

SOHO

Commercial Road

Silvertown Way

Charing Cross

Tower of London

WAPPING

Museum of London Docklands

Canary Wharf Tower

SILVERTOWN

ST JAMES'S PARK

Southbank Centre

Tate Modern

The O₂ Arena

EEN RK

Waterloo

ISLE OF DOGS

Thames Barrier

Westminster Abbey

Houses of Parliament

Imperial War Museum

BERMONDSEY

Mudchute Park and Farm

GREENWICH PENINSULA ECOLOGY PARK

12

Tate Britain

Lambeth Palace

Old Royal Naval College

WOOLWICH

ictoria

LAMBETH

Kennington Pk Rd

Old Kent Road

WALWORTH

DEPTFORD

Thames

Cutty Sark

11

National Maritime Museum

Firepower

Oval Cricket Ground

CAMBERWELL

GREENWICH

GREENWICH PARK

Shooters Hill Road

Camberwell New Rd

PECKHAM

Queen's Rd

New Cross Rd

Royal Observatory

Rochester Way

Brixton Road

Black Cultural Archives

Clapham

Lewisham Way

Shooters Hill Road

Park Rd

Avenue

CLAPHAM

se

BROCKLEY

LEWISHAM

BLACKHEATH

13

Westhorne

ELTHAM

APHAM MMON

BRIXTON

15

Brixton Hill

Lee High Road

Poynders Rd

DULWICH

14

Dulwich Picture Gallery

DULWICH PARK

Horniman Museum

Brownhill Road

Sidcup Road

GROVE PARK

BALHAM

Dulwich Common

FOREST HILL

CATFORD

Eltham Palace, Red House

oting Bec Rd

STREATHAM

Bromley Road

WEST NORWOOD

SYDENHAM

Streatham High Road

CRYSTAL PALACE PARK

Crystal Palace

BECKENHAM PLACE PARK

SUNDRIDGE PARK

UPPER NORWOOD

Bromley Hill

London Road

THORNTON HEATH

BECKENHAM

BROMLEY

SOUTH NORWOOD

Bromley Common

LANGLEY PARK

0

2 miles

Gatwick

0

2 km

see East London map

N

WEST LONDON

West London offers 18th-century mansions, magnificent parks and walks along the River Thames. To the southwest is Henry VIII's great palace, Hampton Court, and Wimbledon, home of the famous tennis championship.

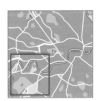

Heading west out of London you can choose between grand riverside mansions, built as country retreats for royals and landed gentry, and wide-open spaces such as Richmond Park and Kew Gardens, the world renowned botanic gardens.

CHISWICK ❶

Although it accommodates the main artery to the M4 and Heathrow Airport, Chiswick has the feel of a small town, with its independent shops, flower stalls, fashionable restaurants and pretty terraces. Near the fragrant Fuller's Brewery (see page 220), off Hogarth roundabout, stands a hidden gem, much loved by locals and at last being given the attention it deserves.

Chiswick House

Address: Burlington Lane, www.english-heritage.org.uk
Tel: 020-8995 0508
Opening Hrs: house Apr–Oct Sun–Wed 10am–5pm, Nov–Mar pre-booked appointments for groups only; gardens daily 7am–dusk
Entrance Fee: gardens free
Transport: train from Waterloo to Chiswick; bus 190
This romantic 18th-century villa was designed by Lord Burlington

(1694–1753), a renowned architect and patron of the arts, who was inspired by classical Rome. Burlington's Palladian house launched a new taste in architecture which was to spread throughout Britain and North America.

The gardens are historically important too, for it was here that the idea of the 'natural style' of gardening – one of England's main contributions to European culture – was conceived. Burlington brought in his friend William Kent to redesign the

Main Attractions
Chiswick House
Hogarth's House
Royal Botanic Gardens, Kew
Syon House and Park
Richmond Park
Hampton Court Palace
Wimbledon Lawn Tennis Museum

Map
Page 216

Chiswick House.

To see how a pint of fine English ale is made, take a tour around Fuller's Griffin Brewery on the Hogarth roundabout. Pre-booking is essential (tel: 8996 2063).

grounds; Kent broke from the rigid formality that had characterised gardens of the early 18th century and created a more natural landscape. Thus the English landscape movement was born. The gardens include an abundance of statuary, a classical bridge, an Ionic temple, and a large conservatory.

Inside the house, the grand rooms are reserved for the first floor, which has a very unusual structure: in the centre is an octagonal room with a lavish domed ceiling – the tribune or saloon. This was the heart of the building and the setting for gatherings and *conversazioni*.

Amongst the celebrated guests welcomed here were Alexander Pope, Jonathan Swift, Handel and several crowned heads of state. The small scale and rounded edges of the rooms in the northern part of the house are intimate and sensual, with the overall symmetry heightened by framed views of the gardens through the doorways of the interconnected rooms. The most sumptuous of the Green, Red and Blue Velvet rooms, so-called because of their vivid wallpaper, is Lord Burlington's study, elegantly adorned in blue. The room's tiny dimensions and rich

Chiswick House gardens.

Hogarth's House.

colours convey an impression of standing inside a jewel box, or inside a Fabergé egg.

Hogarth's House

Address: Hogarth Lane, Great West Road; www.hounslow.info
Tel: 020-8994 6757
Opening Hrs: Tue–Sun noon–5pm
Entrance Fee: free
Transport: train from Waterloo to Chiswick, bus 190

Not far from Chiswick House, sitting incongruously on the six-lane Great West Road, is Hogarth's House, the modest residence of the father of political cartoons, William Hogarth (1697–1764). Hogarth highlighted the ills of society in a series of witty engravings that became bestsellers. The house has recently been restored, and the collection of drawings, including *The Rake's Progress* and *Marriage à la Mode*, is worth seeking out. (Free parking for Chiswick House and Hogarth's House can be found a short distance from the Hogarth roundabout along the A4.)

William Hogarth moved with his family to this three-storey house from busy Leicester Fields (now Leicester Square) in 1749. In a monstrous bit

of irony that would not be lost on the satirist, this 'little country box by the Thames' now lies by the A4 to Heathrow, its owner immortalised in the thundering Hogarth roundabout. The traffic noise is muted in the house though, and a small garden at the back attempts a pastoral charm. The mulberry tree here is said to date from Hogarth's day, one of the few to survive from a time when the trees were brought to England in a vain attempt to get silkworms to breed.

Kew

Downriver from Chiswick is Kew, home to the Royal Botanic Gardens, known as Kew Gardens. The village green gives the place a rural feel, particularly when cricket matches are played here. On the green is St Anne's Church, where the painter Thomas Gainsborough is buried.

Royal Botanic Gardens ❷

Address: Kew, Richmond, www.kew.org
Tel: 020-8332 5655
Opening Hrs: Apr–Aug Mon–Fri 10am–5.30pm, Sat–Sun until 7.30pm; Sept–Oct 10am–6pm; Nov–Jan 10am–4.15pm; last admission 30 minutes before closing
Transport: Kew Gardens, or train from Waterloo to Kew Bridge

Kew Gardens, with 300 acres (120 hectares) of plants from all over the world, were first established in 1759 under the direction of Princess Augusta. In 1772, her son George III put Kew in the hands of the botanist Sir Joseph Banks, who had just returned from a round-the-world expedition to collect plant specimens with Captain Cook. Other explorers and amateur enthusiasts added to the collection over the centuries, so that today Kew is not only a vast botanical garden but also a formidable repository and research centre. In 2003 Kew was added to Unesco's list of World Heritage Sites.

The gardens present a mix of landscaped lawns, wooded areas, formal gardens and glasshouses. Make the most of the map you receive on entering, as it features seasonal highlights and where to find them.

The most famous of Kew's nursery buildings is the Grade I-listed **Palm House**, built in 1844–8. The steamy warmth hits you as you enter this verdant tropical world, in which coconuts, bananas and coffee beans grow. Nearby, the **Waterlily House** (closed Nov–Apr) houses tropical aquatic plants. The **Temperate House**, closed for refurbishment until 2018, is the world's largest surviving Victorian glass structure.

Kew Gardens.

In addition to the glasshouses there are various temples and other follies dating back to the period of royal ownership of the gardens in the 18th and early 19th centuries. The **Chinese Pagoda**, built in 1762, reflects the fashion for chinoiserie in English garden design in the mid-18th century. A 650ft (200-metre)-high treetop walkway allows you to walk above the lime, sweet chestnut and oak trees. The classically styled, Grade I-listed Orangery dating from 1761, too dark to house citrus trees

Kew's Chinese Pagoda.

Kew village green.

as was intended, is now a pleasant café-restaurant.

Kew Palace

Built in 1631 for a Dutch merchant, **Kew Palace** (tel: 020-3166 6000; www. hrp.org.uk; Apr–Sept daily 9.30am–5.30pm) was the country retreat of George III, Queen Charlotte and some of their children from 1801; the king came here during his bouts of supposed madness. The palace has been meticulously restored and brought back to life, revealing aspects of the original Georgian decor and architecture, and many of the family's treasures.

SYON PARK AND MUSEUMS

Across Kew Bridge is the **London Museum of Water & Steam** (Green Dragon Lane; tel: 020-8568 4757; www. waterandsteam.org.uk; daily 11am–4pm), whose original purpose was to supply London's water in the 19th century. It now houses the world's largest collection of steam-pumping engines and a steam railway, which you can ride (Sundays only Easter–Oct). There are also regular events most Sundays throughout the year.

Xstrata treetop walkway, Kew Gardens.

Inside Kew's Palm House.

Further west along the high street is the **Musical Museum** (399 High Street, Brentford; tel: 020-8560 8108; www.musicalmuseum.co.uk; Fri–Sun 11am–5pm, last admission 4pm), which displays a large collection of automatic instruments, from clockwork music boxes to the Mighty Wurlitzer organ.

Syon House

Address: Syon Park, Isleworth, www.syonpark.co.uk
Tel: 020-8560 0882
Opening Hrs: house mid-Mar–Oct Wed–Thu, Sun 11am–5pm; gardens Mar–Oct daily 10.30am–5pm/dusk

Syon House and its 200-acre (80-hectare) park is the London home of the Duke of Northumberland, whose family have lived here for over 400 years. Its 18th-century interior by Robert Adam is unsurpassed, celebrated as the architect's early English masterpiece. From the Long Gallery is a spectacular view over the last tidal water meadow on the Thames. The gardens were created by the great English landscape gardener Capability Brown in the mid-18th century.

Children are well catered for at Syon Park with Snakes and Ladders, a huge indoor play centre.

Further west is another grand house built as a country retreat: Osterley Park House (Jersey Road, Isleworth; tel: 020-8232 5050; www.national trust.org.uk; house Mar–Oct daily noon–4.30pm; garden daily 10am–5pm). This neoclassical mansion has fine interiors by Robert Adam, 18th-century gardens, and a large landscaped park. Regular tours of the house and gardens (charge).

Richmond-upon-Thames ❸

Richmond makes for a pleasant day out, easily reached by District Line Underground or by Overground trains from Waterloo and Vauxhall. Richmond Green is lined with 17th- and 18th-century buildings, while the town centre is good for shopping. Richmond Bridge is the oldest on the river, and the waterfront is always lively, with boats available for hire.

The walk up Richmond Hill to the park leads past views over the Thames and London; in the foreground you may see cows grazing on Petersham Meadows. This view is the only one in England to be protected by an Act of Parliament, passed in 1902.

Richmond Park ❹

Address: Richmond, www.royalparks. org.uk/parks/richmond-park
Tel: 0300 061 2200
Opening Hrs: daily May–Sept 7am–dusk, Oct–Apr 7.30am–dusk
Entrance Fee: free
Transport: Richmond, then No. 371 or 65 bus to Petersham Gate

At 2,500 acres (1,000 hectares), Richmond Park is the largest of all the royal parks. The pastoral landscape of hills, ponds, gardens and grasslands is popular with walkers, cyclists and horse riders. Since 1625, when Charles I brought his court to Richmond Palace (now demolished) to escape the plague, there have been herds of wild red and fallow deer in the park.

The **Isabella Plantation**, an ornamental woodland garden in the southwest corner, has been designed to be interesting all year round, though a favourite time to visit is from April, when the azaleas and rhododendrons bloom. At **Pembroke Lodge**, a Georgian mansion on the western edge of the park, there are fabulous views over west London. There's also a car park here, and refreshments.

The 17th-century Kew Palace.

Deer grazing in Richmond Park.

Ham House

Address: Ham Street, Ham, Richmond, www.nationaltrust.org.uk
Tel: 020-8940 1950
Opening Hrs: house: daily house tours noon–4pm, garden 10am–4.15pm
Transport: District Line to Richmond, then No. 371 bus

About a mile along the Thames Path from Richmond Hill is Ham House, built in 1610 with a sumptuous interior and important collections of textiles, furnishings and paintings. This Stuart mansion is also said to be one of the most haunted houses in the country. The formal garden is being restored to its former splendour.

Across the river is **Marble Hill House** (tel: 020-8892 5115; www.english-heritage.org.uk; house: Apr–Oct guided tours only, Sat–Sun check website for opening times), an elegant Palladian villa set in riverside parkland.

Intended as an Arcadian retreat, the house was built in 1724 for Henrietta Howard, mistress to King George II when he was Prince of Wales. It contains a fine collection of early Georgian paintings.

Hampton Court Palace ❺

Address: East Molesey, Surrey, www.hrp.org.uk
Tel: 0844-482 7777
Opening Hrs: daily Apr–Oct 10am–6pm, Nov–Mar until 4.30pm; last entry to maze 45 minutes before closing
Transport: train from Waterloo to Hampton Court

Surrounded by 60 acres (24 hectares) of magnificent gardens on the banks of the Thames, this vast palace, built to rival Versailles in France, dates from the reign of Henry VIII (reigned 1509–47). In the late 1600s many of the Tudor apartments were rebuilt by Sir Christopher Wren, but the Great Hall and Chapel Royal – the most striking rooms – survive.

Marble Hill House.

THE THAMES PATH

Starting at the Thames Barrier in the east and ending at the river's source in the Cotswolds 180 miles (290km) away, the Thames Path provides some of the best views of London. From Putney the path takes on a rural aspect, passing Barnes Wetland Centre, the grand riverside houses of Chiswick and the pretty cottages of Strand on the Green. After Kew Bridge, the path skirts round Kew Gardens, with Syon Park across the river. At Richmond, with Petersham Meadows on your left and a great sweep of the river ahead of you, it's hard to believe the city is in spitting distance. Along this stretch you'll see Marble Hill House and, a little further along, Ham House.

The Great Hall at Hampton Court Palace.

Start at the introductory exhibition behind the colonnade in Clock Court; here you can decide on your route and find out about activities for children. Costumed guides give entertaining tours of some parts of the palace, including Henry VIII's **State Apartments**.

These you enter through the Great Hall, the last of its kind to be built, and the largest room in the palace.

The hammer-beam roof and richly carved decoration are original. In the **Tudor Kitchens**, you can feel the heat of the massive kitchen fires and smell the meat simmering in the boiling pot, as if in preparation for a feast in Henry VIII's time.

Allow time to visit the riverside gardens, and get lost in the famous maze, planted in 1702 and nowadays enhanced with sound effects such as whispers of conversation and a dog barking.

Wimbledon ⑥

This suburb hosts one of the world's top tennis tournaments in June/July and its history is brought to life in the **Wimbledon Lawn Tennis Museum** (Church Road, Wimbledon; tel: 020-8946 6131; www.wimbledon.com; daily 10am–5pm). The Museum is closed to the public during the Championships.

On the edge of Wimbledon Common, a partly wooded expanse with nature trails, is the **Wimbledon Windmill Museum** (tel: 020-8947 2825; www.wimbledonwindmill.org. uk; Apr–Oct Sat 2–5pm, Sun 11am–5pm), in a disused windmill. Displays illustrate the milling process, with hands-on milling for children.

TIP

To visit Marble Hill House from the Richmond side of the river, take the Hammertons ferry, which runs between the riverbank outside Ham House in Richmond and Marble Hill Park in Twickenham (www.hammer tonsferry.com; tel: 020-8892 9620; Mar–Oct Mon–Fri 10am–6pm, Sat–Sun until 6.30pm; Nov–Mar Sat–Sun only weather permitting).

Hampton Court Palace.

NORTH LONDON

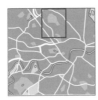

For centuries the well-to-do preferred to live in areas such as Islington, Hampstead and Highgate, away from the brothels and pollution south of the river. These areas still retain a distinct air of superiority.

Main Attractions

Arsenal Emirates
  Stadium
Camden Lock Market
Regent's Canal
Hampstead Heath
Highgate Cemetery

Map
Page 216

I f you have time, there are several interesting areas to visit in north London, all of them most animated at weekends when they are a magnet for Londoners themselves. Choose between Islington with its vibrant eating and shopping scene, Camden with its canal and market, Hampstead with its famous heath, handsome period properties and museums, or Highgate with its overgrown Victorian cemetery containing the remains of many famous figures. They can all be reached on the Northern Line.

ISLINGTON ❼

North of the City of London, City Road rises to the Angel, named after a long-gone coaching inn, marking the start of Islington. In the first half of the 20th century this was a poor and even dangerous area of London. Its once handsome properties were in deep decline, their buddleia-sprouting facades hiding slum conditions and multi-family occupancy.

But as London's Georgian and Victorian dwellings were refurbished in the 1970s, Islington rose phoenix-like from the ashes. It came to epitomise gentrification, and by the 1980s a popular stereotype portrayed it as the happy hunting ground of liberal-minded *bien pensants*. This is where Tony and Cherie Blair lived before moving to 10 Downing Street.

Place of entertainment

In the 18th and 19th centuries Islington was a place of entertainment. It remains a lively area, thronged with visitors both day and night. There are a vast number of restaurants and café-bars on Upper Street alone, a mile-long corridor of consumerism linking Angel Tube station with Highbury and Islington Tube station.

The area also has several theatres, most notably the Almeida Theatre

Arsenal's Emirates Stadium.

Interiors shop on Upper Street.

in Almeida Street, one of London's most innovative small theatres, and, just around the corner, the **King's Head**, which is the best of several pub theatres. At the southern end of Islington on Rosebery Avenue, **Sadler's Wells** is one of London's principal dance venues.

Shopping

Near **Angel**, the crossroads at the top of Islington, the Angel Centre is a small mall of mainstream chain stores. More interesting for visitors is **Chapel Market**, a traditional London street market that retains its working-class character. Camden Passage (on the opposite side of Islington High Street) has elegant buildings and arcades that have become a treasure trove of antiques shops, ranging from simple stalls to grand shops. There is also the Mall Antiques Arcade at 359 Upper Street.

For offbeat individual shops, seek out Cross Street and environs, near the Almeida Theatre halfway along Upper Street.

Islington's classic terraces

Prime examples of terraced houses can be found in **Gibson Square** and also **Canonbury Square**, where authors George Orwell and Evelyn Waugh once lived. At 39a Canonbury Square is the **Estorick Collection** (tel: 020-7704 9522; www.estorickcollection.com; Wed–Sat 11am–6pm, Sun noon–5pm), a collection of Italian Futurist and figurative art in an elegant Georgian house, complete with bookshop.

Last, but to many minds by no means least, Islington is also the home of premier league **Arsenal Football Club**, which in 2006 moved to the new Emirates stadium. Although it is virtually impossible for non-members to obtain tickets for a game, you can take a tour of the stadium and visit the museum (Hornsea Road; tel: 020-7619 5000; www.arsenal.com).

Camden ❽

It's Camden Market that attracts the crowds to Camden, though like Islington it also has many fine period terraces and squares, and a hip pub and club scene. The main market (Camden High Street, Thu–Sun

Vintage fashion in Camden Passage.

KIDS

You can take a 90-minute narrowboat trip from Camden (on the Jenny Wren, tel: 020-7485 4433; www.walkers quay.com). The boat cruises from Camden Town to Little Venice and back daily Apr–Oct, and at weekends in March.

9am–5.30pm) has cheap clothes, and is still a place for street style and cutting-edge fashion. **Camden Lock Market** (off Chalk Farm Road, outdoor stalls Sat–Sun 10am–6pm, indoor stalls Tue–Sun) focuses on crafts (see page 55).

One of the delights of Camden is Camden Lock. A sequence of two locks and a bridge in quick succession, it is one of the most attractive stretches of **Regent's Canal**. From here the towpath, busy with cyclists (including bicycling commuters during the weekday rush hours), walkers and fishermen, heads west to Little Venice and east to Hackney and beyond. The last horse-drawn cargo passed along the canal in 1956.

The Jewish Museum

Address: 128–131 Albert Street, www.jewishmuseum.org.uk
Tel: 020-7284 7384
Opening Hrs: Mon–Thu, Sun 10am–5pm, Fri 10am–2pm
Transport: Camden Town

The Jewish Museum occupies an elegant early Victorian building but the interior is modern with sophisticated displays, including an interactive map showing centres of Jewish

Camden Lock Market.

Amy Winehouse exhibit at the Jewish Museum in Camden.

population in different periods. There is a gallery devoted to Judaica, illustrating religious rituals as passed down the centuries, and exhibitions include the Holocaust Gallery and the story of the Jews in Britain.

HAMPSTEAD ⑨

Hampstead has long been a desirable address and attracts a literary set.

REGENT'S CANAL

This 8.5-mile (14km) stretch of water running from Little Venice near Paddington in west London to Limehouse in Docklands was dug between 1812 and 1820 and drops 86ft (25 metres) through 12 locks beneath 57 bridges. The canal has some delightfully rural stretches and also passes through London Zoo. The stretch between Camden and Victoria Park in Hackney takes around a morning to complete (the towpath is interrupted in Islington, where the canal passes through a 0.75-mile (1.2km) tunnel, but can be picked up again close to Angel). To learn more about the history of the canal visit the **Canal Museum** at 12–13 New Wharf Road, King's Cross (see page 131).

Open spaces predominate. The 3-sq-mile (8-sq-km) **Heath** leads down to **Parliament Hill**, which gives splendid views across London, as does the 112-acre (45-hectare) **Primrose Hill** overlooking Regent's Park. These are all welcome acres over which locals stride, walk dogs, fly kites, skate and swim in the bathing ponds. History-laden pubs near the heath include the **Spaniards Inn** and the congenial **Old Bull and Bush**.

Keats House

Address: Keats Grove, www.cityoflondon.gov.uk/keats
Tel: 020 7332 3868
Opening Hrs: Easter–Oct Tue–Sun 1–5pm, Nov–Easter Fri–Sun 1–5pm
Transport: Hampstead

The poet John Keats (1795–1821) wrote much of his work, including *Ode to a Nightingale*, during the two years he lived in Hampstead. It was here that he met and fell in love with Fanny Brawne, the daughter of his next door neighbour. His house-museum contains memorabilia such as facsimiles of his letters, a lock of his hair and Fanny Brawne's engagement ring. The Regency-style garden is free to visit.

The Freud Museum

Address: 20 Maresfield Gardens, www.freud.org.uk
Tel: 020-7435 2002
Opening Hrs: Wed–Sun noon–5pm
Transport: Finchley Road

Sigmund Freud, fleeing the Nazis in 1938, moved from Vienna to this house in Hampstead. He died just a year later, but his daughter Anna, also a psychoanalyst, looked after it until her own death in 1982.

The museum preserves the house as they left it, and includes many pieces of furniture and other possessions brought over from Vienna. Freud's study on the ground floor includes the couch on which his Viennese patients free-associated, oriental rugs, books and pictures, plus his prize collection of antiquities, including framed Roman frescoes and Greek vases.

Kenwood House

Address: Hampstead Lane, www.english-heritage.org.uk
Tel: 020-8348 1286
Opening Hrs: daily 10am–5pm
Entrance Fee: free
Transport: Archway or Highgate

Looking like a great wedding cake, Kenwood House was remodelled in

Keats House, where the poet lived between 1818 and 1820. In the winter of 1820 he was advised by his physician to leave England for the warmer climate of Italy. He never returned, dying in Rome in 1821, aged 25.

Boats on Regent's Canal.

FACT

Hampstead's elevation gave it a sense of safety. When a great flood that would wipe out London was forecast for 1 February 1524, crowds climbed the hill to observe it. In 1736, the end of the world was predicted and it was here many came to await their doom.

1764–79 by Robert Adam and overlooks Hampstead Heath. Its beautifully maintained rooms reopened in 2013 after extensive refurbishment, and showcase the **Iveagh Bequest**, a major collection with works by Rembrandt, Vermeer, Reynolds, J.M.W. Turner and Gainsborough. The first floor contains many family portraits, and items such as silver tableware and fine furniture. The house is also a backdrop for picnic concerts held during the summer.

Other grand houses

Hampstead has several other ngotable houses open to the public. On Windmill Hill, parallel to Heath Street, **Fenton House** (tel: 020-7435 3471; www.nationaltrust.org.uk; Mar–Oct Wed–Sun 11am–5pm) is a 17th-century mansion containing collections of harpsichords and ceramics. It is noted for its snowdrops in early spring.

Tucked away among the lanes is **Burgh House** (New End Square; tel: 020-7431 0144; www.burghhouse.org.uk; Wed–Fri, Sun noon–5pm, Sat ground

floor gallery only; free), which has a fine music room and library and an award-winning garden. One of London's finest Queen Anne-style houses, it doubles as Hampstead Museum, which has a display on the landscape painter John Constable (1776–1837), a one-time local.

HIGHGATE ⑩

Neighbouring Highgate, a hilltop suburb built round a pretty square, contains London's grandest cemetery. **Highgate Cemetery** (tel: 020-8340 1834; www.highgate-cemetery.org) comprises two sections (see box). The east cemetery (Mon–Fri 10am–4pm, Sat–Sun 11am–4pm) can be visited independently, though guided tours are available The west section, across Swain's Lane, is more atmospheric but can only be visited on a one-hour guided tour (at weekends tours are conducted hourly between 11am and 4.30pm; the weekday tour at 1.45pm should be booked). The cemetery is administered as a museum, with charges for taking photographs.

View from Parliament Hill.

HIGHGATE CEMETERY

As London expanded in the early 19th century, where to bury the dead became a pressing problem. A number of new cemeteries were therefore built on the city's outskirts, including, in 1839, the western section of Highgate Cemetery. In 1854 the cemetery another section was opened on the eastern side of Swain's Lane. These quintessentially Victorian cemeteries are noted for their grandiose mausoleums and statues, artfully covered in creepers and set amidst wild flowers. One of the chief attractions is the rather grim bust of Karl Marx, buried in the eastern section in 1883. There are some 850 notable people buried at Highgate, among them the novelist George Eliot, members of the Rossetti family, and the scientist Michael Faraday.

Highgate Cemetery is full of elaborate memorials and statues, including plenty of weeping angels.

NORTHERN OUTPOSTS

Also worth highlighting are a couple of attractions in suburbs further north. Hendon is reached by the Northern Line.

Hendon

The main reason to visit this northern suburb is the **Royal Air Force Museum** (Grahame Park Way; tel: 020-8205 2266; www.rafmuseum.org.uk; daily 10am–6pm; free). It has a large array of bombers and fighter jets, plus flight simulators and a Battle of Britain Hall with tableaux of scenes from World War II. You can wander among some of the most famous aeroplanes in history.

Walthamstow

An outpost at the far end of the Tube's Victoria line, Walthamstow is not an obvious tourist attraction, but the **William Morris Gallery** (Lloyd Park, Forest Road, Walthamstow, E17; tel: 020-8496 4390; www.wmgallery.org.uk; Wed–Sun 10am–5pm) is well worth the journey. The museum contains an outstanding collection of fabrics, rugs, wallpapers, furniture, glass and tiles, designed by Morris and members of the British Arts and Crafts movement.

A quirky attraction, a 20-minute walk away, is **God's Own Junkyard** (Ravenswood Industrial Estate, Shernhall Street, E17; http://godsownjunkyard.co.uk; Fri–Sat 11am–9pm; Sun 11am–6pm). This warehouse-like 'gallery' shows off the creations of neon and light artist, the late Chris Bracey.

KIDS

Though rather a long trek by Tube to Colindale, plus a 15-minute walk from there, the Royal Air Force Museum is a huge hit with most children. It is also free, as is the Tube journey for children under the age of 11.

The Royal Air Force Museum, Hendon.

EAST LONDON

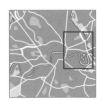

For centuries, waves of immigrants settled in parts of East London such as Bethnal Green and Spitalfields, often in slum conditions. Today, thanks in part to the 2012 Olympic Games held here, redevelopment brought considerable changes for the better.

East London was the first stop for many of the immigrants, whose labour helped fuel the Industrial Revolution and build the docks through which much of the British Empire's trade passed. Poverty and overcrowding were endemic.

Today, this area is a mix of urban poverty and some of the hippest parts of London.

HOXTON

Hoxton, north of Old Street, first became fashionable when young artists such as Damien Hirst and Tracey Emin moved here, creating studios in redundant warehouses. As they became successful, art dealers and web designers followed and urban desolation became urban chic.

Commercial galleries radiate from **Hoxton Square**, the former location of Jay Jopling's White Cube gallery (since moved to Bermondsey Street). Café-bars and clothes shops line the streets around Curtain Road, and the area is one of London's most popular places for a night out. On Sundays Hoxton's **Columbia Road Market** (8am–3pm) specialises in flowers, plants and garden accessories (see page 54).

The Geffrye Museum **A**

Address: 136 Kingsland Rd, www.geffrye-museum.org.uk
Tel: 020-7739 9893
Opening Hrs: Tue–Sun 10am–5pm
Entrance Fee: free except for special exhibitions
Transport: Old Street

This museum charts the interior decorating tastes of the urban middle classes from 1600 to the present day. Housed in a square of former almshouses, it was intended to inspire workers in the East End furniture trade. The rooms – all of

Columbia Road Market.

which are 'sitting' or 'living' rooms – are arranged chronologically from 1620 to 1990. Behind the buildings the museum's gardens comprise period and walled herb gardens (Apr–Oct), overlooked by a pleasant restaurant.

Hackney

East towards Hackney, Broadway Market (Saturdays only) is a great place to come for fabulous food stalls (spices, cheeses, breads, rarebreed meat, luscious cakes and olives), vintage clothes, hip cafés and indie music shops. Walk further east along the Regent's Canal to **Victoria Park**, a lovely big park with ponds, playgrounds, a deer enclosure and the Pavilion Café. In summer music festivals are held here.

BETHNAL GREEN

South of Victoria Park, Bethnal Green has two excellent museums focusing on childhood.

Museum of Childhood **B**

Address: Cambridge Heath Road, www.museumofchildhood.org.uk
Tel: 020-8983 5200
Opening Hrs: daily 10am–5.45pm

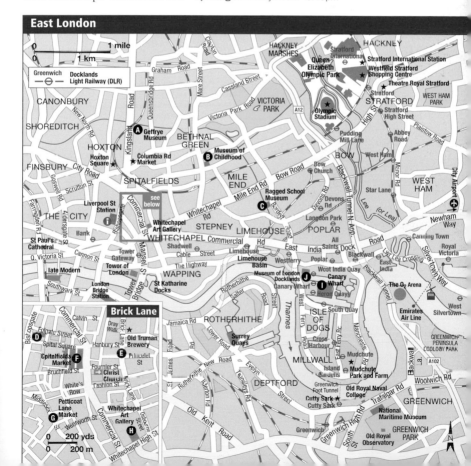

Dennis Severs' House.

The Geffrye Museum.

horse, activate the model railways, rifle through a dressing-up box, and learn through play in the activity corner. There are also some sobering facts to be learnt about childcare and health.

Less than a mile away, the **Ragged School Museum** ⓒ (46–50 Copperfield Road; tel: 020-8980 6405; www.raggedschoolmuseum.org. uk; Wed–Thu 10am–5pm, first Sun of month 2–5pm; free) has a reconstructed kitchen and classroom to show how life was once lived by London's indomitable East Enders. Children can sit at school desks and climb in the tin bath to get a taste of Victorian life.

SPITALFIELDS

Spitalfields contains several streets of fine 18th-century houses that were originally the homes of Huguenot silk weavers.

Dennis Severs' House ⓓ

Address: 18 Folgate Street; www.dennissevershouse.co.uk

Entrance Fee: free
Transport: Bethnal Green
Displays in this outpost of the V&A Museum (see pages 200) range from classic children's toys to the development of nappies and the root of adolescent rebellion. There's much to appeal to children: they can ride a magnificent rocking

At the end of Fournier Street, one of Spitalfields' finest streets, is Christ Church (1729), the greatest of Nicholas Hawksmoor's churches.

Tel: 020-7247 4013
Opening Hrs: every Mon 6–9pm (candlelit tours – booking required); Sun noon–4pm; Mon following the 1st and 3rd Sun of the month noon–2pm
Transport: Liverpool Street

Among the 18th-century properties is this four-storey town house still lit only by gaslight. The late Dennis Severs, an American, laid out the 10 rooms as if they were still occupied by an 18th-century family, and your visit takes you on a sensory journey, room by room.

Markets

Successive waves of immigrants have left their mark on **Brick Lane** Ⓔ. French Huguenots sought refuge here at the end of the 17th century, Jews fleeing the Russian pogroms arrived in the late 19th century, and today the area has a large Bangladeshi community. Famous for its curry houses, it also has some

decent bars and nightclubs, some of which are within the Old Truman Brewery, the self-styled 'creative hub' of the East End. Also here is the Sunday UpMarket (Ely's Yard, Sun 10am–5pm), selling clothes from independent designers and gastronomic treats.

Spitalfields Market Ⓕ (Commercial Street; Mon–Fri 10am 4pm, Sun 9am–5pm), once a wholesale fruit and vegetable market, now sells mainly clothes and crafts, as well as antiques on Thursdays. To the south, centring on Middlesex Street is **Petticoat Lane Market** Ⓖ, packed on Sundays with dozens of stalls flogging cheap clothes.

WHITECHAPEL

To the east is the **Whitechapel Art Gallery** Ⓗ (80–82 Whitechapel High Street; tel: 020-7522 7888; www.whitechapelgallery.org; Tue–Sat 11am–6pm, Thu until 9pm; free), founded by a local vicar and his wife in 1897. The gallery mounts high profile exhibitions of modern and

An incongruous attraction in this over-concreted part of Docklands (known as the Isle of Dogs) is the 35-acre (14-hectare) **Mudchute Park and Farm** (tel: 020-7515 5901; www.mudchute.org; park daily 9am–4.30pm, farm daily 8am–4pm; free) on Pier Street. As well as farm animals and rare breeds, it has llamas, a pets' corner and a riding centre.

The Museum of Childhood in Bethnal Green.

Legacy of the 2012 Olympics

The London 2012 Olympic and Paralympic Games presented Britain – and London in particular – as self-confident, forward-looking and fun.

The games not only exceeded expectations in Great Britain's medal success, but the host city also wowed the world with its sporting arenas.

A major appeal of the successful Olympic bid was the concept of Legacy, that staging the event would be just the starting point for enhancing the nation's love of sport and improved fitness. Several years later it's clear that it was perhaps an ambition too far, as there hasn't been the desired increase in public participation at grass-

Spectators in patriotic attire in the Olympic Park during London 2012.

roots level. However, one undisputed fact is that the Queen Elizabeth Olympic Park has opened up to the public in many contexts.

Venues and facilities

The immense, light-filled Aquatics Centre, designed by the late, great architect Zaha Hadid, is now a public swimming pool plus a special diving pool where Olympic champion Tom Daley trains.

Nearby is the Velodrome – the venue where Britain won so many cycling medals in 2012 – where keen amateurs and novices alike can rent bikes to speed around the track, plus occasional international competitions. The Copper Box Arena hosts regular league matches for the London Lions – London's only professional basketball tea.

The main Olympic stadium itself has been leased out to premier league football team West Ham FC. It also hosts major athletics championships in summer, including the 2017 World Athletics Championships.

The Queen Elizabeth Olympic Park hosts regular events such as monthly 10K races, open to all, plus summer concerts and festivals.

The 2012 Olympics may not have turned the British into a nation of champions, but it has left a fabulous venue in an otherwise forgotten part of London. You can find out all about the events and venues at http://queen elizabetholympicpark.co.uk.

Sculpture, shopping and a cable car across the Thames

Also open to the public is the ArcelorMittal Orbit, the giant twisted sculpture at the heart of the Olympic area, designed by Sir Anish Kapoor and Cecil Balmond.

The Emirates Air Line cable car carries passengers across the Thames from North Greenwich to the Royal Docks (www.emir-atesairline.co.uk).

Westfield Stratford City, Europe's largest urban shopping centre, is the main gateway into the Olympic Park. For a spectacular aerial view of the whole Olympic site, you can abseil from the Orbit on selected dates. In summer 2016, its 'helter-skelter' -type slide opened, whizzing visitors all the way from top to bottom.

contemporary art by non-established artists. Picasso's *Guernica* was on display here in 1939.

DOCKLANDS

London's docks, made derelict by heavy World War II bombing and rendered obsolete by new container ports to the east, were transformed in the 1990s. Their proximity to the financial institutions of the City made them an attractive location for developments such as **Canary Wharf ❶**, whose main tower, One Canada Square, is one of Britain's highest buildings, at 800ft (244 metres). Several national newspapers are based here.

It's worth taking a ride through the area on the Docklands Light Railway (from Bank to Greenwich) to see how property developers turned the place into an architect's adventure playground.

The **Museum of London Docklands ❼** (No 1 Warehouse, West India Quay; tel: 020-7001 9844; www.museum oflondon.org.uk; daily 10am–6pm; free)

recounts 2,000 years of history. It covers the entire history of London, from precious Roman jewellery to the story behind the London 2012 Cauldron, unveiled at the Olympics opening ceremony. There's also some surprising history, such as the gallery on London, Sugar and Slavery, revealing the complexities of the city's involvement in the slave trade.

Model at the Museum of London Docklands.

Canary Wharf.

SOUTH LONDON

South London's suburban 'villages' include Greenwich and Woolwich, with their distinguished naval and military heritage, historic Blackheath, leafy Dulwich and, in the southwest, vibrant Brixton.

Neighbourhoods and communities on the southern bank of the Thames offer parkland, museums, art galleries and great places to eat out. They are connected by a spaghetti of overground railway lines emanating from London Bridge and Charing Cross railway stations.

GREENWICH

A good way of getting to Greenwich is the time-honoured tradition of arriving at this maritime centre by water. Boats leave Westminster Pier daily from 10am (10.20am in winter) and take about 60 minutes. The quickest alternative is via the Docklands Light Railway.

Cutty Sark

Address: King William Walk; www.rmg.co.uk/cuttysark
Tel: 020-8312 6608
Opening Hrs: daily 10am–5pm
Transport: DLR Cutty Sark

Near the waterfront at Greenwich the **Cutty Sark** makes a handsome sight. The sailing ship from the great days of the 19th-century tea clippers, now a fascinating museum, has been beautifully restored (see box).

Built at a Dumbarton shipyard in 1869 the vessel was only expected to last about 30 years, but it has outlived

its builders and crews. It opened as a museum in 1957 and was a popular London icon until old age began to show. The world's last tea clipper, the ship was named after one of the witches in Robert Burns' poem, Tam O'Shanter: 'She wore a short petticoat, a "cutty sark"'.

National Maritime Museum

Address: Park Row; www.rmg.co.uk
Tel: 020-8858 4422
Opening Hrs: daily 10am–5pm

View from Greenwich Park.

Cutty Sark.

National Maritime Museum exhibit.

Entrance Fee: free
Transport: DLR Cutty Sark

Located in Greenwich Royal Park, the National Maritime Museum was opened in 1937, displays an unrivalled collection of maritime art and artefacts, reflecting on its maritime history. There are 10 galleries set around the Neptune Courtyard.

Ground Floor

The Explorers Gallery looks at the history of sea exploration, covering early explorers such as the Vikings, Magellan's first circumnavigation of the earth, and the Europeans who sailed to America. The Maritime London gallery explores the city's naval heritage. Star item is the uniform coat worn by Admiral Horatio Nelson on HMS *Victory* during the Battle of Trafalgar. The fatal bullet hole at the shoulder is clearly visible.

In the slick Sammy Ofer wing visitors will find the Voyagers gallery, which looks at Britons and the sea. Focussing on the personal stories of this maritime nation, items on display include a letter from Nelson to Emma Hamilton, a sword and scabbard that belonged to Captain Bligh, and a watch worn by a passenger on the *Titanic*. This new wing also houses hi-tech exhibitions and a café.

First Floor

The new Traders gallery explores Britain's maritime trade with Asia, looking at the mighty East India Company and the tea trade. Artefacts on display include journals kept by sailors and a portrait of Robert Knox

---

RESTORATION AND DEVASTATION

The *Cutty Sark* is the last ship of its kind in the world and for that reason the old tea clipper was made the subject of a £25-million restoration project in 2006. It was temporarily dismantled so that the hull and other valuable parts could be restored by a specialist team.

Then, in May 2007, midway through the project, there was a devastating early-morning fire at the site. The flames took two hours to contain. Although many sections of the ship, including the masts, were in safe storage at the time, the stern, considered too fragile to move, suffered acute damage, and about 50 percent of the hull's ironwork and timber were destroyed.

However, the Cutty Sark has been restored to her former glory, using only materials and techniques contemporary to the 19th century when she was built. She was officially reopened by the Queen in 2012. After the fire it was decided to raise the ship up 10ft (3 metres) on giant steel props, so you can now walk right beneath the iron hull, as well as exploring the cargo and lower decks, and trying out the cabins.

– the man said to have been the inspiration for Robinson Crusoe.

The Atlantic Worlds gallery deals with issues of trade and slavery, looking at the movement of people, goods and ideas across the Atlantic between the 17th and 19th centuries.

Second Floor

The Navigators gallery looks at how maps were developed, the use of scientific instruments in sea voyages, underwater exploration, and the discovery of the polar regions. There are also interactive galleries aimed at children, one with a simulator allowing visitors to take the helm of a ship and steer it into port.

The Queen's House

Completed in 1637, the Queen's House, showcasing the museum's art collections, was designed as a summer palace for Queen Anne of Denmark, the wife of James I. Designed by Inigo Jones, it was England's first classical Renaissance building. It reopened in 2016 after extensive renovation, and celebrated its 400th anniversary the same year.

Royal Observatory

Address: Greenwich Park, Blackheath Avenue, www.rmg.co.uk
Tel: 020-8858 4422
Opening Hrs: daily 10am–5pm, summer until 6pm
Entrance Fee: free; charge for Flamsteed House and Meridian Courtyard
Transport: DLR Greenwich

It's a steep climb through the park – but worth it – to the **Royal Observatory**. Greenwich Mean Time was established here in 1884, and the observatory has Britain's largest refracting telescope. A brass rule on the ground marks the line between the Eastern and Western hemispheres.

Flamsteed House, designed by Sir Christopher Wren (himself a keen astronomer), contains exhibits tracing the history of astronomy from its earliest origins in the ancient civilisations of Sumeria and Egypt. Valuable items on display include a Chinese sundial and a lodestone, an ore used for magnetising compass needles.

The pièce de résistance is a complete collection of John Harrison's ornate sea clocks, designed to remain

TIP

An alternative way to reach central London from Greenwich is to walk through a foot tunnel under the Thames and board a Docklands Light Railway train at Island Gardens. The 1,217ft (365-metre) -long tunnel, built in 1897–1902, enabled local workers to reach the West India Docks on the north bank of the river.

Looking across to Canary Wharf from the Greenwich foot tunnel.

accurate through the heat and cold, humidity and constant motion experienced on a ship at sea. They allowed mariners to determine their position east or west – an achievement chronicled in Dava Sobel's 1995 non-fiction bestseller Longitude.

A short distance from the main complex is the state-of-the-art **Peter Harrison Planetarium** (tel: 020-8312 6608; times of shows vary). It includes interactive exhibits and an education centre, and offers a variety of shows.

Old Royal Naval College

Address: 2 Cutty Sark Gardens, www.ornc.org
Tel: 020-8269 4747
Opening Hrs: college daily 10am–5pm; grounds daily 8am–11pm
Entrance Fee: free
Transport: DLR Greenwich

The Old Royal Naval College begun by Sir Christopher Wren in 1696 was built in two halves to preserve the view from Queen's House to the river. Originally a royal palace, it was given over to the training of naval officers in 1873. The chapel, where regular Sunday services are held, is full of decorative touches, and the ceiling of the Painted Hall, originally a sailors' dining room, displays a celebrated painting of William and Mary (who reigned 1689–1702) handing Liberty and Peace to Europe.

In 2006, during routine maintenance work, Tudor brickwork was unearthed in the grounds. Subsequent excavations revealed the remains of the palace chapel and vestry. The Discover Greenwich visitor centre has exhibitions, a shop and brewery café.

Greenwich centre

The heart of Greenwich lies just to the west of the park. The town centre has interesting restaurants and shops, as well as **Greenwich Market** around Greenwich Church Street (see page 242). On the same street is **St Alfege's Church**, built in 1712–18 by Nicholas Hawksmoor to replace an earlier church in which Henry VIII had been baptised. It was restored in 1952 after being badly bombed during World War II.

In an elegant period house is the **Fan Museum** (12 Croom's Hill; tel: 020-8305 1441; www.thefanmuseum. org.uk; Tue–Sat 11am–5pm, Sun noon–5pm) displaying an unusual

The Old Royal Naval College.

The Painted Hall at the Old Royal Naval College.

collection of hand-held fans from the worlds of fashion and the stage.

WOOLWICH ⑫

River trips continue downriver from Greenwich, sweeping back up the eastern side of the Isle of Dogs to **Blackwall Reach**, around The O2, an exhibition arena built for the year 2000, and once known as the Millennium Dome (www.theo2.co.uk). It is now a venue hosting everything from comedy and music gigs to ballet and the tennis ATP World Tour Finals. This is also where the Emirates Air Line departs, London's only cable car (www.tfl.gov.uk). As it climbs high above the river you get fabulous views of the sweep of the Thames and beyond to the new Olympic Park.

THAMES BARRIER

Address: 1 Unity Way;
www.environment agency.gov.uk
Tel: 020-8305 4188
Opening Hrs: Thu–Sun 10.30am–5pm
Entrance Fee: charge for information centre

Beyond The O2 is the massive **Thames Barrier**, which protects 45 sq miles (117 sq km) of London from the very real danger of flooding. In 1953, 300 people died in floods and the threat of tidal surges remains. The giant gates of the £435 million barrier, finished in 1982, can rise to 60ft (21 metres) high. The barrier has been closed 119 times in defence since its completion, and is raised once a month for tests (phone for times). You can reach the visitor centre on the south side by boat or bus from Greenwich.

Beyond is Woolwich, once the Royal Navy's dockyards and arsenal. The main attraction at the Royal Arsenal is **Firepower** (tel: 020-8855 7755; www.firepower.org.uk; Tue–Sat 10am–5pm), also known as the Royal Artillery Museum.

The centrepiece of this military museum is the ground-shaking 'Field of Fire', which puts viewers in the midst of battle. Bombs and shells whizz overhead, guns roar and smoke fills the room. There is also a large two-level gunnery gallery which has an impressive display of artillery and 'have a go' simulator.

TIP

There are excellent views of the Thames Barrier from a small urban park on the northern bank of the river. Thames Barrier Park on North Woolwich Road has a visitor café, a children's playground and paths lined with shrubs and flowers. Transport: Pontoon Dock DLR.

The Thames Barrier.

Horniman Museum.

Restaurants in Brixton Village.

BLACKHEATH ⑬

A few miles south of Greenwich is **Blackheath**, one of London's neat middle-class villages. The windy heath is where Henry V was welcomed home after beating the French at Agincourt in 1415. Overlooking the heath is the Paragon, a crescent of colonnaded houses. **St Michael's Church** (1829) has a severely tapering spire known as 'the needle of Kent.'

DULWICH ⑭

With leafy streets, elegant houses and a spacious park, Dulwich is an oasis of calm. It is largely the creation of one man, Edward Alleyn, an Elizabethan actor-manager who bought land in the area in 1605 and established an estate to administer a chapel, almshouses and a school for the sons of the poor.

Today, the estate has more than 15,000 homes, Dulwich College, Alleyn's School and James Allen's Girls' School.

Dulwich Picture Gallery

Address: Gallery Road;
www.dulwichpicturegallery.org.uk
Tel: 020-8693 5254
Opening Hrs: Tue–Sun 10am–5pm
Transport: mainline train from Victoria to West Dulwich or London Bridge to North Dulwich

Dulwich College, which schooled the writers P.G. Wodehouse and Raymond Chandler, spawned the **Dulwich Picture Gallery** by combining Edward Alleyn's collection with a bequest of paintings intended for a Polish National Gallery but diverted when the King of Poland was forced to abdicate.

The magnificent building, designed by Sir John Soane, opened in 1811 as the country's first major public art gallery. It contains 300 works by Rembrandt, Rubens, Van Dyck, Gainsborough and Murillo. A highlight is seven paintings by Poussin, including *The Roman Road*.

Horniman Museum

Address: 100 London Road;
www.horniman.ac.uk
Tel: 020-8699 1872
Opening Hrs: daily 10.30am–5.30pm
Entrance Fee: free

Transport: mainline train from London Bridge to Forest Hill

A mile to the east of the gallery is the **Horniman Museum**, one of south London's unsung treasures. Combining rich collections of ethnography and natural history, it was founded in 1901 by a wealthy tea merchant, Frederick Horniman, and is set in 16 acres (6.5 hectares) of parkland.

Highlights include a spectacular collection of African masks, bronze plaques from Benin, a large aquarium (charge) and a reptiles area. There are also over 7,000 unusual and historical musical instruments.

BRIXTON ⑮

It's not the architecture but the people who give **Brixton** its character. The population is around 60 percent white, and the balance includes Vietnamese, Chinese, Africans and Caribbeans. Its laid-back attitude to recreational drugs gets it a bad press, but the area has been steadily gentrified, and attracts plenty of affluent young professionals.

Brixton Market (Mon–Sat 8am–6pm, Wed until 3pm), running from Electric Avenue to Brixton Station Road, mixes Caribbean produce with fruit, vegetables and fish, plus stalls of second-hand clothes, music and junk. Brixton Village Market in Coldharbour Lane, not so long ago a rundown arcade, is the new culinary and cultural hub of Brixton, with vintage shops, boutiques, live music and lots of great places to eat. It's open late Thursday and Fridays and gets very busy, with a real community buzz.

Nightlife is lively here too. The five-screen **Ritzy** cinema in Coldharbour Lane is popular (the area was focal point of street parties following the death of David Bowie, who was born there), as are edgy dance clubs such as **Electric Brixton** (1 Town Hall Parade), and DJ bars/clubs such as **Dogstar** (389 Coldharbour Lane).

Lively restaurants and bars line the high street of nearby Clapham.

THE SOUTHEAST

The National Trust-owned **Red House** (Red House Lane; tel: 020-8304 9878; www.nationaltrust.org.uk/red-house; Mar–mid-Nov Wed–Sun 11am–5pm; book a guided tour if you wish to visit 11am–1pm, unguided from 1.30pm) is the only house commissioned by William Morris and is a temple to the Arts and Crafts movement. Built in 1859 by his friend Philip Webb, it contains furniture by Morris and Webb, and paintings and stained glass by Burne-Jones. Morris lived here for five years and the house was central to the lives of many of the Pre-Raphaelites. Trains depart from Charing Cross to Bexleyheath.

Eltham Palace (off Court Road; tel: 020-8294 2548; www.english-heritage.org.uk; Apr–Oct Mon–Wed, Sun 10am–5pm, Nov–Mar check website for opening times) is a stunning Art Deco mansion. It was built in the 1930s for the Courtaulds, onto the existing Great Hall of the medieval palace (built for Edward IV in the 1470s). The lavish rooms include a bathroom with gold-plated taps, and a centrally heated area for the Courtaulds' pet ring-tailed lemur. After a major refurbishment, five new rooms opened in 2015. Trains run from London Bridge to Eltham and Mottingham stations.

Entrance hall of Eltham Palace.

Winchester Cathedral.

DAY TRIPS

Within striking distance of the capital is a vast range of places to visit, from castles to country houses, from theme parks to seaside resorts. Bath, Oxford, Cambridge and Canterbury are within reach, too.

The roads around the capital are as busy as any European city's and, unless you are following a complex itinerary, it is best to travel by train or coach. For directions on how to reach places in this chapter, see page 260.

WINDSOR

Just 25 miles (40km) from central London is **Windsor Castle ❶** (tel: 01753-831118; www.royalcollection.org. uk; daily Mar–Oct 9.45am–5.15pm, Nov–Feb 9.45am–4.15pm, last admission one hour and 15 minutes before closing), still a favourite residence of the Royal Family. William the Conqueror began fortification here in 1066, immediately after defeating King Harold at the Battle of Hastings. There are temporary exhibitions also.

The present stone castle was started 100 years later by Henry II. Queen Victoria had a special love for Windsor and is buried, along with her husband, Albert, at Frogmore (www.royal.gov.uk/TheRoyalResidences/ Frogmore/History.aspx; limited opening times), a former royal residence, set among sweeping lawns and exotic trees, about a mile (1.6km) away.

Though overshadowed by its vast castle, Windsor is a pleasant town, with lovely walks among deer and ancient trees in Windsor Great Park, which spreads south from the castle, and along the River Thames.

A great draw for children is **Legoland Windsor ❷** (2 miles/3km from the town centre on the B3022 Bracknell/Ascot road; tel: 0871-222 2001; www.legoland.co.uk; daily mid Mar–Oct, closed selected weekdays in Apr, May, Sept and Oct). This theme park is based on the children's building blocks – in this case, millions of them, creating famous characters and landmarks. Its 150 acres (60 hectares)

Main Attractions
Windsor Castle
Blenheim Palace
Canterbury
Brighton
Bath
Cambridge
Oxford
Stratford-upon-Avon

Map
Page 248

Changing the Guard, Windsor Castle.

Harry Potter fans young and old will love the **Warner Bros. Studio Tour** (www.wbstudiotour.co.uk; advance booking essential). Here you can discover the magic behind the film franchise by exploring the sets and a fascinating collection of props and costumes. It's located 20 miles northwest of London near Watford; the nearest station is Watford Junction where a shuttle bus will take you to the tour.

of wooded landscape also has rides for all age groups, ranging from roller-coasters for teenagers to gentle jaunts for toddlers.

More sedate, but also very popular with children, is **Bekonscot Model Village** and **Railway** (tel: 01494-672919; www.bekonscot.co.uk; Mar–Oct daily 10am–5pm), near Beaconsfield, just north of the M40 (junction 2). This delightful attraction, rich in detail, has been expanding since 1929.

Six miles east of Windsor, on the other side of the river, is **Runnymede** (tel: 01784-432891; www.nationaltrust.org.uk/runnymede; dawn–dusk; charge for car park). This riverside meadow is where King John signed the Magna Carta in 1215.

GREAT HOUSES AND GARDENS

The largest private house in England, **Blenheim Palace** ❸ (tel: 0800-849 6500/01993-810530; www.blenheimpalace.com; mid-Feb–Oct daily 10.30am–4.45pm, Nov–early Dec Wed–Sun only) is just outside the Oxfordshire village of Woodstock (8 miles/13km north of Oxford on the A44 Evesham Road).

The palace was built by John Vanbrugh for the first Duke of Marlborough as a reward for his victory over the French at the Battle of Blenheim (1704). Winston Churchill was born here in 1874. He is buried in the church at nearby Bladon, on the edge of the Blenheim estate.

One of the country's most popular gardens is in Kent. **Sissinghurst Castle** ❹ (tel: 01580-710701; www.nationaltrust.org.uk; mid-Mar–Oct daily 11am–5pm) has the famous garden created in the 1930s by the English aristocrats Vita Sackville-West and her husband, Harold Nicolson.

Winston Churchill's country home at **Chartwell** ❺ (tel: 01732-868381; www.nationaltrust.org.uk/chartwell; Mar–Oct daily 11am–5pm; entry by timed ticket) at Westerham, close

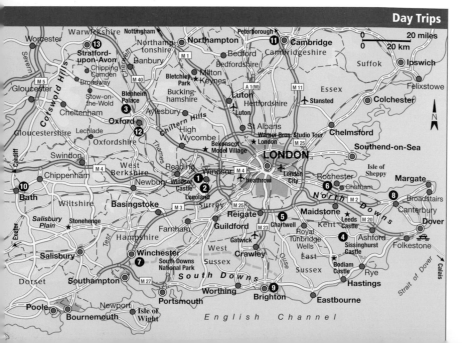

Day Trips

Canterbury Cathedral.

to the M25, has a water garden, rose garden and stunning views, and you can visit Churchill's studio.

Cathedrals and Dickens

Rochester ❻ has a lovely Norman cathedral, and its huge castle, a gaunt ruin, stands brooding over the River Medway, 30 miles (48km) east of London. For many years the town was home to Charles Dickens, and in nearby Chatham is **Dickens World** (tel: 01634-890421; www.dickensworld. co.uk; daily 10am–5.30pm, last tour 3.30pm), with 90-minute guided interactive tours through a re crea tion of Victorian London complete with Dickensian characters and an atmospheric boat ride.

Winchester ❼, a refined country town 66 miles (106km) southwest of London, was the capital of England in Saxon times. Its cathedral has a fine English Perpendicular interior.

 is also famous for its cathedral, where Thomas à Becket was martyred in 1170.

SEASIDE EXCURSION

Brighton ❾, 59 miles (95km) south of London, is a perennially popular spot. The old-fashioned pedestrianised streets known as The Lanes are a maze of antiques shops, book-sellers and souvenir stores, and much of the enjoyment to be had is in wandering. The jewel of Brighton is the exotic **Royal Pavilion** (tel: 0300-029 0900; http:// brightonmuseums.org.uk/royalpavilion;

Blenheim Palace, one of England's finest stately homes, was built in the early 18th century by John Vanbrugh and is the birthplace of Winston Churchill.

The Bridge of Sighs, Hertford College, Oxford.

Brighton beach and pier.

is a Georgian masterpiece and well worth a visit. Although 116 miles (187km) from London, it can be reached in 80 minutes by fast train from Paddington. At its elegant heart are the impressive **Roman Baths** (tel: 01225-477785; www.romanbaths. co.uk; daily Jan–Feb and Nov–Dec 9.30am–6pm, July–Aug 9am–10pm, Mar–June and Sept–Oct 9am–6pm; last admission one hour before closing) to which has been added a new complex utilising the mineral-rich, soothing hot springs (see tip).

The adjacent Pump Room was built in the 1790s as an elegant antechamber to the baths where visitors could sample the water, promenade and listen to musical entertainment. Today it is a restaurant and a lovely spot to have lunch or tea. You can still try the spa water, too.

Other architectural highlights of the city include the sweeping **Royal Crescent, Queen Square**, the Circus, the **Assembly Rooms** (which contain an excellent Museum of Costume) and pretty **Pulteney Bridge**, which is lined, like the Ponte Vecchio in Florence, with tiny shops.

daily Apr–Sept 9.30am–5.45pm, Oct–Mar 10am–5.15pm; last admission 45 minutes before closing), built in the architectural style of Mughal India by Henry Holland and John Nash for the Prince Regent at the end of the 18th century. The brilliant oriental interiors are decorated with golden dragons, chinoiserie, burnished palms and coloured glass. There is an ice rink in the grounds in winter.

ROMAN BATH

Bath ⑩, with its beautifully integrated crescents, squares and terraces,

UNIVERSITY TOWNS

Within easy reach of the capital are the UK's finest university towns, each of which offers tours around the historic colleges, a pleasant city centre and that quintessentially Oxbridge pastime, punting on the river Cam or Isis.

Cambridge ⓫, 61 miles (98km) from London is compact and best explored on foot. It gained its first college, Peterhouse, in 1284, but undoubtedly the finest of all the college buildings is **King's College Chapel**, which boasts magnificent fan vaulting, 16th-century stained-glass windows and Rubens' painting *Adoration of the Magi*.

The college is also famous for the King's College Choir, whose carol performance is broadcast live across the world on Christmas Eve.

Among the other historic colleges, Sidney Sussex College in Sidney Street is remarkable for being the last resting place of the head of Oliver Cromwell, leader of the Roundheads in the English Civil War (1642–49), who had briefly been a student here.

Like Cambridge, **Oxford** ⓬, 56 miles (90km) from London, is also easily explored on foot. There's something about the light in Oxford, reflecting off the ancient stones, that gives the town a unique allure. Indeed, it was regarded by the poet John Keats as 'the finest city in the world.'

Coach-loads of tourists come to visit, trooping respectfully round the university's three dozen colleges, a few of which have been centres of learning for up to seven centuries.

The best place to start a tour is Carfax Tower, at the crossroads of the four main streets: Cornmarket, High Street, Queen Street and St Aldate's. On St Aldate's is **Christ Church**, the grandest of Oxford's colleges, founded in 1525 by Cardinal Wolsey, Henry VIII's chancellor, on the site of an earlier priory.

For drivers, the Cotswolds to the west of Oxford beckon, their quaint showpiece villages seeming to grow out of the earth, so perfect is their relationship with the landscape. Tourism is intensive here, though it is possible to get off the beaten track with your own transport. Among the prettiest villages are Lechlade, Stow-on-the-Wold, Broadway and Chipping Campden.

TIP

You can sample Bath's spa facilities at Thermae Bath Spa, a luxurious and architecturally inspiring complex utilising two of the historic spa buildings. It offers an extensive range of pampering treatments to both men and women, and incorporates a rooftop pool with lovely views (tel: 01225-331234 or 0844-888 0844 from the UK; www.thermaebathspa.com).

Royal Crescent, Bath.

TIP

The RSC (Royal Shakespeare Company) presents a varied programme of Shakespeare and other plays at its venues in Stratford (the Royal Shakespeare Theatre and the Elizabethan-style Swan Theatre). Check its website for details: www.rsc.org.uk.

To the northeast of Oxford, at Bletchley around 40 miles (64km) away, is a place that was once the best-kept secret in Britain. **Bletchley Park** (tel: 01908-640404; www.bletchleypark.org.uk; daily Mar–Oct 9.30am–5pm, Nov–Feb 9.30am–4pm; last admission one hour before closing) was a rambling country estate that became the heart of Britain's code-breaking operations in World War II. It was here that Germany's seemingly impenetrable Enigma code was broken, and here that the genius Alan Turing worked to build the Bombe, the machine that helped to crack it. You can see operational rebuilds of the Bombe, and the Colossus, the first semi-programmable electronic computer, built by the Post Office engineer Tommy Flowers to break another German cipher. Many of the original huts are still standing. If travelling from London, you may reach Bletchley by direct train from Euston in 40 minutes.

SHAKESPEARE COUNTRY

**Stratford-upon-Avon **, birthplace of Shakespeare, is 40 miles (64km) north of Oxford. The Shakespeare Centre (tel: 01789-204016; www.shakespeare.org.uk) in Henley Street is the headquarters of The Shakespeare Birthplace Trust, which administers five properties associated with the Shakespeare family (each with its own opening times, check website for details; money-saving multi-house tickets available).

Shakespeare's Birthplace, adjacent to the centre, was the Shakespeare family home and business premises – his father was a glove maker, wool merchant and money-lender, and became mayor in 1568. Like the other period properties run by the Trust, it has been authentically restored and furnished.

Ann Hathaway's Cottage, the childhood home of Shakespeare's wife, is in Shottery, about 1 mile (1.6km) west of town. It is an idyllic timber-framed thatched cottage with a pretty garden rather than the working farmyard it would have been in Shakespeare's day. The other properties are Mary Arden's Farm, Hall's Croft, and Nash's House and New Place.

Trinity College fountain, Cambridge.

Ann Hathaway's Cottage, Stratford-upon-Avon.

INSIGHT GUIDES TRAVEL TIPS
LONDON

TRANSPORT

GETTING THERE AND GETTING AROUND

Note: London telephone numbers are shown as 8-digit numbers. If dialling from elsewhere in the UK, precede these with the code 020. If outside the UK, dial +44 20 and then the 8 digits.

GETTING THERE

By Air

London is served by two major international airports: Heathrow, 15 miles (24km) to the west (mainly scheduled flights); and Gatwick, 28 miles (45km) to the south (scheduled, charter and low-cost flights). The smaller airports of Stansted and Luton, both to the north of London, are used by many European low-cost airlines, but have some long-haul flights. The tiny London City Airport in Docklands is used by small aircraft connecting London with some European cities.

Heathrow Airport

Heathrow can be a daunting place at which to arrive, but it's straightforward to reach central London from. For further information on all airport services, see www.heathrowairport.com.
Train The fastest route is the **Heathrow Express** (www.heathrowexpress.com) to Paddington Station, which runs every 15 minutes and takes 15 minutes. Paddington connects with several Underground (Tube) lines. The fare is £22 single (£36 return) – it is an expensive journey although you can get cheaper tickets if you book in advance online. A cheaper option is the 25-minute **Heathrow Connect** service (www.heathrowconnect.com), which stops at several stations en route to Paddington, and costs £10.20.
Underground The cheapest, albeit slowest, way of reaching central London and most parts of the city is the Underground. The airport's terminals are on the Piccadilly Line, which reaches the West End in around 50 minutes. It goes directly to Kensington, Park Lane (Hyde Park Corner), Piccadilly, Covent Garden and King's Cross, and operates from 5am (6am on Sunday) until 12.30am daily. A single fare to central London will cost £5.50 at peak times; keep your ticket, as you need it to exit the station. There are four terminals (T1 closed in 2015): Heathrow Terminals 2 and 3 all connect to the same Tube station, but there are separate ones for T4 and T5.
Bus National Express runs coaches from Heathrow to Victoria Coach Station; the journey takes between 45 and 80 minutes, depending on traffic, and the single fare is £6. The bus station is at Terminals 1, 2 and 3;

from Terminals 4 and 5, take the free Heathrow Connect train to the bus station. For information, tel: 0871-781 8178; www.nationalexpress.com
Taxis Heathrow is well-served by taxis. A ride into town in a London 'black cab' will cost £45–85 (plus small tip), depending on destination and traffic.
Car Hire Heathrow offices of major car rental firms are:
Alamo, tel: 0800-028 2390; www.alamo.co.uk
Avis, tel: 0808-284 0014; www.avis.co.uk
Budget, tel: 0808-284 4444; www.budget.co.uk
Hertz, tel: 020-7365 3369; www.hertz.co.uk

Gatwick Airport

Gatwick airport, 28 miles (45km) from the city centre, isn't on the Underground network, but trains

FLIGHT INFO

Heathrow Airport, tel: 0844-335 1801
Gatwick Airport, tel: 0844-892 0322
Luton Airport, tel: 01582-405 100
Stansted Airport, tel: 0844-335 1803
London City Airport, tel: 020-7646 0088

COACH CONNECTIONS

National Express coach (long-distance bus) services connect Heathrow, Gatwick, Stansted and Luton airports with one another and with Victoria coach station. There are also direct bus services from all the main airports and destinations around Britain. For details and bookings, tel: 0871-781 8181, www.national express.com.

and buses run to and from Victoria rail and coach stations. For further information, see www.gatwick airport.com.

The Gatwick Express train leaves every 15 minutes from 3.30am to 12.35am; it takes 30 minutes and for a single journey costs £17.70 online or £19.90 from the ticket office. Children under five travel free; children aged 5–15 travel for half the adult fare. For more details tel: 0845-850 1530 or see www.gatwickexpress.com. Passengers can also use their Oyster card or contactless payment card between the airport and London. You can buy Oyster cards at the airport.

Southern Railway also run services from Gatwick to Victoria, with stops en route: journey time is 30–40 minutes, and the fare £14.40 (online advance fares cheaper; www.southernrailway.com)

EasyBus (www.easybus.co.uk) run services from Gatwick to West London (fares are cheaper the earlier tickets are booked). National Express bus services (tel: 0871-781 8181) operate the 32-mile (51km) journey between Heathrow and Gatwick (£25 single), taking between 60 and 90 minutes.
Car Hire from Gatwick:
Alamo, tel: 0870-400 4562; www.alamo.co.uk
Avis, tel: 0844-544 6007; www.avis.co.uk
Enterprise, tel: 0870-350 3000; www.enterprise.com.
Hertz, tel: 0843-309 3099; www.hertz.co.uk

Luton Airport

Luton is linked by First Capital Connect rail services with London St Pancras; some trains continue to Gatwick via Blackfriars. There is a

shuttle bus between the airport and Luton train station. The journey to St Pancras takes about 40 minutes, and trains run every 7–15 minutes. Green Line buses (route 757) run to Victoria in London, and take about 90 minutes (tel: 0344-801 7261, www.greenline.co.uk).

Stansted Airport

Stansted Express trains run to Liverpool Street Station in London every 15 minutes; journey time is 45 minutes, and a single ticket is £19 (online; www.stanstedexpress. com). Buses run from Stansted to several destinations in London, notably the A50 bus direct to Victoria. It runs every 30 minutes, and tickets cost £12 (cheaper with advanced online booking; www.nationalexpress.com).

London City Airport

London City Airport is mainly used by business travellers. The airport has its own station on the Docklands Light Railway (DLR), which connects with the Underground network at Bank station. For airport and flight enquiries, tel: 020-7646 0088; www.londoncityairport.com.

By Channel Tunnel

The London terminus for **Eurostar** passenger trains from Paris and Brussels is London St Pancras International (King's Cross). Journey times are about 2 hours 15 minutes from Paris, or 1 hour 50 minutes from Brussels. For information and reservations, tel: 03432-186186 (UK) or 00 44 1233 617575 (from outside the UK), or check www.eurostar.com.

Vehicles are also carried by **Le Shuttle** trains through the tunnel between Folkestone in Kent and

Calais in France. There are two to four departures each hour, and the trip takes 35 minutes. Bookings are not essential, but advisable at peak times. Fares vary according to the time of travel: late night or early morning crossings are cheaper and there are often cheap offers. Taking a car (with any number of passengers) through the tunnel costs from about £120 return, depending on availability. For information and reservations, tel: 08443-353535 (UK), or see www.eurotunnel.com.

By Ferry

Ferries operate between many British and Continental ports. Calais–Dover is the shortest crossing (75–90 minutes). Some of the main companies are:
Brittany Ferries, tel: 0330-159 7000 (UK), www.brittany-ferries. co.uk, Sail from Portsmouth to Caen, Le Havre, Cherbourg or St-Malo, Poole–Cherbourg and Plymouth–Roscoff.
Norfolk Line, tel: 08/1-574 7235 (UK), www.norfolkline.com. Dover–Dunkirk, Dover–Calais
P&O Ferries, tel: 0800-130 0030, www.poferries.com. Dover–Calais.
SeaFrance, tel: 0844-493 0651 (UK), www.seafrance.co.uk. Frequent sailings from Dover to Calais.

GETTING AROUND

Public Transport

The Tube

The Underground (known as the Tube) is the quickest way across town, but is often very busy. In rush hours (8am–9.30am and 5–7pm) every station is packed with commuters. Trains run from

TRANSPORT

A – Z

Docklands Light Railway.

5.30am to around midnight. If you're heading for the end of a line, or on Sunday, the last train may leave closer to 11pm.

Make sure you have a valid ticket and keep hold of it after you have passed through the electronic barrier – you will need it to exit at your destination. If you have an Oyster card (see page 259), be sure to touch in on entry and on exit, or you will be charged the maximum fare for the line. You can also use a contactless debit or credit card in the same way, and the same price for a single fare, as an Oyster card. Stations are divided into one of nine zones, spreading out from the centre; the minimum adult fare for a single ticket in zones 1–2 is £4.70, but much less with an Oyster card. A single ticket from Heathrow to the centre will cost £6 (regardless of time of day), and £5.10 with an Oyster card at peak time (6.30–9.30am), and £3.10 off peak.

It is illegal to smoke anywhere on the London transport system. You can print out itineraries from www.tfl.gov.uk.

Docklands Light Railway

Known as the DLR, this is a fully automated railway that runs through redeveloped areas of east London and to Greenwich, and connects with the Tube net-

work at Bank, Tower Gateway, Stratford and a few other stations. Tickets and fares are the same as the Tube.

Buses

Bus routes run throughout the city day and night. You cannot pay cash on the bus and and there are no longer any single-tickets for sale. Single fares cost £1.50 for

Oyster and contactless card users, or use a Travelcard or one day bus pass.

A new model of Routemaster double decker buses replaced the old hop-on hop-off buses in 2012, with a few sleek modifications from the original from 50 years ago. By 2016 more than 800 Routemasters operate on around 20 routes throughout the city.

Several bus routes run 24 hours a day, and on others Night Buses (identified by an N before the number) run about every 30 minutes from midnight to 6am. Most Night Bus routes run through Trafalgar Square. A full bus route map is available from London's six Travel Information Centres.

Taxis

London's **taxis** ('black cabs') are licensed and display the regulated charges on a meter. They can be hailed in the street (an orange roof-light is displayed when they are free) or you will find them at railways stations, airports

RAILWAY STATION TERMINALS

Britain's rail services are run by a variety of private companies. These are the principal mainline stations, with the areas they serve:

Charing Cross Station. Services to south London and southeast England: Canterbury, Folkestone, Hastings, Dover Priory.

Euston Station. Services to northwest London and beyond to Birmingham and the northwest: Liverpool, Manchester, Glasgow.

King's Cross Station. Services to north London and beyond to the northeast: Leeds, York, Newcastle, Edinburgh and Aberdeen.

St Pancras Station. Points not quite so far north, such as Nottingham, Derby and Sheffield, plus the Eurostar terminal for trains to and from Paris and Brussels.

Liverpool Street Station and **Fenchurch Street**. To east and northeast London, Cambridge and East Anglia.

Paddington Station. Services to west London and to Oxford, Bath, Bristol, the west, and South Wales.

Victoria Station. Services to south London and southeast England, including Gatwick airport, Brighton, Newhaven and Dover.

Waterloo Station. To southwest London, Southampton, and southern England as far as Exeter, including Richmond, Windsor and Ascot.

Other terminals, such as **Marylebone, London Bridge, Cannon Street** and **Blackfriars**, are mainly commuter stations, used for destinations around London. For information on **train times**, tel: 03457-484 950.

and taxi ranks. You can book a taxi in advance at www.tfl.gov.uk (comments and complaints can be registered here too), or by using the smart phone app Hailo.

Minicabs are cheaper than black cabs, but can only be hired by telephoning for one, as they're not allowed to pick up passengers on the street. Book only licensed cabs and do not use any of the unlicensed cabs that tout for business on the street late at night in central London. Check the price before you travel. To receive the telephone numbers of the two nearest minicabs and one black cab number, text CAB to 60835 from your smartphone (charge applies).

Cable Car

The newest addition to London's public transport network is the Emirates Air Line, a cable car which runs between North Greenwich (near the O2) and the Royal Docks. It's a great way to get fabulous views of east London, including the new Olympic park, and the sweep of the Thames as it heads out to sea. Cash fares are £4.50 for single, or you can use your Oyster card (cheaper). For more information, check www.tfl.gov.uk.

Coaches

Coach (long-distance bus) travel is generally cheaper than travelling by train. National Express

Licensed taxis are reliable.

Single tickets on London's transport networks are very expensive, so it's best to buy one of several multi-journey passes. Travelcards give unlimited travel on the Tube, buses, DLR and local rail services. London is divided into nine fare zones, with zones 1–2 covering all of central London. A one-day Travelcard for zones 1–4 costs £12.10 (child aged 11–15 £6). You can also buy seven-day Travelcards.

Oyster cards are smart cards that you charge up with however much you wish to pay,

runs services throughout the country from Victoria Coach Station on Buckingham Palace Road, tel: 0871-781 8181, www.nationalexpress.com.

Central London is a challenge to drive in, with its maze of one-way streets, poor signposting, impatient drivers, and pedestrians often crossing the road without looking for traffic. Drive on the left and observe speed limits (police detection cameras are common). Do not drive in bus lanes at the hours signposted. There are heavy penalties for driving after

then touch in on card readers at Tube and rail stations and on buses, so that an amount is deducted for each journey. They are cheaper than Travelcards if you only travel a few times daily, and the daily amount is capped at £6.50 for zones 1–2.

Oyster cards can be bought from Tube or DLR stations. Visitors can order them from www.visitbritainshop.com. Children aged 11–15 travel free on buses with an Oyster photocard, and under-11s travel free on the Tube and DLR at off-peak times, provided they are with an adult.

drinking over the limit. Drivers and passengers (front and back) must use seat belts.

Parking

Meters are slightly cheaper than car parks, but allow only for a stay of two to four hours. Wardens are strict. Some meter parking is free after 6.30pm each evening and after 1.30pm in many areas on Saturday afternoons and all day Sunday. However, always check the details given on the meter. Many areas of central London operate 'pay by phone' parking only, for which you will need a credit or debit card. Penalty tickets cost £80 or £130 and reclaiming your vehicle once it has been towed away can set you back over £200.

Congestion Charge

Cars driving into the clearly marked Congestion Zone in cen-

To arrange for a licensed black cab by phone, call 07519-055 741.
Minicab Companies
Addison Lee
Tel: 0844-800 6677
London Cabs
Tel: 020-7205 2677

tral London between 7am and 6pm Mon–Fri are filmed and their owners fined if a £11.50 payment is not made by 10pm the same day. You can pay at many small shops (newsagents, off licences/ liquor stores) or by telephoning 0343-222 2222. See www.tfl.gov. uk for details.

Car Hire

To rent a car you must be over 21 years old and have held a full driving licence for more than a year. The cost usually includes insurance and unlimited mileage.
Alamo, tel: 0800-028 2390
Avis, tel: 0808-284 0014
Budget, tel: 0808-284 4444
Hertz, tel: 0843-309 3049 (Marble Arch branch)

Trips out of London

This section details how to reach day-trip destinations.
Windsor
Either take the train from Paddington, journey time 30–50 minutes, or from Waterloo, journey time about 55 minutes. Green Line coaches (tel: 0844-801 7261; www.greenline.co.uk) depart from Victoria approx. every hour, journey time about 1 hour.

CYCLING

Cycling in London can be intimidating, but a bike is often the quickest means of getting around the city. Extensive information on cycling in London can be found on the Transport for London website, www.tfl.gov.uk, which has information on the Santander Cycles hire scheme (found all over the city). You can pay at docking stations with a credit or debit card. More information is available from the London Cycle Network (www.londoncyclenetwork.org. uk) and the London Cycling Campaign (www.lcc.org.uk).

Blenheim Palace
Trains from Paddington to Oxford, journey time 1 hour (see also under Oxford). Bus No. S3 from Oxford to Woodstock at approx. 30-minute intervals.
Sissinghurst Castle
Trains from Charing Cross to Staplehurst Station, journey time 1 hour. A bus link from Staplehurst to the castle runs Tue and Sun only from May (tel: 01580-710 700). Or take Arriva bus No.5 Maidstone–Hastings alighting at Sissinghurst.
By road, it is 2 miles (3km) northeast of Cranbrook, 1 mile (1.6km) east of Sissinghurst village.
Chartwell
Take a train from Victoria to Bromley South, and then take bus no.246. Alternatively, catch a train from from Charing Cross or London Bridge to Sevenoaks, then take bus no.238.
By road, it is 2 miles/3km south of Westerham, fork left off B2026.
Rochester
Trains from Victoria, journey time 40 minutes–1 hour; high-speed trains from St Pancras, journey time 35 minutes.
Winchester
Trains from Waterloo, journey time 1 hour.
National Express coaches from

Santander Cycles hire points can be found all over the city.

CYCLE HIRE

Velorution
tel: 020-7637 4004
www.velorution.com
18 Great Titchfield Street, W1.
London Bicycle Tour Company
tel: 020-7928 6838
www.londonbicycle.com

Victoria, journey approx. 90 minutes–2 hours.
Canterbury
Trains from Victoria and Charing Cross, journey time 90–105 minutes; high-speed trains from St Pancras, journey time 55 minutes.
National Express coaches depart from Victoria, journey time 110 minutes.
Brighton
Trains from Victoria or London Bridge, journey time 50 minutes–1 hour.
National Express coaches from Victoria stopping at Gatwick and elsewhere, journey time 2 hours.
Bath
Trains from Paddington, journey time 90 minutes.
National Express coaches from Victoria; direct-service journey time around 3 hours and 10 minutes.
Cambridge
Trains from King's Cross, journey time 50–80 minutes; a slower service runs from Liverpool Street Station.
National Express coaches from Victoria, journey time 2 hours.
Oxford
Trains from Paddington, journey time 60–100 minutes.
Two competing bus lines (Oxford Tube and Oxford Bus Company) run from Victoria bus station; they have services every 12 to 20 minutes.
Stratford-upon-Avon
Trains from Marylebone station, direct-service, journey time 2–3 hours.
National Express coaches from Victoria: three services a day, journey time around 3 hours.

A – Z

AN ALPHABETICAL SUMMARY OF PRACTICAL INFORMATION

A

Accommodation

London has everything from grand hotels of international renown to family-run hotels, guesthouses, self-catering flats and youth hostels with more modest prices. The choice of accommodation can make or break a visit to the capital.

However, there are bargains to be had. As with most things, you need to shop around. If a clean room and a hot breakfast are all you want, a small hotel may offer them for about a sixth of the price of a top hotel. The smaller hotels are often more friendly, making up in the welcome what they may lack in facilities. Just don't expect a lot of space – the cheaper rooms really are often cell-like. If you are a light sleeper, bear in mind that central London is quite noisy, both by day and night. Enquire about noise levels and remember that in small hotels, rooms at the rear, or on higher floors, are often quieter.

There are hotels everywhere in London, but some areas have more than others. The main concentrations tend to be around Victoria, Earl's Court/Kensington, the West End and Bayswater. There are some delightfully

old-fashioned hotels in Victoria, in most price brackets, and the streets close to Victoria Station are full of terraced bed-and-breakfast accommodation. There are also streets full of terraced (or rather town house, for this is Kensington) hotels in SW5 (Earl's Court) and SW7 (South Kensington), major centres for medium-range hotels of dependable comfort.

The West End is the third area and the best-known zone. You'll pay more for budget or moderate accommodation here than you will in SW1 or SW5. W1 hotels at the bottom end of the price range can be very humble. WC1 (Russell Square and Holborn) is a clever choice: it's central and has reasonable prices, and there is still some dignity, even romance, in Bloomsbury.

The area between Edgware Road, Bayswater Road, Paddington and Queensway, is full of hotels. It does have a few large, expensive hotels on its fringes, but has a greater concentration of moderate and budget accommodation. Quality and prices vary enormously but the area is convenient for the West End.

Budget Chains

Premier Inn is Britain's biggest budget hotel chain, with several outposts in central London,

including County Hall (by Westminster Bridge), St Pancras, Euston, Kensington, Southwark, Tower Bridge and Old Street. There are also branches close to Gatwick and Heathrow. They are clean, modern and cost between £80 and £100 per night. Central reservations: 0871 527 9222, www.premier inn.com

The **Travelodge** chain does a similar job at similar prices; book early for good deals: www. travelodge.co.uk. Other reputable chains include **Best Western** (tel: 0845-776 7676; www.best western.co.uk), Holiday Inn (tel: 0871-423 4896; www.holiday inn.com) and **Thistle** (tel: 0871-376 9099; www.thistle.com), which often have hotels in prime locations.

Booking Accommodation

Book ahead. London fills up with tourists in the summer months (May and September are also crowded because of conference traffic), and, conversely, busiest the rest of the year on weekdays with business visitors. If you arrive without a reservation, you can call **Visit London's** telephone accommodation booking service on 020-3320 2609 and book by credit card, or book online at www.visitlondon.com.

Youth Hostels

English Youth Hostels tend to be extremely basic but the price is low, especially if you book reasonably far in advance or for several nights; it will often include breakfast.

The **Youth Hostelling Association** (YHA) has six London locations, including St Paul's (36 Carter Lane, EC4V 5AB, tel: 0845-371 9012), St Pancras (Euston Road, NW1 2QE, tel: 0845-371 9344) and Earl's Court (38 Bolton Gardens, SW5 0AQ, tel: 0845-371 9114).

Accommodation prices for members are about £20–25; non-members pay slightly more. To join, visit www.yha.org.uk.

Bed and Breakfasts

Staying in a private home ensures that you meet at least one London family. The **London Bed & Breakfast Agency** specialises in such accommodation, with prices from £37–55 per person per night, based on double occupancy, or £50–90, based on single occupancy, depending on the area. Tel: 020-7586 2768; www.londonbb. com. Other bed and breakfast options include: **At Home in London** (70 Black Lion Lane, W6 9BE, tel: 020-8748 1943, www.athome inlondon.co.uk) and **London Home-to-Home** (42 Dahomey Road, London, SW16 6ND, tel: 020-8769 3500, www.london-hometohome.com)

Halls of Residence

University halls of residence offer some of the best value for money accommodation i n central London from mid-June to the end of September during college vacation. The **London School of Economics** (LSE) for example, has a number of residences that are centrally situated. Tel: 020-7955 7676; www. lsevacations.co.uk.

Admission Charges

Major state-owned museums in London are free of charge but a

Posing with police officers outside Buckingham Palace.

donation is much appreciated. You usually have to pay for special exhibitions. Museums and galleries which do charge usually offer reductions for families, children, students, pensioners and the unemployed. For some attractions, online booking is often cheaper.

B

Budgeting for a Trip

London is a very expensive city. You'll be lucky to find a conveniently located double room for less than £100 a night and prices soar to well over £400. Breakfast is often included in the price, but if not, a full English Breakfast will start at around £8 and a Continental breakfast at £5. Expect to pay from £30 to £55 each for a three-course dinner, including a modest wine, at a mid-range restaurant. Most cinema tickets cost £10–15, and a good seat for a West End musical is about £50. Taxis aren't cheap, especially at night, but neither is the Underground, with a short Tube journey costing from £4.50 if you buy single tick-

ets – check out the special passes available. For more information see page 259.

C

Children

For ideas on museums and other attractions suitable for children of various ages, see page 8.

Accommodation. Some hotels do not accept children under a certain age, so be sure to check when you book.

Restaurants and bars. Most restaurants accept well-behaved children, but only those that want to encourage families have children's menus and baby-changing facilities. Some pubs will allow children, with adults, although this will usually apply only in daytime hours, and maybe only certain areas. Publicans, like restaurateurs, reserve the right to refuse entry.

Public transport. Up to four children aged 11 or under can travel free on the Tube if accompanied by a ticket-holding adult. 11 to 15-year-olds can get unlimited free travel on buses, and child rates on the Tube, DLR and London Overground, providing they have a photo Oyster card (this can take up to two weeks to obtain). Alternatively, they can buy a special child's Oyster card with discounted journey prices.

Buses are free for all children under 16, but those over 10 years need an Oyster photocard if unaccompanied. Buses can take up to two unfolded pushchairs (buggies) at one time. They must be parked in a special area halfway down the bus. Any further pushchairs must be folded. Visit www.tfl.gov.uk.

Supplies. Infant formula and nappies (diapers) can be found in chemists (pharmacies), supermarkets and some general stores.

Hospitals. In a medical emergency, take your child to the Accident & Emergency department of the nearest hospital. If you require over-the-counter medications such as Calpol (liquid paracetamol) late at night, check the nearest Boots, which will have the address of the nearest late-night chemist posted on the door. Zafash Pharmacy (233 Old Brompton Rd, SW5; tel: 020-7373 2798) is open 24 hours a day.

Climate and Clothing

The climate in London is mild, with the warming effects of the city itself keeping off the worst of the cold in winter. Snow and temperatures below freezing are unusual, with January temperatures averaging 43°F/6°C. Consequently, if it does snow hard, London is unprepared. Temperatures in the summer months average 64°F/18°C, but they can soar, causing the city to become airlessly hot (air conditioning is not universal). Rainfall is unpredictable, and it's wise, even in summer, to keep a fold-up umbrella close by.

What to Wear

Between the stuffy Tube and often damp weather, it's best to dress in light layers. A cool, rainy day can turn beautiful unexpectedly and vice versa. In general, short sleeves and a jacket are recommended for summer and a warm coat and woollens for winter.

While a few of the traditional restaurants retain a dress code, smart casual is generally the norm for restaurants and theatres. In general, Londoners are quite style conscious but also practical; most getting around will be on foot or via public transport, so wearing comfortable shoes is wise.

Crime

Serious crime is low for a city of this size, but the Dickensian tradition of pickpocketing is alive and well. Hold on tightly to purses and handbags, do not put wallets in back pockets, and do not place handbags on the floor or the back of your chair in busy restaurants and pubs.

In a genuine emergency, dial 999 from any telephone (no cash required). Report routine thefts to a police station (address found under Police in a telephone directory). The threat of terrorism has led to an increase in police patrols, so don't hesitate to report any suspicious packages – and don't add to any fears by leaving unattended bags.

Customs Regulations

There are no official restrictions on the movement of goods within the European Union, provided those goods were purchased within the EU. However, British Customs have set the following personal use 'guide levels'.
Tobacco 3,800 cigarettes or 400 cigarillos or 200 cigars or 1kg tobacco.
Alcohol 10 litres spirits, 20 litres fortified wines, 90 litres wine, 110 litres beer.
Those entering from a non-EU state are subject to these limits: Tobacco 200 cigarettes or 100 cigarillos or 50 cigars or 250g of tobacco are permitted.
Alcohol 1 litre of spirits, 2 litres of fortified or sparkling wine, or 2 litres of table wine (an additional 2 litres of still wine is allowed if no spirits are bought).
£390-worth of other goods, such as perfume and sunglasses, are also permitted.
Animals Cats and dogs may enter Britain from EU countries providing they have the appropriate documentation. All unauthorised pets are placed in quarantine upon arrival at the owner's expense. For further details, log on to www.gov.uk/defra
The following are prohibited entry into the United Kingdom:
Plants and **perishable foods**, such as meats and meat products, eggs, fruit; some drugs (check with your doctor if you need to carry strong medication. You may need to carry a letter from them).
Firearms and ammunition (without special arrangement).
Obscene film or written material. There are no restrictions on the amount of currency you can bring into the country.

Disabled Access

Venues. Artsline (www.artsline. org.uk), London's information and advice service on disability

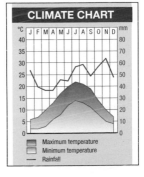

CLIMATE CHART

°C | J F M A M J J A S O N D | mm

Maximum temperature
Minimum temperature
Rainfall

TRANSPORT

A – Z

access to arts and entertainment events, provides detailed access information for venues across London, including theatres, cinemas, museums, arts centres, tourist attractions, comedy and music venues, and selected restaurants.

Advice. William Forrester is a museum lecturer, co-author of Access in London, a trained guide and wheelchair user. He offers tailor-made tours of London and Britain including well-known sights. He operates an advice and guiding service for anyone planning to visit the UK in a wheelchair. Tel: 01483-575 401. Email: wforrester@hotmail.co.uk

Toilets. Most attractions, hotels, restaurants, train stations (not underground stations) and shopping centres have accessible toilets. Britain has a system of keys to open many of the public toilets available for disabled people. You can get a list of these accessible toilets for £3.50, and a key for £4.50. Contact Disability Rights UK on 020-7250 8181; or visit the website (www.disability rightsuk.org).

Public transport. Wheelchair-friendly buses have been progressively introduced across the transport network; almost all are accessible via low-floor vehicles or retractable ramps. Tubes are more difficult as entry is mainly by steps; for exceptions, look for the stations' 'step-free access' symbol on the tube maps. The Jubilee Line has lifts. Ticket offices can provide a free leaflet on Access to the Underground or alternatively call 0343 222 1234 or visit https://tfl.gov.uk/transport-accessibility for help planning an accessible route.

River cruises. Step-free access is available from most major piers and newer boats have designated wheelchair spaces. Mobility-impaired groups can obtain information and advice by telephoning London River Services on 0343 222 1234.

E

Electricity

230 volts. Square, three-pin plugs are used and virtually all visitors will need to bring or buy adaptors if planning to plug in their own equipment.

Embassies & High Commissions

Australia Australia House, Strand, WC2B 4LA. Tel: 020-7379 4334
Canada Canada House, Trafalgar Square, SW1Y 5BJ. Tel: 020-7004 6000
India India House, Aldwych, WC2B 4NA. Tel: 020-7632 3070
Ireland 17 Grosvenor Place, SW1X 7HR. Tel: 020-7235 2171
Jamaica 1 Prince Consort Road, SW7 2BZ. Tel: 020-7823 9911
New Zealand 80 Haymarket, SW1Y 4TQ. Tel: 020-7930 8422
South Africa South Africa House, Trafalgar Square, WC2N 5DP. Tel: 020-7451 7299
United States 24 Grosvenor Square, W1K 6AH. Tel: 020-7499 9000.

Emergencies

Call 999 for all emergency services (no charge) and ask for fire, police or ambulance.

Entry Requirements

To enter Britain you will need a valid passport. Visas are not needed if you are from the USA, a Commonwealth citizen or an EU national (or from most other European or South American countries). Health certificates are not required unless you have arrived from Asia, Africa or South America. If you wish to stay for a protracted period or apply for work, contact the Border and Immigration Agency after checking the website www.ind.homeoffice.gov.uk. London's nearest Home Office Public Enquiry Office (PEO) is at Lunar House, 40 Wellesley Road, Croydon, CR9 2BY, tel: 0300-123 2241.

G

Gay and Lesbian

With Europe's largest gay and lesbian population, London has an abundance of bars, restaurants and clubs to cater for most tastes. Many of them will make space for one or more of London's free gay weekly magazines, *Boyz* and *QX*. Monthly magazines on sale at newsstands include *Gay Times*, *Diva* and *Attitude*.

GETTING TICKETS

The only way to get a ticket at face value is to buy it from the theatre box office. Most open 10am–mid-evening. You can pay by credit card over the phone for most theatres, or reserve seats three days in advance before paying. A ticket booth (TKTS) on the south side of Leicester Square offers unsold seats at half price or three-quarter price (plus booking fee) on the day of performance (Mon–Sat 10am–7pm, Sun 11am–4.30pm). You can also buy advanced tickets on their website www.officiallondontheatre.co.uk.

There are booking agents throughout London (and quite a few unofficial kiosks around Leicester Square), but beware: some charge high fees. It's sensible to ask what the face value of a ticket is before parting with your money. Two reputable agents are **Ticketmaster** at www.ticketmaster.co.uk and www.seetickets.com.

Ignore ticket touts unless you're prepared to pay several times a ticket's face value for sell-out performances.

Two established websites for meeting other gay people in London are www.gaydar.co.uk and the female version, www.gaydargirls.com. Other websites reflecting the gay scene include www.lgbtlondon.com and www.londonfriend.org.uk.

Useful telephone contacts for advice and counselling include **London Lesbian and Gay Switchboard** (tel: 0300-330 0630) and London Friend (7.30–10pm, tel: 020-7837 3337). **Pride in London** (Gay Pride) takes place in June.

H

Health & Medical Care

Newsstands abound, but free newspapers are also plentiful.

If you fall ill and are a national of the European Union, you are entitled to free emergency medical treatment for illnesses arising while in the UK. Many other countries also have reciprocal arrangements for free treatment. However, most visitors will be liable for medical and dental treatment so will have to pay for any non-emergency treatment. They should ensure they have adequate health insurance.

Major hospitals include Charing Cross Hospital (Fulham Palace Road, W6, tel: 020-3311 1234), St Mary's Hospital (Praed Street, W2, tel: 020-3312 6666), and St Thomas's (Westminster Bridge Road, SE1, tel: 020-7188 7188).

Emergency dental treatment is available on weekdays 9am–5pm (queuing begins at 8am; last patient accepted at 3pm) at Guy's Hospital, St Thomas Street, SE1, tel: 020-7188 7188.

Chemists (pharmacists). Boots is a large chain of pharmacies with branches throughout London that will make up prescriptions. The branch at 114 Queensway, W2 is open until 10pm daily, whilst Bliss Chemist at 5 Marble Arch is open until midnight daily.

Accidents: in the case of an emergency, dial 999.

L

Left Luggage

Most of the main railway stations have left luggage departments where you can leave your suitcases on a short-term basis, although all are very sensitive to potential terrorist bombs. Left luggage offices are generally open 24 hours a day, but at Heathrow they close at 11pm.

Lost Property

For all possessions lost on public transport or in taxis, contact Transport for London's central Lost Property (200 Baker Street, NW1 5RZ, tel: 0343-222 1234; www.tfl.gov.uk/lostproperty) Mon–Fri 8.30am–4pm, or fill in an enquiry form, available from any London Underground station or bus garage. It can take two to four days for items left on a Tube train or bus to reach the office and more than a week for items a taxi driver has handed in at a police station. It is therefore advisable to wait several days before visiting or phoning the office, which can search for your property while you are on the phone. It can also post your prop-

erty back to you for a fee. The office receives 600 items a day.

M

Maps

Insight Guides' *FlexiMap London* is laminated for durability and easy folding. For detailed exploration of the city centre and suburbs, the London A–Z books come in various formats. Free Tube maps are available at Underground stations. Map lovers should head for Stanford's flagship shop (12–14 Long Acre, WC2), one of the world's top map and guidebook stores.

Money

The pound sterling (GBP) is the currency. Each pound is made up of 100 pennies. Many large London stores will accept euros.

Most **banks** open Mon–Fri 9.30am–5pm (or even later) and Saturdays until midday. Major British banks tend to offer similar exchange rates; it's only worth shopping around if you have large amounts of money to change. There will be a charge for changing cash into another currency. The easiest way to get cash out is through a cash machine (ATM).

Some high street travel agents, such as Thomas Cook, operate **bureaux de change** at comparable rates. There are also private bureaux de change (some are open 24 hours) where rates can be very low and commissions high. Chequepoint (www.chequepoint.com) is a reputable chain with branches at 222 Earl's Court, 71 Gloucester Road, 2 Queensway and 550 Oxford Circus.

International **credit cards** are almost universally accepted. However, a few stores and restaurants do not accept them, so check for signs at the entrance first. Another option is a currency card, which you load up online from your bank account and then use to take out cash from an ATM, with low commission charges.

Tax refunds enable visitors from outside the European Union to reclaim the 20 percent value-added tax when spending over a certain amount. Stores can supply VAT refund forms which should be presented to Customs officials when leaving the country.

Money-saving Passes

Although national museums and galleries are free, most others have entrance charges. Energetic visitors will benefit from the London Pass, which allows free entry to several dozen attractions. Free travel on the Tube and buses is also included. At press time, prices ranged from £55 for a one-day pass to £121 for a six-day pass (children £37–84). For details tel: 020-7293 0972 or check www.london pass.com.

Launched in 2016, the Where Pass is a unique debit card that can be loaded with spending money, buying discounted tickets and accessing offers at attractions, restaurants and shops in a single currency transaction. It can also be used

across London's public transport system. Details at www.where passlondon.com.

Joining the Art Fund costs £62 a year and provides free admission to more than 200 museums, galleries and historic houses around the country, plus discounts on some exhibitions. Details on 0844-415 4100 or from www.artfund.org

N

Newspapers

Politically speaking, the *Daily Telegraph* and *The Times* are on the right of the political spectrum, *The Guardian* is on the left and *The Independent* has a liberal, international slant. To appeal to commuters, most are printed in a compact (tabloid) format rather than the traditional full-size broadsheet. On Sunday *The Observer* is the sister newspaper of *The Guardian*; likewise there are the *Sunday Times*, *Independent on Sunday* and *Sunday Telegraph*. The *Financial Times* is renowned for the clearest, most unslanted headlines in its general news pages – plus, of course, its financial coverage.

Among the mass-market tabloids, *The Sun* and *The Star* are traditionally on the right (and obsessed with royalty, soap operas and sex), as is the Express. The *Daily Mirror* and *Sunday Mirror* are on the left, as is the *Sunday People*. The right-wing *Daily Mail* and *Mail on Sunday* are considered slightly more up-market.

Editions of the free, London-only *Evening Standard* come out Mon–Fri mid-afternoon and are good for London news, cinema and theatre listings. The free tabloid *Metro* can be picked up at stations in the morning from Mon–Fri. Both of these contain useful but not comprehensive listings sections.

Listings magazines. Supreme in this field is the long-established free weekly Time Out.

Foreign newspapers and magazines can be found at many street newsstands, at mainline stations, and at these outlets:
A. Moroni & Son: 68 Old Compton Street, W1.
Compton News: 48 Old Compton Street, W1.
Selfridges: Oxford Street, W1.
Victoria Place Shopping Centre: Victoria Station, SW1.

O

Opening Hours

Most shops open Monday to Saturday between 9am and 10am and close around 5.30pm to 6pm. In commercial areas such as Oxford Street shops stay open until 8pm Monday to Saturday (until 9pm on Thursdays). On Sundays major shops are only allowed six hours of trading between 10am and 6pm. The large shopping centres such as Westfield Stratford and Westfield White City have longer opening hours during the week, and are open noon–6pm on Sundays.

For post office opening hours, see Postal Services.

For bank opening hours, see Money.

P

Police

Don't call the emergency number 999 unless there has been a serious crime or accident. For non-emergencies, the Metropolitan Police number is 101. If you can't find a policeman and it's not urgent, check http://content.met. police.uk for the location and number of your nearest local station. If your passport has been lost, you must also let your embassy know.

Postal Services

Post offices open Mon–Fri 9am–5pm and Sat 9am–noon.

Stamps are available from post offices and many other shops, usually newsagents, and from machines outside some post offices. There is a two-tier service within the UK: first class is supposed to reach a UK destination the next day, second class will take at least a day or two longer. London's main post office is at Trafalgar Square, behind the church of St Martin-in-the-Fields. It stays open until 6.30pm Mon–Fri.

The cost of sending a letter or parcel depends on weight as well as size. Queues tend to be long over the lunch period (1–2pm).

Postcodes

The first half of London postcodes indicates the general area (WC = West Central, SE = Southeast etc) and the second half, used only for mail, identifies the exact block. Here is a key to some of the more common codes:
W1 Mayfair, Marylebone, Soho; **W2** Bayswater; **W4** Chiswick; **W8** Kensington; **W11** Notting Hill; **WC1** Bloomsbury; **WC2** Covent Garden, Strand; **E1** Whitechapel; **EC1** Clerkenwell; **EC2** Bank, Barbican; **EC4** St Paul's, Blackfriars; **SW1** St James's, Belgravia; **SW3** Chelsea; **SW7** Knightsbridge, South Kensington; **SW19** Wimbledon; **SE1** Lambeth, Southwark; **SE10** Greenwich; **SE21** Dulwich; **N1** Hoxton, Islington; **N6** Highgate; **NW3** Hampstead.

Public Holidays

Compared to most European countries, the UK has few public holidays:
January New Year's Day (1st)
March/April Good Friday, Easter Monday
May May Day (first Monday of the month), Spring Bank Holiday (last Monday)
August Summer Bank Holiday (last Monday)
December Christmas Day (25th), Boxing Day (26th).

A British icon, sadly becoming less common.

Radio Stations

You can receive national stations as well as many targeted specifically at London:

Commercial Stations
Capital FM – 95.8FM, 24-hour pop music.
Classic FM – 100.9FM, 24-hour light classical music.
Choice FM – 96.9FM, soul music.
Heart – 106.2FM, classic rock.
Kiss FM – 100FM, 24-hour dance music.
LBC – 97.3FM, 24-hour chat, showbiz, opinion, news.
Smooth FM – 102.2FM, bland playlist of jazz, soul and blues and middle-of-the-road.
Virgin – 105.8FM, adult-oriented rock.

BBC Stations.
Radio 1 – 98.8FM, mainstream pop.
Radio 2 – 89.2FM, easy-listening music, chat shows.
Radio 3 – 91.3FM, 24-hour classical music, plus drama and serious talks.

Radio 4 – 93.5FM, heavyweight news, current affairs, plays.
Radio Five Live – 909MW, rolling news, sport.
BBC 6 Music – cutting-edge dedicated music channel (digital only)
BBC Radio London – 94.9FM, London-oriented music, chat and sports station.
BBC World Service – 648 kHz, international news.

S

Smoking

In July 2007 England imposed a ban on smoking in all enclosed public spaces, including pubs, clubs and bars (though not in outside beer gardens). This extends to railway platforms. E-cigarettes are also banned on public transport and many bars and restaurants.

Student Travellers

International students can obtain various discounts at attractions, on travel services (including Eurostar) and in some shops by showing a valid ISIC card. Visit www.isiccard.com for more details.

T

Telephones

Despite the ubiquity of mobile phones, London still has an adequate number of public kiosks and public phones in pubs. It is cheaper to use a public phone than one in your hotel as many hotels still make an outrageous charge for calls from your room.

British Telecom (BT) is the main telephone operating company. The smallest coin accepted is 10p, and the minimum cost for making a call is 60p. Most kiosks and private phones will also accept phone cards, which are widely available from post offices and newsagents in varying amounts between £5 and £20. Credit card phones can be found at major transport terminals and on busy streets.

Phoning Abroad

You can telephone abroad directly from any phone. Dial 00 followed by the international code for the country you want, and then the number. Some country codes: **Australia** (61); **Hong Kong** (852); **Ireland** (353); **New Zealand** (64); **Singapore** (65); **South Africa** (27); **US** and **Canada** (1).

If you are using a US credit phone card, first dial the company's access number as follows: **Sprint**, tel: 0800-890877 **MCI**, tel: 0800-279 5088 **AT&T**, tel: 0800-890 011

Useful Numbers

Emergency – police, fire, ambulance: 999
Operator (for difficulties in getting through): 100
International Operator: 155
Directory Enquiries (UK): For a free service (with a sponsored ad) phone 0800 118 3733, 118 500, 118 888 or 118 118. Charges are high if you ask to be connected directly.
International Directory Enquiries 118 505 or 118 866 or 118 899. Again, these can be expensive calls. Use www.thephonebook. bt.com for free.
Transport for London 24-hour information: 0343-222 1234
Rail information for all stations: 03457-484 950
Accommodation bookings: Visit London on 020-3320 2609

Television Stations

The BBC (British Broadcasting Corporation) is financed by compulsory annual television licences and is advertising-free. The independent channels (ITV1, Channel 4 and Channel Five) are funded by commercials.

In recent years the choice of channels has expanded expo-

nentially as cable, satellite and digital channels have joined the small number of terrestrial channels. The BBC has several digital channels, including the round-the-clock BBC News 24, the youth-oriented BBC3 and the arts-oriented BBC4. In 2012, analogue television transmissions were shut down, and even BBC1, BBC2 and the terrestrial commercial channels are now only available through digital technology. Other digital channels include ITV2, ITV3, ITV4, Film4 and more. All of the major UK independent channels have catch-up services available online: BBC iPlayer, 4OD, ITV Player and Demand 5.

Time

British Summer Time (one hour ahead of Greenwich Mean Time) operates from the last Sunday in March until the last Sunday in October. Greenwich Mean Time is 8 hours in front of Los Angeles, 5 hours in front of New York and Montreal, and 10 hours behind Sydney.

Tipping

Most hotels and many restaurants automatically add a 10–12 percent service charge to your bill. It's your right to deduct it if you are not happy with the service. If you pay by chip and PIN, the machine will often require you to add or decline to add a tip before you insert your PIN number, which feels rather cheeky when the waitress or waiter is standing in front of you. If a service charge has already been included in the bill, you shouldn't feel obliged to add anything extra. If you choose to leave a tip, pay this by cash as the waiting and kitchen staff are more likely to receive the full amount.

It is not customary to tip in pubs, cinemas, theatres or elevators, but you should tip sightseeing guides (about 10 percent) and hotel porters. It is also usual to tip

cab drivers if they've been particularly helpful or assisted with your bags.

Tour Operators

Bus Tours

A guided tour of London by bus is the best way for visitors to familiarise themselves with the city. All tours that are registered with the London Tourist Board use Blue Badge Guides, whose ranks number around 1,000.
The Big Bus Company, tel: 020-7808 6753; www.bigbustours. com. Open-top bus tours over a choice of two routes lasting 2.5 to 3.5 hours. You are free to hop on or hop off at any of the 70 stops. Buses run every 5–15 minutes. Tours have live commentary in English or recorded commentary in seven languages as well as English. Tickets are valid for 24 hours (sometimes they are valid for 48 hours in winter); buses operate 8.30am–8pm in the summer and until 6pm in the winter. Cost: £30 for adults and £12 for children.
Duck Tours use World War II amphibious vehicles which drive past famous London landmarks before taking to the water. It's expensive, but great for children. Departure is from County Hall. Tel: 020-7928 3132; www.london ducktours.co.uk
Evan Evans, tel: 020-7950 1777; www.evanevanstours.co. uk. A variety of tours giving a comprehensive introduction to the city, with emphasis on historic sites. Admittance to St Paul's Cathedral, the Royal Albert Hall and the Tower of London are part of some tours. Picks up from many hotels. Cost: £89 (£79 for children 3–16) for a full day.
Golden Tours, tel: 020-7630 2028; www.goldentours.com. Various tours of the city in air-conditioned coaches accompanied by guides who hold the coveted Blue Badge. The London Experience full-day tour takes in major sights such as the Tower and St Paul's,

and includes a London Eye ride and lunch. Cost: £104 (£94 for children).

The Original London Sightseeing Tour, tel: 020-8877 1722; www.theoriginaltour.com. A choice of three different tours in traditional red double-decker buses, some of which are open-top. The Original tour features live commentary in English; the other two have recorded commentary in a choice of seven languages. A unique feature is the recorded children's commentary – by kids for kids (suitable for ages 5–11). Tours run from 9am approximately every 15–20 minutes and passengers can hop on and off at any of the 90 stops. Tickets cost £30 for adults and £15 for children under 16, and are valid for 24 hours (often discounted in winter). There are departure points throughout central London. A free river cruise from Embankment is included in the price.

Boat Tours

Bateaux London, tel: 020-7695 1800; www.bateauxlondon.com. Romantic dinner cruises along the Thames with cabaret and dancing. From £49 for a Sunday lunch jazz cruise, from £79 per person for a dinner cruise (including wine).

Thames River Services, tel: 020-7930 4097; www.thamesriver services.co.uk. Trips between Westminster and Greenwich piers every 30 minutes (£16 return, child £8). Tours go beyond Greenwich to the O2 Arena and the Thames Flood Barrier.

Walking Tours

Some walking tour operators use London Tourist Board-trained **Blue Badge Guides** – a guarantee of quality. Walks generally last one or two hours. Visit London lists recommended walking tours on their website www.visitlondon. com.

City Walks, www.walklondon-uk. com. Tailor-made tours of London and the City.

Ghost Walk, tel: 020-8530 8443, www.london-ghost-walk.co. uk. Explores the graveyards, nooks and crannies of the City of London, focussing on the paranormal.

Jack the Ripper Tours, tel: 020-8530 8443, www.jack-the-ripper-tour.com. Author Richard Jones devised these successful two-hour after dark tour (which he sometimes leads), exploring London's more murky past and shady courtyards of Whitechapel. Adult £10.

Original London Walks, tel: 020-7624 3978; www.walks.com. More than 200 walks, including Along the Thames Pub Walk, Hidden London, Hampstead, Historic Westminster, Little Venice and Ghost walks. Adults £10, under 15s free with an adult.

Theatre Tours

National Theatre, tel: 020-7452 3400. Daily backstage tours and workshops. Up to five times a day (Mon–Sat), with each tour lasting 1.25 hours. Cost: £9. Booking: tours@nationaltheatre.org.uk

Shakespeare's Globe Theatre, tel: 020-7902 1400. Daily (9.30am–5pm) 40-minute tours. Adults £15, children £9.

Royal Opera House, tel: 020-7304 4000. A variety of themed tours (Mon–Fri) three times a day. Not suitable for children under 8. Cost: £12.

BBC Television Tours, Broadcasting House, Portland Place, W1A, tel: 0370-901 1227; www. bbc.co.uk/tours. Tours of Broadcasting House, home to BBC Radio and all the BBC television news programmes. Pre-booking essential. Adults £15, children (9–15) £10.

Tourist Offices

The official tourist board maintains a website at www.visitlondon. com. It contains a huge amount of information on attractions, upcoming events and festivals, as well as practical information and a hotel booking service.

Tourist information centres are located at:

City of London Information Centre, St Paul's Churchyard, EC4M 8BX. Tel: 020-7332 1456. Open Mon–Sat 9.30am–5.30pm, Sun 10am–4pm.

Greenwich TIC, Pepys House, 2 Cutty Sark Gardens, Greenwich SE10 9LW. Tel: 0870-608 2000. Open daily 10am–5pm. Email: tic@greenwich.gov.uk.

Visas and Passports

EU nationals will need their **passport** or **national ID card** (issued by an European Economic Area (EEA) country) to enter the UK. Non-EU nationals may also require a **visa** in addition to their passport.

Loss or theft should be reported to the appropriate embassy or consulate, and to the local police. It is sensible to photocopy the relevant pages of your passport and keep the photocopy separate from the passport itself.

A visa to visit the United Kingdom is not required by nationals of member states of the EEA, the Commonwealth (including Australia, Canada, New Zealand and South Africa), and the USA. Nationals of other countries should check with the British Embassy and apply for a visa, if necessary, in good time.

Entry visas are required by Australian, New Zealand, Canadian and US nationals for a stay exceeding three months. All visitors from areas outside the EEA must apply for a visa before travelling if they plan to stay for more than six months.

For up-to-date official information on visas, visit www.gov.uk/check uk-visa.

US citizens should view tips for traveling abroad online (travel. state.gov) for general information on visa requirements, customs regulations and medical care.

TRANSPORT

A – Z

FURTHER READING

GOOD COMPANIONS

London: A Literary Companion by Peter Vansittart. A journey around the capital with the literary luminaries.

Secret London by Andrew Duncan. Uncovers London's hidden landscape from abandoned tube stations to the gentlemen's club.

The London Blue Plaque Guide by Nick Rennison. Details the lives of more than 700 individuals who have been commemorated with a blue plaque on their houses.

A Literary Guide to London by Ed Glinert. A very detailed, street-by-street guide to literary lives.

London on Film by Colin Sorensen. How the cinema has portrayed the city.

HISTORY

The Concise Pepys by Samuel Pepys. Read a first-hand account of the Great Fire of London and find out about daily life in 17th-century England.

Dr Johnson's London by Liza Picard. Brings 18th-century London to life.

London: The Biography by Peter Ackroyd. Anecdotal and entertaining history.

London: A Social History by Roy Porter. Less quirky than Ackroyd but a telling account of how badly the capital has been governed over the centuries.

The Story of the British Museum by Marjorie Caygill. A fascinating tale, authoritatively told, featuring an astonishing variety of heroes and villains.

London Villages by John Wittich. A walker's notes on his travels through village London.

Thames: Sacred River by Peter Ackroyd. Social history of London's famous river.

MEMOIRS

The Shorter Pepys by Samuel Pepys. A distillation of 11 volumes of diaries describing London life, including the Great Fire and the plague, from 1660 to 1669.

84, Charing Cross Road by Helene Hanff. Touching book-lover's correspondence with a London bookseller.

London Orbital by Iain Sinclair. A walk round the M25, exploring little-known parts of London's periphery.

The Oxford Book of London edited by Paul Bailey. A bran-dip of observations by famous visitors over eight centuries.

ART AND ARCHITECTURE

London's Contemporary Architecture by Ken Allinson and Victoria Thornton. Covers buildings since the 1980s; black-and-white pictures.

London Under London: A Subterranean Guide by Richard Trench and Ellis Hillman. Traces the astonishing maze of railway lines, sewers and utilities that lies beneath the streets.

LONDON STREET ATLAS

The key map shows the area of London covered by the atlas section. An index of street names and places of interest shown on the maps can be found on the following pages. For each entry there is a page number and grid reference

Map Legend

Motorway	⊖ Underground	Motorway with junction	✈ Airport
Dual carriageway	⊖ Docklands Light Rail (DLR)	Motorway (under construction)	✝ Church (ruins)
Main roads	⇌ National rail	Dual carriageway	✝ Monastery
	🚌 Bus station	Main road	Castle (ruins)
Minor roads	⊕ Tourist information	Secondary road	∴ Archaeological site
	✉ Main post office	Minor road	⋂ Cave
Footpath	✚ Cathedral / Church	Track	★ Place of interest
Railway	☾ Mosque	International boundary	🏠 Mansion / Stately home
Pedestrian area	✡ Synagogue	Province boundary	✳ Viewpoint
Important building	⚊ Statue / Monument	National park / Reserve	Beach
Park		Ferry route	

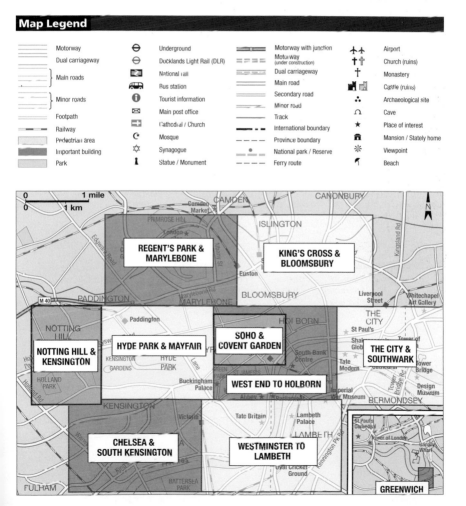

A · B

0   100   200 yds
0   100   200 m

1

Margaret Street

John Prince's St

Regent Street

Great Portland Street

Great Titchfield St

Castle Street

Great Street

Topshop

Oxford Circus

Oxford Circus

Market Place

Hills Place

Eastcastle Street

Winsley St

Ramillies St

Wells Mews

Wells Street

Berners Street

Berners Pl.

Berners Street

Newman Street

Oxford Street

Gresse Street

Rathbone Place

Hanway Place

Hanway St

St Patrick

Soho Square

St Barnaba in-So

St Anne's Court

Dean Street

Carlisle

Square

Frith

Bateman

Ronnie Scott's Jazz Club

French House

St Anne's

Romi

Old Compton

2

Princes Street

Apple

Regent Street

Hanover Square

Hanover Street

Argyll Street

Liberty

Kingly Street

Carnaby Street

Foubert's Place

Marshall Street

Broadwick

Lexington Street

Ingestre Place

Hopkins Street

Peter Street

Walkers Court

Dick La.

Berwick Street

Wardour Street

Poland Street

D'arblay Street

Noel Street

Photographers' Gallery

Palladium Theatre

Ramillies Pl.

Ramillies St

Great Marlborough Street

Hamleys

Broadwick Street

James Street

Golden Square

Bridle Lane

Great Pulteney Street

Brewer Street

Berwick St Market ★

SOHO

Greens Ct

Rupert Street

Archer St

Shaftesbury Avenue

Wardour St

Gerr

St

3

St George Street

Maddox Street

Mill St

Conduit Street

Boyle St

Saville Row

Old Burlington Street

Clifford Street

Cork Street

Heddon St

Regent Street

Warwick Street

John Street

Denman Street

Glasshouse Street

Air Street

Trocadero Centre

Ripley's Believe it or not

Piccadilly Circus

Coventry St

Prince of Wales Theatre

Haymarket

4

New Bond Street

Faraday Museum

Albemarle Street

Old Bond Street

Dover Street

Stafford Street

Vigo Street

Sackville Street

Burlington Gdns

Burlington Arcade

Royal Academy of Arts

The Albany

Fortnum & Mason

Piccadilly Arcade

Piccadilly

Jermyn Street

St James's Piccadilly

Duke Street

Bury Street

Duke St.

St James's Square

Duke of York St.

St James's Sq.

ST JAMES'S SQUARE GARDENS

Charles II St.

Charles II St

Pall Mall

Panton

Haymarket

Harold Pinter Theatre

Aquascutim

Piccadilly Circus

Eros

Criterion Theatre

Green Park

Ritz Hotel

Berkeley Street

Arlington Street

St James's Street

Regent St

A · B

HOLBORN

COVENT GARDEN

CHINATOWN

STRAND

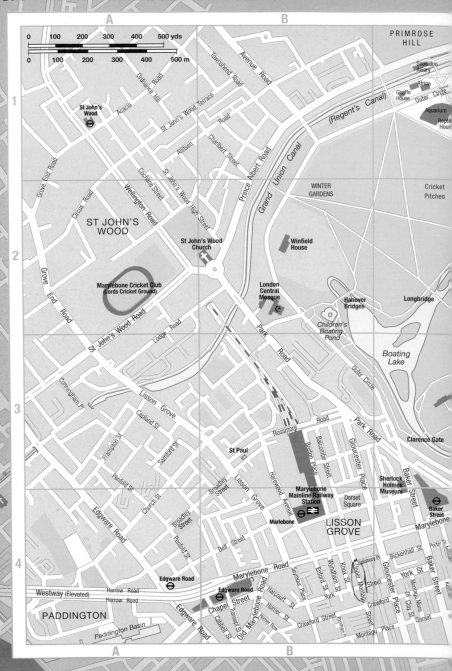

PRIMROSE
HILL

Snowdon
Aviary

Africa

Giraffe
House

Aquarium

Repti
Hous

0   100   200   300   400   500 yds
0   100   200   300   400   500 m

Townshend Road

Avenue Road

(Regent's Canal)

Outer Circle

St John's
Wood

Ordnance Hill

Acacia

St John's Wood Terrace

Road

Charlbert Street

Prince Albert Road

Grand Union Canal

Cricket
Pitches

Grove End Road

Allitsen

Cochrane Street

St John's Wood High Street

WINTER
GARDENS

ST JOHN'S
WOOD

Circus Road

Wellington Road

St John's Wood
Church

Winfield
House

Marylebone Cricket Club
(Lords Cricket Ground)

London
Central
Mosque

Hanover
Bridges

Longbridge

Grove End Road

St John's Wood Road

Lodge Road

Park Road

Children's
Boating
Pond

Outer Circle

Boating
Lake

Cunningham Pl

Lisson Grove

Rossmore

Road

Park Road

Clarence Gate

Capland St

Frampton St

Samford St

St Paul

Boston Place

Balcombe Street

Gloucester Place

Sherlock
Holmes
Museum

Baker Street

Penfold St

Broadley
Street

Harewood Avenue

Lisson Grove

Marylebone
Mainline Railway
Station

Dorset
Square

Baker
Street

Edgware Road

Church St

Broadley Street

Marlebone

LISSON
GROVE

Marylebone

Bell Street

Penfold St

Bickenhall St

York St

Baker Street

Edgware Road

Marylebone Road

Salisbury Pl

Upper Montagu Street

Gloucester Place

Montagu Mews

Clay St

Westway (Elevated)

Harrow Road

Harrow Road

Edgware Road

Chapel Street

Old Marylebone Road

Harcourt St

Seymour Place

Enford St

Knox St

Wyndham Place

York

Crawford

Dorset

Montagu Place

PADDINGTON

Paddington Basin

Edgware Road

Cabbell St

Transept St

Homer St

Homer Row

Crawford Street

Wyndham Pl

A   B

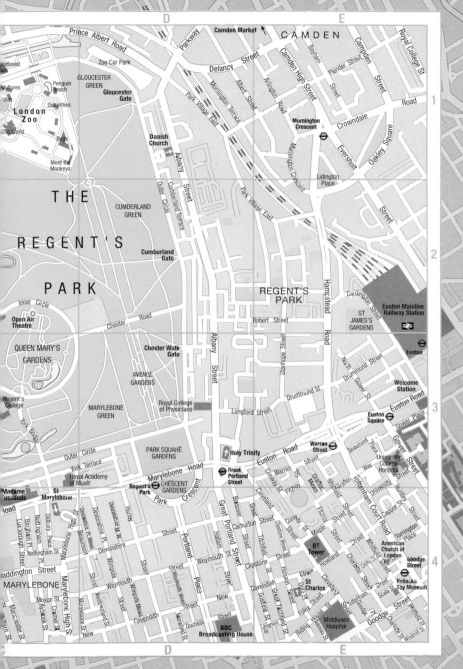

CAMDEN

Prince Albert Road
Camden Market
Parkway
Delancy Street
Zoo Car Park
Camden High Street
Barham Street
Plender Street
Camden Street
Royal College St
Road

GLOUCESTER GREEN
Park Village East
Mornington Terrace
Albert Street
Arlington Road
Crowndale

Rainforest
Vultures
Villas
London Zoo
Zoo World
Penguin Beach
Butterflies
Bugs
Meet the Monkeys

Gloucester Gate

Danish Church

Mornington Crescent
Eversholt Street
Oakley Square

THE

CUMBERLAND GREEN

Outer Circle
Cumberland Terrace
Albany Street
Mornington Crescent
Lidington Place

REGENT'S

Cumberland Gate

PARK

Inner Circle
Open Air Theatre

REGENT'S PARK

Chester Road

Robert Street

Hampstead Road

Cardington Street
ST JAMES'S GARDENS

Euston Mainline Railway Station

Euston

QUEEN MARY'S GARDENS

Chester Walk Gate

Albany Street
Stanhope Street

North Gower St
Drummond Street
Gower St

Welcome Station

Regent's College

AVENUE GARDENS

MARYLEBONE GREEN
Royal College of Physicians

Drummond St
Longford Street

Euston Square
Gower Place

York Bridge

Outer Circle
York Terrace
Royal Academy of Music

PARK SQUARE GARDENS

Holy Trinity
Great Portland Street

Euston Road
Warren Street
Warren St
Beaumont Place
University College Hospital

Madame Tussauds
St Marylebone
Regent's Park
CRESCENT GARDENS
Marylebone Road
Conway St
Fitzroy St

Gower Street

Road

MARYLEBONE
Moxon St
Aybrook St
Nottingham Pl
Luxborough Street
Nottingham St
Paddington Street
Weymouth
New
Cavendish
Devonshire M.W.
Devonshire
Wimpole Street
Harley Street
Portland Place
Great Portland Street
Hallam Street
Carburton
Clipstone Street
Weymouth Street
Bolsover Street
Great Titchfield Street
Cleveland Street
Cleveland Mews
Great Portland
Maple St
Conway
Fitzroy Street
Whitfield Street
Grafton Way
University Street
Huntley Street
Capper St
Tottenham Court Road
Torrington Place
American Church of London
Goodge Street
Pollock's Toy Museum

BT Tower

St Charles

Cavendish
Crawford Street
Foley Street
Riding House Street
Langham
Mortimer Street
Nassau St
Howland
Charlotte Street
Tottenham Street
Scala St
Charlotte Cross St
Whitfield Street
Windmill St
Goodge Street

BBC Broadcasting House

Middlesex Hospital

1

2

3

4

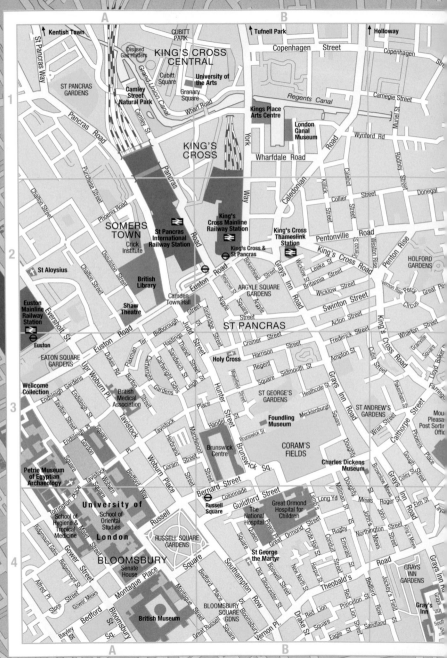

ARNARD
PARK

↑Highbury   Theberton St.

Celestial Church
of Christ

ISLINGTON

ISLINGTON
GREEN

Upper Street

Business
Design
Centre

Islington Grn

Essex Road

Cloudesley Pl.

Liverpool

St Mary's

Camden Passage

Colebrooke Row

Cruden St.

St. Peter's Street

Arlington
Square

Packington Square

Tolpuddle Street

Upper Street

Road

Duncan St.

Gerrard Road

Devonia Road

Danbury Street

Eagle Wharf Rd

PENTONVILLE

Noel Road
Regents Canal

Napier Grove

Street

Duncan Terrace

Colebrooke Row

Vincent Terrace

Wenlock Basin

Wharf Road

SHEPHERDESS
WALK PARK

Angel

City Road Basin

Wenlock St.

Pentonville   Road

St John   Street

Goswell   Road

City   Road

Graham Street

Wenlock Rd.

Micawber St.

Shepherdess Walk

Murray Grove

Claremont

Square

Myddelton

Chadwell St.

Friend St.

Sadler's Wells
Theatre

Rawstorne   St.

City   Road

Moreland Street

Central   Street

Dingley Rd.

Amwell

Street

River St.

Myddelton Pge

FINSBURY

St John   Street

Wynyatt St.

Spencer
Street

King Square
Gardens

Lever   Street

Galway St.

Lloyds R.

The City
University

Northampton

Ashby St.

Radnor   St.

Bath St.

Merlin's St.

Hardwick St.

Rosebery   Avenue

Gloucester Way

Wyclif St.

Square

Sebastian St.

ST LUKE'S
GARDEN

Tysoe St.

Finsbury
Town Hall

Myddelton Rd.

CLERKENWELL

Skinner   Street

Percival Street

Seward Street

ST LUKE'S
GARDEN

Easton St.

Exmouth Market

Pine St.

Northampton Rd

Cyrus Street

Pear Tree   Street

Central   Street

Old   Street

Banner St.

Bowling Green Lane

Sans   Walk

Compton

Goswell   Road

Bastwick Street

Gee Street

Golden   Lane

Bunhill   Row

Farringdon   Road

St John   Street

Dallington St.

Dufferin St.

Warner   Street

Clerkenwell   Cl.

St James

Aylesbury Street

Harwood Pl.

Northburgh St.

Rosebery   Avenue

Ray St.

Herbal Hill

St John

Great Sutton   Street

FORTUNE STREET
PARK

Clerkenwell   Road

Hatton

Clerkenwell   Close

Briset Street

Road

Barts
Medical
College

Aldersgate   Street

Ben Johnson
House

Exhibition
Hallo

Chiswell Street

Cross

Kirby St.

Turnmill   Street

St John's Lane

Charterhouse

St John   Street

Beech

Defoe
House

Arts Centre

Silk   Street

Milton   Street

Baldwin's Gdns

Hatton Gdn

Greville   Street

Farringdon
Station

Albion Pl.
Gate Cl.

Charterhouse
Sq.

Barbican

Aldersgate   St.

BARBICAN

Guildhall School
of Music & Drama

Moor   Lane

St
Etheldreda

Brooke St.

Saffron Hill

Farringdon   Road

Cowcross   Street

Smithfield
Central Market

Long   Lane

Cloth Fair

Charterhouse   Street

T. More
House

St Giles

PENTONVILLE

A　　　　　**B**

PADDINGTON

Gloucester Terrace
Westbourne Bridge
Orsett Terrace
Porchester Rd
Bishop's Bridge Rd
Eastbourne Terrace
Paddington Basin
South Wharf Road
St Michael's Street
Star Street
Praed Street
Norfolk Pl
Norfolk Square
Sussex Gardens

1

Paddington Mainline Railway Station

🚇 Paddington

Inverness Terrace
Queensway
Porchester Gdns
Leinster Pl
Cleveland Terrace
Gloucester Terrace
Westbourne Terrace
Chilworth Street
Cleveland Sq
Queen's Gardens
Craven Road
Westbourne Ter
Gloucester Terrace
London Street
Sussex Gardens
Gloucester Square
Sussex Square
Hyde Park

🚇 Bayswater

Queensborough Terrace
Porchester Terrace
Leinster Terrace
Craven Hill
Lancaster Ter
Westbourne St
Bayswater

2

🚇 Queensway

Lancaster Gate
Marlborough Gate
🚇 Lancaster Gate
Westbourne Gate
Victoria Gate

Lancaster Gate
ITALIAN GARDENS
The Fountains
West Carriage Drive

🎗 Speke's Monument
🎗 Peter Pan
BUCKHILL

THE PADDOCK
KENSINGTON
Longwater
🎗 Rima

Serpentine Sackler Gallery

3

Sunken Garden
The Broad Walk
🎗 Physical Energy
Temple Lodge
🎗 Norwegian/ British Monument

Kensington Palace
Round Pond

GARDENS
Serpentine Gallery
Princess Diana Memorial Fountain
The Lido

Kensington Palace Gardens
Palace Avenue
Rotton Row
West Carriage Drive

Bandstand
Tennis Courts
Bowling Green

King's Arms Gate
South Flower Walk
Albert Memorial
Alexandra Gate
Prince of Wales Gate
Rutland Gate

4

🚇 Kensington High St
Kensington Rd
Palace Gate
Hyde Park Gate
Queen's Gate
Kensington Road
Russian Orthodo Cathedral

Victoria Rd
De Vere Gardens
Palace Gate
Hyde Park Gate
Kensington Gore
Royal College of Art
Royal Albert Hall
Royal Geographical Sociey
KNIGHTSBRIDGE

Queen's Gate Ter
Exhibition Road
Prince Consort Road
Princess Gardens

0　100　200　300　400　500 yds
0　100　200　300　400　500 m

A　　　　　**B**

MARYLEBONE

St Mark

St John

St John

Wallace Collection

St Paul

Wigmore Hall

Marble Arch Synagogue

Selfridges

Bond Street

Marble Arch

Oxford Street

Marble Arch

Cumberland Gate

Speakers' Corner

American Embassy

Roosevelt

MAYFAIR

Immaculate Conception

Brook Gate

THE MEADOW

Grosvenor Chapel

Nursery

New Lodge

Grosvenor Gate

Thomas Goode & Company

HYDE PARK

Shepherd Market

THE COCKPIT

7/7 Memorial

Christ Church

Boathouse

Curzon Gate

The Serpentine

Serpentine Road

War Memorial

Achilles

Piccadilly

THE DELL

NANNIES LAWN

Rotton Row

Apsley House

GREEN PARK

site of The Great Exhibition

Edinburgh Gate

Albert Gate

Wellington Monument

Wellington Arch

Hyde Park Barracks

South Carriage Drive

Kensington Road

Knightsbridge

Knightsbridge

Hyde Park Corner

Constitution Hill

DUCKINGHAM PALACE GARDENS (not open to the public)

Knightsbridge

Harvey Nichols

St Paul's

Harrods

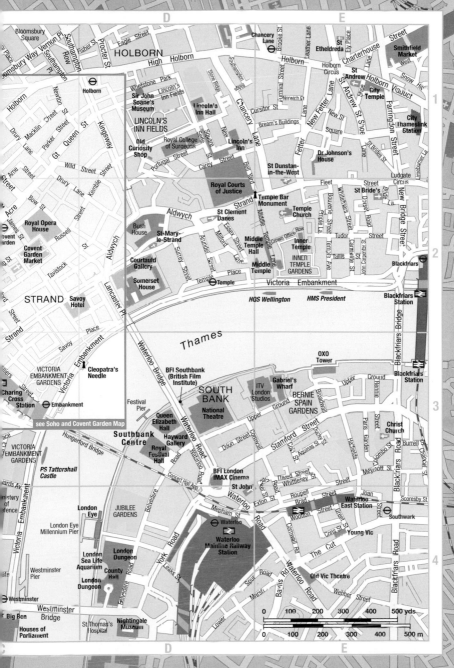

Bloomsbury Square
Bloomsbury Way
Vernon Pl.
Southampton Row
Fisher St.
Procter St.
Eagle Street
Chancery Lane
Brooke St.
Feather Lane
Ely Place
Charterhouse Street
Smithfield Market
West

HOLBORN
High Holborn
Holborn
St Etheldreda
Holborn Circus
Holborn Viaduct
St Andrew
City Temple
Snow Hill
City Thameslink Station

Holborn
Newton Street
Macklin Street
Parker Street
Gt. Queen St.
Kingsway
Whetstone Park
Lincoln's Inn Fields
Sir John Soane's Museum
Lincoln's Inn Hall
Stone Bldgs
Southampton Bldgs
Cursitor St.
Furnival Street
Norwich St.
New Fetter Lane
St Andrew St.
St Andrew St.
Shoe Lane
Farringdon Street

Drury Lane
Queen St.
LINCOLN'S INN FIELDS
Old Curiosity Shop
Royal College of Surgeons
Lincoln's Inn
Bream's Buildings
New St.
Fetter Lane
St Bride's
Dr. Johnson's House
Square
Ludgate Circus
New Bridge Street

Gt. Wild Street
Kemble Street
Drury Lane
Russell St.
Portugal Street
Carey Street
Bell Yard
St Dunstan-in-the-West
Fleet
Street
St Bride's
Whitefriars Street
Bouverie Street
Dorset Street
Tudor
St.

Arne Street
Bow St.
Aldwych
Royal Courts of Justice
Strand
Temple Bar Monument
Temple Church
Carmelite St.
Tallis
St.
Blackfriars

Acre
Royal Opera House
Covent Garden Market
Tavistock
Aldwych
Bush House
St-Mary-le-Strand
St Clement Danes
Essex Street
Milford
Crown Office Row
Middle Temple Hall
Inner Temple
Middle Temple La.
Temple
Pl.
INNER TEMPLE GARDENS
Middle Temple
INNER TEMPLE GARDENS
Blackfriars

Covent Garden
Russell St.
Courtauld Gallery
Somerset House
Surrey Street
Arundel
Temple Place
Temple
Victoria Embankment
Blackfriars Station

STRAND
Savoy Hotel
Lancaster Pl.
HQS Wellington
HMS President
Blackfriars Station

Strand
Savoy Place
Embankment
Cleopatra's Needle
Thames
OXO Tower
Blackfriars Bridge
Blackfriars Station

Charing Cross Station
VICTORIA EMBANKMENT GARDENS
Victoria Embankment
Embankment
Waterloo Bridge
BFI Southbank (British Film Institute)
SOUTH BANK
Gabriel's Wharf
Upper Ground
Ground
Christ Church

see Soho and Covent Garden Map
Festival Pier
ITV London Studios
BERNIE SPAIN GARDENS
Paris Garden
Burrell St.

VICTORIA EMBANKMENT GARDENS
PS Tattershall Castle
Hungerford Bridge
Southbank Centre
Queen Elizabeth Hall
National Theatre
Upper Ground
Stamford Street
Meymott St.
Colombo St.
Blackfriars Road
Christ Church

London Eye
JUBILEE GARDENS
Hayward Gallery
Royal Festival Hall
Waterloo Road
BFI London IMAX Cinema
St John
Mitred Street
Whittlesey St.
Street
Waterloo East Station
Scoresby St.
Southwark

London Eye Millennium Pier
Belvedere Road
Concert Hall App.
Mepham St.
Exton St.
Roupell St.
Brad
Joan Street
Young Vic

Westminster Pier
London Sea Life Aquarium
London Dungeon
County Hall
London Dungeon
Waterloo
Waterloo Mainline Railway Station
York Road
Leake St.
Cornwall Rd
The Cut
Old Vic Theatre

Westminster
Big Ben
Houses of Parliament
Westminster Bridge
St Thomas's Hospital
Nightingale Museum
Lower
Leake St.
Sour
Marsh
Bayliss
Road
Waterloo Road
Webber Street
Blackfriars Road

0 100 200 300 400 500 yds
0 100 200 300 400 500 m

WHITECHAPEL

SHADWELL

Liverpool Street Station
Liverpool Street
Heron Tower
St Helen
30 St Mary Axe (The Gherkin)
Lloyds of London
Fenchurch Street Station
St Margaret Pattens
Corn Exchange
Tower Hill
All Hallows
Custom House
Tower Pier
HMS Belfast
Crown Court
MORE London
City Hall
Unicorn Theatre
Fashion and Textile Museum

Spitalfields Market
Christ Church
Old Truman Brewery
East London Mosque
Whitechapel Art Gallery
Petticoat Lane Market
St Botolph-without-Aldgate
Aldgate
Aldgate East
Tower Gateway
Trinity House Square
World Trade Centre
Tower of London
Traitors Gate
St Katherine Dock
St Katherine's Way
St Katherine's Pier
LONDON BRIDGE CITY PARK
Tower Bridge Experience
Butler's Wharf
St Savior's Dock
Rotherhide

Brushfield Street
Artillery
White's Row
Brune St
Fashion Street
Thrawl St
Old Montague Street
Chicksand St
Brick Lane
Fournier Street
Wentworth Street
Gouston Street
Old Castle
Harrow Pl
White Kennett St
Duke's St
Aldgate High St
Mansell Street
Alie Street
Leman Street
Prescot Street
Chamber Street
Royal Mint Street
Cable St
Goodmans Yd
Shorter St
Tower Hill
Byward Street
Mark Lane
Mincing Lane
Seething La
Crutched
Crosswall
Coopers Row
Pepys Street
Trinity
Vine Street
Minories
Haydon Street
Portsoken Street
Scarborough St
South Tenter St
West Tenter St
Tower's Walk
Commercial Road
Fairclough St
Boyd St
Ellen St
Back Church Lane
Christian St
Pinchin St
Burslem St
Ponier St
Carnon St Rd
Golding St
Settles Street
Greenfield Road
Myrdle St
Fordham St
New Road
Bethnal Green
Swedenborg Gardens
SWEDENBORG GARDENS
Pennington St
Thomas More Street
East Smithfield
Kennet St
Vaughan Way
Hermitage Wall
Wapping High Street
Tower Bridge Approach
Tower Bridge
Shad Thames
Queen Elizabeth Street
Gainsford
Curlew
Maguire St
Bermondsey Wall West
Jacob Street
Wolseley Street
Chambers St
George Row
Mill
Dockhead
Jamaica Rd
Tooley Street
Druid Street
Crucifix La.
Bermondsey Street
Weavers La
Barnham St
Fair Street
Crowns La.
Horselydown La.
Boss St
Bishopsgate
Camomile St
Houndsditch
Bevis Marks
Bury St
Leadenhall Street
Fenchurch Street
Lloyd's Ave
Aldgate
Mitre St
Commercial Street
Whitechapel High St
Alie Street
Whitechapel Road
Greatorex St
Casson St
Osborn Street
Turnthorpe St
Old Castle
Wentworth
Commercial Road
Fenchurch Avenue
THE DITCH

KENSINGTON

St Margarets Lane

Kensington Parish Park

St Stephen

Stamford Road
Victoria Road
Launceston Place
Gloucester Road
Queen's Gate Terrace
Elvaston Place

Royal College of Music

Imperial College

Imperial College Road

Science Museum

Natural History Museum

Victoria & Albert Museum

Princes Gdns

Exhibition Road

Cornwall Gardens

Cornwall Gardens

Lexham Gardens

Queen's Gate Gardens

Queen's Gdns

Cromwell Road

Cromwell Road

Cromwell Gdns

Cromwell Road

Thurloe Place

Thurloe Square

Thurloe Street

Hammersmith

EARL'S COURT

St Jude's

Gloucester Road

Courtfield Gdns

Collingham Road

Courtfield Road

Harrington Road

South Kensington

Pelham Street

SOUTH KENSINGTON

Stanhope Gdns

Harrington Gardens

Wetherby Gardens

Queen's Gate Mews

Sumner Place

Onslow Square

Onslow Gardens

Fulham Road

St Paul

Earl's Court

Barkston Gardens

Bramham Gdns

Bolton Gardens

Laverton Place

Gloucester Road

Cranley Gardens

Onslow Gardens

Old Brompton Road

Cranley Pl

Neville St

Paul's Terrace

Selwood Terrace

Fulham Road

Sydney

Chelsea Farmer's Market

Earl's Court Road

Old Brompton Road

Old Brompton Rd

Colherne Road

Redcliffe Gardens

Finborough Road

St Luke's

Redcliffe Square

Hardcourt Terrace

The Little Boltons

The Boltons

Tregunter Road

Drayton Gardens

Roland Gardens

Cranley Gardens

St Yeghiche

Evelyn Gardens

Elm Park Gdns

Beaufort Street

Old Church Street

Chelsea Square

Dovehouse Street

Manresa Rd

Carlyle Square

King's Road

WEST BROMPTON

Cathcart Road

Hollywood Road

Redcliffe Road

Gilston Road

Drayton Gardens

Fulham Road

Elm Park Road

Park Walk

BROMPTON CEMETERY

Cemetery Chapel

Ifield Road

Finborough Road

Redcliffe Gardens

Nightingale Pl

Limerston St

Gertrude St

Hobury St

Slaycomb St

Langton St

WORLD'S END

Milman's Square

Pultons Square

Denver's Street

Old Church Street

Chelsea Old Church

Chelsea

Stamford Bridge (Chelsea Football Club)

Fulham

Fulham Road

Gunter Grove

Hortensia Road

Edith Grove

King's

King's Road

Cheyne Walk

Battersea Bridge

A   B

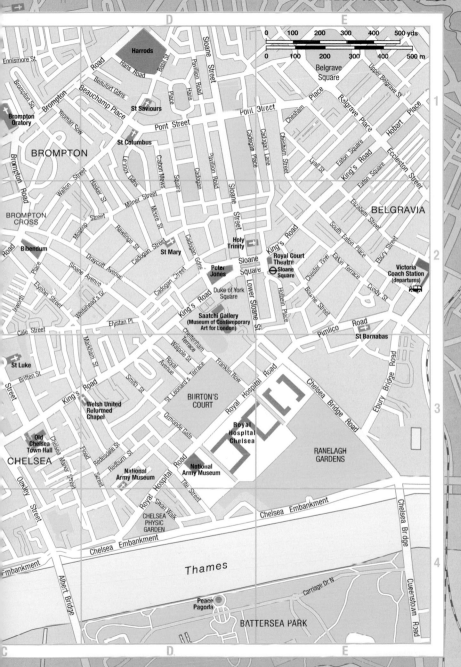

0   100   200   300   400   500 yds
0   100   200   300   400   500 m

Ennismore St

Brompton Sq

Brompton Road

Brompton Oratory

BROMPTON

BROMPTON CROSS

Road

Bibendum

Ixworth

Elysian Street

Cale Street

St Luke

Britten St

Street

CHELSEA

Oakley Street

Albert Bridge

Embankment

Beaufort Gdns

Beauchamp Place

Yeoman Row

Walton Street

Hasker St

Milner Street

Mossop

Rawlings St

Draycott Avenue

Sloane Avenue

Whitehead's Gr

Elysan Pl.

Markham St

King's

Road

Smith St

Redesdale St

Radnor St

Chelsea Manor Street

Old Chelsea Town Hall

Welsh United Reformed Chapel

National Museum

Royal Hospital

Road

Swan Walk

CHELSEA PHYSIC GARDEN

Chelsea Embankment

Harrods

Hans Road

Beauls St

Pavilion Road

Hans Place

St Saviours

Pont Street

St Columbus

Lennox Mews

Cadogan Square

Cadogan Gdns

Cadogan Street

Cadogan Gdns

St Mary

Cadogan Street

Sloane Street

Pavilion Road

Sloane Street

Sloane Street

Sloane Square

King's Road

Lower Sloane St

King's Road

Duke of York Square

Holy Trinity

Peter Jones

Saatchi Gallery
(Museum of Contemporary
Art for London)

Chiltenham Terrace

Walpole St

Royal Avenue

St Leonard's Terrace

Franklin Row

BURTON'S COURT

Ormonde Gate

Royal Hospital Road

Royal Hospital Chelsea

National Army Museum

Tite Street

Royal Hospital Road

Belgrave Square

Pont Street

Chesham Place

Belgrave Place

Upper Belgrave St

Lyall St

Eaton Square

King's Road

Eaton Square

Eaton Square

Hobart Place

Eccleston Street

BELGRAVIA

Elizabeth Street

South Eaton Place

Eaton Terrace

Chester Row

Ebury Street

Ebury Street

Victoria Coach Station
(departures)

Chester Row

Eaton Terrace

Bourne Street

Holbein Place

Cundy St

Pimlico

Road

St Barnabas

King's Road

Royal Hospital Road

Chelsea Bridge Road

RANELAGH GARDENS

Ebury Bridge Road

Chelsea Embankment

Chelsea Bridge

Carriage Dr N

Queenstown Road

Chelsea Embankment

Thames

Peace Pagoda

BATTERSEA PARK

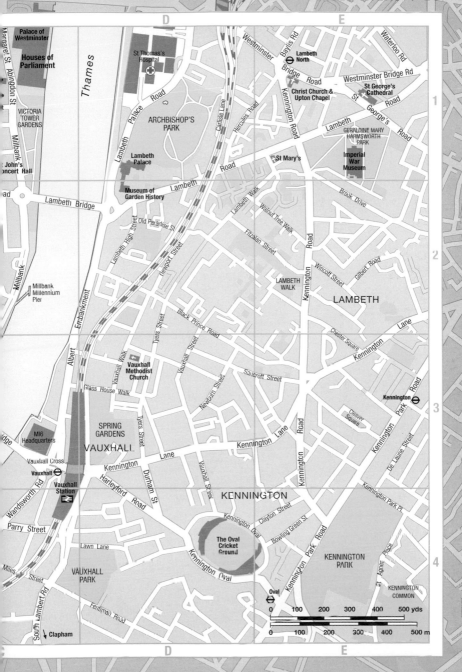

Palace of Westminster
Houses of Parliament
St Thomas's Hospital
Westminster Bridge Road
Lambeth North
Baylis Rd
Waterloo Rd
Christ Church & Upton Chapel
St George's Cathedral
Westminster Bridge Rd
Margaret St
Abingdon St
VICTORIA TOWER GARDENS
Millbank
Thames
Palace Road
ARCHBISHOP'S PARK
Lambeth
Carlisle Lane
Hercules Road
Kennington Road
Lambeth Road
St George's Road
St John's Concert Hall
Lambeth Palace
St Mary's
GERALDINE MARY HARMSWORTH PARK
Imperial War Museum
Museum of Garden History
Lambeth
Lambeth Bridge
Old Paradise St
Lambeth High Street
Newport Street
Lambeth Walk
Walnut Tree Walk
Fitzalan Street
Road
Brook Drive
Millbank
Millbank Millennium Pier
Embankment
Black Prince Road
Tyers Street
Vauxhall Street
Newburn Street
LAMBETH WALK
Kennington Road
Wincott Street
Gilbert Road
LAMBETH
Chester Square
Lane
Albert
Vauxhall Walk
Vauxhall Methodist Church
Glass House Walk
Sancroft Street
Kennington Lane
Kennington
Cleaver Square
Kennington Park Road
Kennington ⊖
De Laune Street
MI6 Headquarters
SPRING GARDENS
VAUXHALL
Tyers Street
Vauxhall Cross
Vauxhall ⊖
Kennington Lane
Durham St
Harleyford Road
Vauxhall Street
KENNINGTON
Kennington Road
Kennington Park Rd
Kennington Park Pl
Cleaver Square
Wandsworth Rd
Vauxhall Station
Parry Street
Lawn Lane
Kennington Oval
Clayton Street
Bowling Green St
KENNINGTON PARK
Agnes Place
KENNINGTON COMMON
The Oval Cricket Ground
VAUXHALL PARK
Miles Street
South Lambeth Rd
Fentiman Road
Kennington Oval
Oval ⊖
↓ Clapham

0   100   200   300   400   500 yds
0   100   200   300   400   500 m

D   E   1   2   3   4

0   100 200 300 400 500 yds
0   100 200 300 400 500 m

A   **B**

Cambridge Gardens

Westway (elevated)   ◆ Ladbroke Grove

Porchester Oak

Westbourne Park Villas

Westbourne Park Road

Lancaster

Tavistock Road   All Saints Road   St Luke's Road   St Luke's Mews   Leamington Rd Villas   Aldridge Rd Villas   Westbourne Park Road   Westbourne Park Villas   Queensway

1

St Marks Road   Cornwall Crescent   Ladbroke Grove   Westbourne Park Road   Basing Road   Powis   Westbourne Park Road   Powis Terrace   Colville   Talbot Courtnell St   Talbot Road   Moorhouse Rd   Ledbury Rd   Northumberland Pl   Chepstow Road   Shrewsbury Road   Hereford Road   Bridstow Place   Newton Rd   Westbourne Grove   Kensington Gardens Square   Garway Road   Recent Place   Whiteley's Shopping Centre

Blenheim Crescent   Talbot Road   Colville   Artesian Mews

Elgin Cres.   Portobello Road Market   Lonsdale Rd   Westbourne Grove   Leinster Square   Greek Orthodox

Walmer Road   Clarendon Road   Elgin Crescent   Arundel Gdns   Portobello Road   Westbourne Grove   Denbigh Rd   Chepstow Villas   Pembridge Villas   Chepstow Place   Hereford Road   Princes Square   Bayswater

2

Lansdowne Rise   Lansdowne Road   Ladbroke Gardens   Stanley Crescent   Kensington Park Gardens   Pembridge Cres.   Portobello Road   **NOTTING HILL**   Pembridge Rd   Dawson Place   Moscow Road   St Petersburgh Place   Place Court   Ossington Street   Queensway

St John's Gdns   Lansdowne Crescent   Ladbroke Grove   Ladbroke   Ladbroke Road   Ladbroke Ter   Pembridge Gdns   Linden Gdns   Bark Pl.

Portland Road   Clarendon Road   Lansdowne Walk   Ladbroke Walk   Ladbroke Road   Kensington Park Road   Pembridge Square   Pembridge Rd   **Notting Hill Gate**   Bayswater Road

Princedale Rd   Addison Rd   Notland Square   Ladbroke Road   **Notting Hill Gate**   **Diana Memorial Playground**

Holland Park ◆   Holland Park Avenue   Campden Hill Square   Hillsleigh Road   Campden Hill Road   Kensington Place   **KENSINGTON GARDENS**   Elfin Oak

Holland Park   Aubrey Road   Aubrey Walk   Peel Street   Campden Street   Kensington Church Street   Palace Gardens Ter.   Brunswick Gardens   Kensington Palace Gardens   **Sunken Garden**

3

Holland Park Mews   Tennis Courts   Bedford Gardens   Sheffield Terrace   Gloucester Walk   Kensington Palace Gardens   **Kensington Palace**

Holland Park   Holland Park   Abbotsbury Road   Camden Hill   Camden Gr.   Pitt St   Horton Pl   Holland Street   **Royal Garden Hotel**

HOLLAND   Duchess of Bedford's Walk   Pike's La.

PARK   **Holland House**   Youth Hostel   **KENSINGTON**   **St Mary Abbots**   Kensington Road

Open Air Theatre   Upr Phillimore Gdns   Phillimore Pl   **Kensington Town Hall**   **High Street Kensington**   Kensington Square   Wright's Lane

Tennis Courts   Ilchester Place   Holland Walk   Phillimore Gdns   Argyll Rd   Essex Villas   Stafford Ter   Campden Hill Road   **High Street Kensington**

4

Addison Road   Oakwood Court   Melbury Road   Holland Park Road   Cricket Pitch   **Design Museum**   Phillimore Walk   Phillimore   Allen Street   Young St   Iverna Gdns   Marloes Road   Stanford Road

Kensington (Olympia) ◆   **Leighton House**   Kensington High   Street   Earls Court Road   Abingdon Rd   Abingdon Villas   Scarsdale Villas

Kensington (Olympia) Mainline Railway Station

Russell Road   Holland Road   Addison Road   St Edwardes Square

Olympia Exhibition Halls   ← **Hammersmith**

A   **B**

Thames

D

Greenwich Foot Tunnel

Greenwich
Pier

Crane St

Eastney

Prime Meridian Line

E

1

Old Woolwich Road

Queen Anne
Court

Greenwich Foot Tunnel
Southern Entrance

Park Row

Trinity College
of Music

Trafalgar

Road

Greenwich Pk St

Cutty
Sark

University of Greenwich

Queen Mary
College

Street

Trafalgar Dr

Thames Street

Thames Street

College
Approach

King William

Old
Royal Naval
College

Romney

Road

Park Row

Park Vista

Cutty
Sark

Dreadnought
Library

Feathers Pl

Creek   Road

Durnford
St

Queen's
House

Park Row
Gate

Bardsley Lane

Church

Nelson Rd

St Mary's
Gate

National
Maritime Museum

Boating
Lake

2

GREENWICH

St Alfege's
Church

Street

Cooper
Building

ONE TREE
HILL

Ryan
Street

Walk

Randall Place

Stockwell St

Nevada St

HERB
GARDEN

GREENWICH
PARK

Straightsmouth

Burney
Street

Circus Gate

Croom's Hill

The Avenue

Prime Meridian Line

THE
GARDENS

Greenwich Mainline
Railway Station

Gloucester Circus

Old Royal
Observatory

Blackheath Ave

3

Greenwich

Greenwich High Rd

Royal Hill

King George
Street Gate

Planetarium

Circus Street

Brand Street

Prior Street

King

George   Street

Our Ladye
Star of the Sea

Croom's Hill

Royal
Observatory

Greenwich South Street

Blissett Street

Winforton Street

Point Hill

Diamond Terrace

Hyde Vale

Charlton Way

Croom's Hill
Gate

Maidenstone

Hill

BLACKHEATH
THE POINT

West Grove

BLACKHEATH

Gate Road

Gloucester Wolfe Road

Rangers House

4

Blackheath

Hill

Shooters   Hill   Road

0   100   200 yds

0   100   200 m

C

D

E

STREET INDEX

ART AND PHOTO CREDITS

INDEX

ABOUT THIS BOOK

INSIGHT GUIDES

LONDON

Editor: Rachel Lawrence
Author: Emma Levine
Head of Production: Rebeka Davies
Picture Editor: Tom Smyth
Cartography: original cartography based on OSM data, (c) OpenStreetMap contributors (CC BY-SA) Styled by Phoenix Mapping Ltd, updated by Carte

What makes an Insight Guide different? Since our first book pioneered the use of creative full-colour photography in travel guides in 1970, we have aimed to provide not only reliable information but also the key to a real understanding of a destination and its people. To achieve this, our books rely on the authority of locally based writers and photographers.

The Contributors

This fully updated edition of *City Guide London* was commissioned by **Rachel Lawrence** at Insight's London editorial office.

The entire book has been comprehensively updated by **Emma Levine**, a travel writer based in Walthamstow, northeast London.

The fifteenth edition of this book builds on previous editions produced by **Catherine Dreghorn**, **Rachel Lawrence**, **Sian Lezard**, **Tom Stainer**, **Dorothy Stannard**, **Brian Bell**, **Roger Williams** and **Andrew Eames**. Past contributors whose work is still evident here include **Roland Collins** (history), **Srinvasa Rao** (Who Lives in London?), **Rebecca Ford**, **Allison Lobbett** and **Tim Grimwade**.

The design was created by Klaus Geisler and the principal photographer was **Lydia Evans**, a regular contributor to Insight Guides.

The book was copy-edited by **Tom Fleming** and the index compiled by **Penny Phenix**.

Distribution

UK, Ireland and Europe
Apa Publications (UK) Ltd
sales@insightguides.com

United States and Canada
Ingram Publisher Services
ips@ingramcontent.com

Australia and New Zealand
Woodslane
info@woodslane.com.au

Southeast Asia
Apa Publications (SN) Pte
singaporeoffice@insightguides.com

Hong Kong, Taiwan and China
Apa Publications (HK) Ltd
hongkongoffice@insightguides.com

Worldwide
Apa Publications (UK) Ltd
sales@insightguides.com

Special Sales, Content Licensing and CoPublishing

Insight Guides can be purchased in bulk quantities at discounted prices. We can create special editions, personalised jackets and corporate imprints tailored to your needs.
sales@insightguides.com;
www.insightguides.biz

Printing

CTPS-China

SEND US YOUR THOUGHTS

We do our best to ensure the information in our books is as accurate and up-to-date as possible. The books are updated on a regular basis using local contacts, who painstakingly add, amend, and correct as required. However, some details (such as telephone numbers and opening times) are liable to change, and we are ultimately reliant on our readers to put us in the picture.

We welcome your feedback, especially your experience of using the book "on the road". Maybe we recommended a hotel that you liked (or another that you didn't), or you came across a great bar or new attraction that we missed.

We will acknowledge all contributions, and we'll offer an Insight Guide to the best letters received.

Please write to us at:
Insight Guides
PO Box 7910, London SE1 1WE
Or email us at:
hello@insightguides.com